ROUTLEDGE LIBRARY EDITIONS:
WOMEN AND BUSINESS

Volume 12

WOMEN IN TOP JOBS

WOMEN IN TOP JOBS

Four Studies in Achievement

MICHAEL P. FOGARTY, A.J. ALLEN,
ISOBEL ALLEN AND PATRICIA WALTERS

Routledge
Taylor & Francis Group
LONDON AND NEW YORK

First published in 1971 by George Allen & Unwin Ltd

This edition first published in 2017
by Routledge
2 Park Square, Milton Park, Abingdon, Oxon OX14 4RN

and by Routledge
711 Third Avenue, New York, NY 10017

Routledge is an imprint of the Taylor & Francis Group, an informa business

British Library Cataloguing in Publication Data
A catalogue record for this book is available from the British Library

ISBN: 978-1-138-23710-0 (Set)
ISBN: 978-1-315-27106-4 (Set) (ebk)
ISBN: 978-1-138-24318-7 (Volume 12) (hbk)
ISBN: 978-1-138-28065-6 (Volume 12) (pbk)
ISBN: 978-1-315-27653-3 (Volume 12) (ebk)

Publisher's Note
The publisher has gone to great lengths to ensure the quality of this reprint but points out that some imperfections in the original copies may be apparent.

Disclaimer
The publisher has made every effort to trace copyright holders and would welcome correspondence from those they have been unable to trace.

WOMEN IN TOP JOBS

Four Studies in Achievement

POLITICAL AND ECONOMIC PLANNING

London

GEORGE ALLEN & UNWIN LTD

RUSKIN HOUSE MUSEUM STREET

FIRST PUBLISHED IN 1971

ISBN 0 04 331046 X

PRINTED IN GREAT BRITAIN
in 10 point Times Roman type
BY THE ALDEN PRESS, OXFORD

Acknowledgements

The four Parts of this book are the result of four studies which were part of a large study of women and their careers, sponsored by the Leverhulme Trust and undertaken by PEP in collaboration with the Tavistock Institute. The study as a whole was under the direction of Michael P. Fogarty and Robert and Rhona Rapoport. Parts One and Three of this volume, on Women in Two Large Companies and Women in the BBC, are by Isobel Allen. Part Two, on The Woman Director, is by A. J. Allen. Part Four, on Women in The Administrative Class of the Civil Service is by Patricia A. Walters of the Department of Sociology, Government and Administration at the University of Salford.

We are grateful to the many informants in the organizations concerned, who gave their time and help to the studies. Particular thanks are due to the Civil Service Commission, the BBC, the managements of the two large companies, and the Institute of Directors, who facilitated the work in many ways. The production, printing and distribution of the questionnaire and much other work in the survey of women directors was done by the Institute of Directors, and the staff of the Institute and of its Medical Centre were a constant source of help in this part of the work. It must be made clear, however, that none of these organizations has any responsibility for what is written in this book.

PEP and the authors express their gratitude also to the members of the Advisory Group and others who gave valuable advice throughout the study; and to those who typed and edited the drafts.

Finally, PEP acknowledges the generous grant from the Leverhulme Trust which made the whole study possible.

Contents

Foreword

The four studies published together here form part of a larger project on women's prospects in higher professional and managerial work, and related aspects of family life, which have resulted in several volumes and papers. The occupations chosen for special study here were selected for two reasons. Much less material on women's progress and prospects in these occupations has hitherto been available than in such fields as school and university teaching, medicine or social work, so that studies on them were an opportunity to break new ground and not merely to go over old. Secondly, they cover between them the three main types of occupational situation which it was wished to study:

1. The independent professional practitioner, head of a business, or freelance writer or producer, in control of her own time and with final responsibility for her own decisions.
2. The 'entrepreneurial bureaucrat', in a policy-making position in a large company or public service organization.
3. The professional employee or manager below policy-making level.

The findings from the five occupational studies are developed and discussed more fully, in combination with findings from occupational studies other than those of the present project, in *Career, Family and Sex Roles*. Here, therefore, only a brief introduction to them will be made.

Statistical analysis has been used where possible but, because of the small number and scattered distribution of women in these occupations, it has been possible to rely on it only to a limited extent. Much of the material gathered has been qualitative. Special attention was paid to three groups of informants:

1. Women, and comparable men, in the age group from roughly 35 to 45: old enough to have reached senior positions, but young enough still to be involved, in many cases, in the problems of growing families, and not so old as to belong to a generation which grew up under conditions wholly different from those of today.
2. Young women management trainees (or in corresponding grades in other occupations), having their careers to make, but recog-

nized by the organizations which have recruited them as having high promise. Women in this group were contacted preferably at the point where they had two or three years' working experience, but were not yet finally settled into a career line.

3. Establishment officers, personnel managers, and, generally, senior managers (men and women, line and functional) in a position to take an overall view of men's and women's career patterns and prospects.

As already stated the occupations were selected to cover a wide variety of working environments. This difference of environments naturally reflects itself in differences in women's progress and prospects in the various fields. In the private sector, as the studies in this volume bring out, women have often found it easier to reach the top of small businesses or independent professional practices than to climb to policy-making levels in large bureaucracies. Public sector organizations such as the BBC or the Administrative Civil Service have made a more deliberate effort than private enterprise to give women an equal chance. But this is cross-cut by differences in the character of these organizations' work. In the BBC, given the competitive and other characteristics of the communications industry, posts at even moderately senior levels may require more of the qualities of the 'entrepreneurial bureaucrat'—with the accent on 'entrepreneurial'—than would be expected in the Civil Service. Women's relative progress and prospects in these two branches of the public service have differed accordingly.

But, over and above differences arising from different occupational environments, the studies reported here highlight certain common factors both in women themselves and in employers' and colleagues' attitudes to them.

1. *Common factors in women's performance compared to men's*

The studies show no basic difference between the level and style—or rather the range of levels and styles—of work performance of the women who in present conditions have reached top jobs and those of men in similar positions. As regards highly qualified women generally, these studies support the finding from studies in other fields that the abilities and interests of men and women overlap considerably. They are not two separate worlds. They also indicate that the interests and abilities of women in the professions and management tend to differ from those of men in certain respects; so long as it is remembered that the differences are comparative, and that the point is not that all men and women have, or lack, certain characteristics but that the chances are rather greater that men will have some characteristics and women others. Women are more likely than men to have what might be called a general rather than a specialized (or a 'horizontal' rather than a 'vertical') type of ambition; to be interested in balancing family or leisure interests against work, and to settle for a satisfying job which leaves room for this rather than to drive towards the peaks of a profession. They tend to be less interested in empire-building, office politics, and administration. They are less likely than men to be forceful and competitive whether in their jobs or in promoting their own careers. They are seen as more likely to adopt an informal, personal, expressive style of management or professional approach, and as more tense, self-conscious, meticulous in details, and reluctant to delegate than men. In some circles—broadly speaking, the more traditional and the less educated, and among people of lower ability—they tend still to arouse resentment on the part of men customers, colleagues, or subordinates.

These characteristics, as they stand, have both positive and negative aspects. A number of them read like a specification for a middle, as apart from a top, manager. A fair comment on the statistics of women's employment in British business and in some branches of the public service is that, given the characteristics which well-qualified women are perceived as having here and now, many more of them should be holding posts at middle management and corresponding professional levels than are in fact doing so. On the other hand the list of characteristics reads less well as a specification for top management, or at least for top management in its traditional bureaucratic forms. For 'democratic', 'network', or group-centred styles of management, of the kind that have developed rapidly in recent years, women's tendency to an informal, unbureaucratic style of working might seem to fit them very well. Sometimes the point is simply a difference of which account needs to be taken, but which in itself is neither positive nor negative; for example that women seem often to be as capable as men of filling a top job if promoted into it, but may need more than men to be pulled up to it rather than be left to find their way to it themselves.

It also appears however from the studies that many of the characteristics of work performance now commonly found among women are culturally determined, have changed and can well change or be made to change again. The characteristics of young highly qualified women today are described as being different from those of women of similar abilities and qualifications who are now middle-aged, and these again as different from those of the generation of career women now moving into retirement. Comparisons between occupations or organizations, or even between departments of the same firm, show how women's career commitment, work performance, and job stability can be influenced by employers' greater or lesser willingness to take them and give them responsibility. A historical view shows how often the beliefs once held in these occupations about women's unsuitability for this or that job have collapsed under the test of experience.

The implication is not that typical differences between the work styles of men and women will or should disappear. On the contrary: the impression from the studies is that there is something (though one should be careful not to exaggerate this) in the idea of a 'feminine vision' of many work problems complementary to that of men, and that a certain complementarity is valuable and should be preserved. But it does seem likely that the overlap between the work abilities and interests of highly qualified men and women will and should become even greater than now. This can happen not only through women developing skills and attitudes traditionally found among men but through men taking up those once characteristic of women; for example by their developing the informal, loose style of working appropriate to 'democratic' or 'network' management, or taking a more relaxed attitude to work and moving towards a more equal balance between work, family, and leisure interests. Bearing in mind these possibilities, the studies make it clear that it would be wrong to assume for the future any general permanent difference between the level or style of men's and women's performance when actually in a job—as apart from the questions about availability for work dealt with below—such as would justify treating them as two classes apart. Decisions about the appointment or promotion of a woman as opposed to a man, or *vice versa*—so far as they depend on work performance—are more likely to be sound if made, like similar decisions comparing one man or one woman with another, in terms of individual merit and not of class characteristics.

2. *Women's availability—the different life cycles of women and men*

It is on the other hand very near the truth to say that women, at any rate that great majority of them who marry and have children, do need to be treated as a class in respect of the timing of their careers, as distinct from the level or style of their performance in whatever job they currently hold. The pressure on them both from social exactions and from their own attitudes, to slow down or drop out of their careers during the time when their children are young is severe.

Men too may have broken careers or need to go slow or drop out for a time, perhaps to study or because of illness, but for women the problems of maternity and availability for work are general ones. Issues arising out of this for the family and, generally, on sex roles are discussed in the light of the project's other evidence in *Career, Family and Sex Roles.* A main purpose of the occupational studies has been to establish, not whether the different timing and shape of women's careers does at present limit their chances of promotion to and employment in senior levels—this hardly needs to be argued—but whether and how far it need do so in future.

The answer from the studies is clear; it need not do so. In this respect it is particularly worth drawing attention to the study of architects which PEP is publishing separately, for in architecture, with its small, informal units and with its many husband-and-wife partnerships, the conditions are particularly favourable for experiment and informal adaptation; indeed much interesting experience has accumulated as a result. Taking the experience of all five professions together two things are clear. First, it is practicable and economic to make the adaptations needed to let able women combine having children with a chance of promotion to senior posts: but secondly, in none of the occupations studied have such measures been clearly thought out. It is practicable and economic to guarantee mothers security in their jobs, as well as a reasonable maternity break, at the time of a birth, to arrange for them spells of part-time work while their children are young and they themselves are working at relatively junior levels; and to ensure for them opportunities to reenter work (not necessarily to their old job or employer), retrain, and to accelerate back up to the level which they might have reached had they not made a break. In a number of occupations it can be practicable to offer part-time work, or at any rate work not tied to an ordinary office timetable, even at senior levels; though this tends to be particularly difficult in top administrative and managerial posts. But though there has been enough informal, unplanned experiment to show that these things are possible, in none of the five occupations have full-scale policies to that effect been worked out.

3. *The need for a planned approach*

This need for forethought and a planned approach to the career problems of highly qualified women, and the absence of this at present, is the third general finding of the occupational studies. It has become apparent, not that the problems raised by women's careers are insoluble, but that insufficient thought has been given to them.

There appears to be a general tendency on the part of employers to underestimate the career commitment of highly qualified women, who today are more likely than not to be lifetime workers. This leads, as the studies show, to using well-qualified women in jobs below their ability, to low morale and high turnover and to their exclusion from many opportunities and job rotations usually forming part of a career pattern at the top. Employers have grown used to the idea that an able young man is worth having even though he is likely to change employers, perhaps several times, before he settles down. One employer's loss is another's gain. The employer who loses a trained male graduate to another firm may well be able to replace him with another trained at the expense of a third firm. Where women are concerned employers are still inclined to assume, consciously or unconsciously, that maternity ends an able young woman's serious working career, and that if she leaves work for family reasons the loss is final and irrecoverable.

To this can be added the point just made that employers and, generally, management planners have not yet thought seriously about how to adapt the timetabling and techniques of recruitment planning and promotion to a situation in which women now provide many of the ablest candidates for high-level careers; women with a strong career commitment and a capacity for job performance in the same range as that of men, but with a different life-cycle and timetable of availability for work.

Career, Family and Sex Roles makes a double point in the light of the whole material of the PEP studies. On the one hand it is still through pioneering by individuals and by individual enterprise that many of the changes in family and working life and, generally, in sex roles which need to follow from the fact of women's careers can best come about, as they often have done in the past. But, on the other hand, these changes are too complex, with progress on one front dependent upon progress on another, to be left to individual enterprise alone. Overall planning and action are needed as well.

The occupational studies provide a substantial part of the justification for this point of view. The changes which they show to be needed to bring about the fuller use of women's abilities in senior jobs appear from the employer's point of view—or rather would do so if employers perceived them more clearly—in the same light as measures of industrial planning such as those required for the Industrial Training Act of 1964. It is clearly to employers' advantage that they should have a highly qualified work force and, generally, that responsible jobs should be filled by the people of the greatest ability. But, as with industrial planning, it may happen that individual employers see no advantage to themselves in pioneering the training and utilization of new sources of labour. It may happen, as it did in the past in many branches of industrial training and is now doing over bringing women into the field of selection for senior jobs, that the amount of training and other opportunities made available by enterprises become stabilized below the level ultimately in the employers' own interest. An overall authority will then have to step in (as suggested by the Industrial Training Act) to persuade, encourage or even compel employers to cross the threshold and do what their own ultimate interests require.

Some employers will take action themselves, once they are made clearly aware what it is practicable and economic for them to do and what they will gain by doing it; in the case of women's higher careers, this point about the need to inform employers is important. To persuade others to follow them may require more pressure. *Career, Family and Sex Roles* suggests a number of ways in which information might be disseminated and pressure be applied. But in both cases the intention is not to compel employers to do something which would be in the interests of others rather than in their own. From the employers' point of view, the message of the occupational studies is that the utilization of Britain's largest reserve of under-employed high-grade ability is likely to prove both practicable and profitable, and that what has stood in its way in the last few years is not some solid and permanent obstacle of difficulty and cost but thoughtlessness, tradition, and threshold difficulties of the kind which may hold people back from pioneering a new development but no longer count for much once the first steps have been taken.

It is of course true that questions about higher qualified women's, or any women's, careers cannot be settled on grounds of manpower planning and employers' interests alone. Wider considerations have to be taken into account about the family and the whole future pattern of living; about the future pattern of sex roles or the question of 'one-dimensional' versus 'multi-dimensional' roles. Considerations of these wider issues are explored in *Career, Family and Sex Roles*. The object of the occupational studies, however, was first and foremost to consider not this wider context, but what problems arise in the whole process of women's high-level careers: problems of availability, of recruitment, promotion and job performance. The task for the occupational studies was to identify these problems and see whether they could be economically solved. The answer is clearly in the affirmative; they can.

Part One

WOMEN IN TWO LARGE COMPANIES

Chapter I
REPORT ON COMPANIES A AND B

1. *Structure and organization*

In view of the desire on the part of both companies to remain anonymous, it has not been possible to look at their structure and organization in the same way as those of the BBC or the Civil Service. However, some brief description is necessary, so that the careers and experience both of men and women can be seen against an organizational background.

Company A is a large international organization with a number of departments and divisions. These are involved in manufacturing, marketing, sales, distribution, market research, scientific research, advertising, personnel, finance and all the other service departments which go to make up a large organization.

Company B is also a large company with international links, but it is a much more directly science-based organization. It too has manufacturing, marketing, sales, distribution, market research, advertising, personnel and finance departments, but its scientific research department has a much greater proportion of its staff than in the case of Company A. Company B is not as large or diversified as Company A, and the links between the different departments and the centre are much closer than those in Company A.

2. *Where the senior women are in Companies A and B*

This analysis can only be given in fairly broad terms, since greater detail would identify the companies.

In Company A, women account for approximately 3 per cent of all managers—those members of staff holding managerial responsibility and earning over £2,000 a year. Company A divides its managers into three categories—senior, middle and junior managers. Women account for less than 1 per cent of managers at the most senior level, 1·6 per cent of middle managers, and 3·3 per cent of the junior managers.

Some broad analysis can be made of where the women are in the company. In the largest area of the company—the operational side, which is mainly concerned with manufacturing and marketing—women account for only 2 per cent of all managers. Within this group there are some significant variations. For example, there is a much higher proportion of women among the managers in the market research and advertising departments than in the marketing departments. In the scientific research department, women account for 5 per cent of the managers, and in certain service departments in the head office, for example, in personnel departments, the proportion of women managers is even greater. However, there are certain areas of the business where women managers do not exist at all.

In Company B, the picture is not quite so clear, since there is not the straightforward division of senior staff into managers and non-managers as there is in Company A. There is a high proportion of senior staff who have great responsibility, but are not called managers in Company B, although it is possible that they would have this title if they worked for Company A.

Of the top management in Company B—the Executive grade—3 per cent are women. This Executive grade covers all areas of the company—manufacturing, marketing, personnel and so on, and including scientific research. Since most of the women interviewed were involved in scientific research, some analysis of their performance was thought to be useful. The scientific grades are divided into Senior Scientific Officer 1, Senior Scientific Officer 2, Scientific Officer, and Junior Scientific Officer. The proportion of women on each of these grades is as follows: Senior Scientific Officer 1: approximately 10 per cent; Senior Scientific Officer 2: approximately 10 per cent; Scientific Officer: approximately 11 per cent; Junior Scientific Officer: nearly 50 per cent. Some of the scientists on the top scientific grade are also classified as managers. Over a third of the SSO 1 men are managers and half the SSO 1 women are managers. However, the figures here are very small and not really statistically significant.

What emerges from all the figures for both companies is that top women are in a distinct minority. It is also clear from the figures that the higher up the management scale, the smaller the proportion of women. This report will look at the evidence and analyse the reasons for this poor performance of women in the management structure of two large companies.

3. *Comparison of men and women managers in Company A*

Company A made some information available on a sample of its managers—96 men and 96 women. This represented a 100 per cent sample of the women managers at the time, and a random sample of the same number of men managers. The information made available consisted of date of birth, date of entry to the company, date at which management status was achieved and date of appointment to present job. It also showed post at entry, post when management status was achieved, and present post. The information did not include details of department, so that movement within the organization was impossible to judge. It also gave no real indication of the level of seniority reached, either by salary level or job description. However, it was possible to use the information to classify the entry gates of the managers. These fell into four main categories, but the present posts held were impossible to classify. This information is perhaps better illustrated by the figures already given on the proportion of women in top, middle and junior management.

The first piece of information was a comparison of the dates of birth of the men and women (Table 1). This table shows that the men

TABLE 1 *Year of birth (numbers)*

	Women	Men
1901–10	4	8
1911–20	16	15
1921–30	26	29
1931–40	34	31
1941–50	16	13
Total	96	96

tend to be slightly older than the women, but not very significantly. What is most interesting is that the spread of age among both men and women is very similar. There is no gap among the women where the women who have dropped out for domestic reasons might have been. It is in the total numbers that this gap is reflected—in the fact that only 3 per cent of managers are women.

The second table shows the entry gates of men and women. These entry gates were classified into four categories:

1. coming in with some expertise already established as a result of specialist training or experience in other work—often shown by fact that first post a management appointment;
2. coming in with some expertise or training, but with no definite indication that would achieve management status;

3. coming in as a trainee—usually of graduate calibre;
4. no qualifications for management. This group includes secretaries who may have had some training or even have been graduates, but would not normally be regarded as potential managers.

Table 2 shows quite clearly that more women than men were recruited with an expertise—and probably for their expertise. Far fewer women came in as totally unqualified for management, and most of the women falling into Category 4 were in fact secretaries, some of whom may well have been graduates before the war. It is interesting, too, that a slightly larger proportion of women than men came in as trainees, particularly since one of the criticisms of women in trainee schemes, whether run by the company as a whole or by individual departments, is that there is no point in training women because they leave. The figures appear to show that the opposite may be true.

TABLE 2 *Entry gates (numbers)*

Category	Women	Men
1	39	25
2	20	27
3	18	13
4	19	31
Total	96	96

Table 3 looks at the length of time between the managers' first appointment to the company and their first management appointment. This information is not surprising in view of the fact that the women who became managers were generally better initially qualified than their male counterparts. This would mean that they were likely to take less time to achieve management status, if they were going to achieve it, than the large proportion of men plodding up the ladder from the humble beginnings of errand boy or junior clerk. There were no women managers who had come in as the equivalent of errand boy. Although some of the men had taken a long time to reach management status, they had eventually reached it, and in many cases must have been very highly motivated. Thirty-three men had taken more than ten years to achieve management status in comparison with only 17 women. It looks as though women who enter on a very junior level have had neither the opportunities nor the motivation to move into management in the past.

TABLE 3 *Length of time between first appointment and management appointment (numbers)*

Years	Women	Men
0	29	16
1–5	33	27
6–10	14	17
11–15	5	7
16–20	7	9
21–25	3	9
26–30	1	6
31–35	1	0
35–40	0	2
Total	93[1]	93[2]

[1] Numbers only add up to 93 because 3 women are still in management training and have not yet been appointed to their first management post.

[2] Numbers only add up to 93 because 2 men have had broken careers in Company A and 1 man is still in management training.

Table 4 relates the information given in the last two tables. This table shows what might be expected—that women because of their greater expertise reached management status more quickly than men. However, it must be remembered that these figures show only what has happened to managers. There is no evidence to suggest whether there are less qualified women in Company A, who, had they been men, would have had the opportunities that some of the men in Categories 2 and 4 have had. As it is, on the evidence of these figures, the women appear to be a much better qualified group than the men, This, of course, only takes into consideration paper qualifications and acquired expertise, and does not consider the imponderable qualities of managerial and administrative ability.

Table 5 shows entry gate by date of birth. Again, it shows what might be expected—that it is the older men and women managers who came in on Category 4, and that it appears to be increasingly difficult for men or women to work their way up. It could be that there are a number of potential managers in the younger age groups moving up the ladder who are not yet shown statistically, but it appears unlikely that they are a significant number. The table also shows that the younger age groups of both men and women are

TABLE 4 *Entry gates by length of time between first appointment and management appointment*

WOMEN

		Entry gates			
Years	Numbers	1	2	3	4
0	29	29	0	0	0
1–5	33	9	8	14	2
6–10	14	1	8	0	5
11–15	5	0	1	1	3
16–20	7	0	2	0	5
21–25	3	0	0	0	3
26–30	1	0	0	0	1
31–35	1	0	1	0	0
36–40	0	0	0	0	0
	93				

MEN

		Entry gates			
Years	Numbers	1	2	3	4
0	16	16	0	0	0
1–5	27	5	12	9	1
6–10	17	2	7	2	6
11–15	7	0	4	0	3
16–20	9	1	2	1	5
21–25	9	0	0	0	9
26–30	6	1	1	0	4
31–35	0	0	0	0	0
36–40	2	0	1	0	1
	93				

better qualified than the older age groups. About 40 per cent of the women managers are under 38 and came in as experts or as graduate trainees. The proportion of men falling into the same category is, however, only about 30 per cent. The older men are less well qualified than the older women.

The figures in Table 6, showing the age at which the managers achieved management status, are extremely interesting. The bulk of the women—a third—reached management status in their early thirties. It looks as if either their management status was delayed until it seemed clear that they were going to stay with the firm, or that they came to the firm having achieved management status elsewhere. The number of women under 24 reaching management status is also striking—twice the number of men in the same age group. It is interesting that there are more men in the 25–29 age group than women. It could be interpreted as showing that if women do not achieve management status in their early twenties, they may well be less persistent than the men, and may leave. It is also possible that the relatively fewer women in this age group reflect the fact that a number of potential or actual women managers do in fact leave at this time for domestic reasons. However, the pattern shows that 63 of the women and 65 of the men achieved managerial status between the ages of 25 and 39, with women bunching in the middle of this age group, and the men tending to bunch a little more at the younger end of this age group.

TABLE 5 *Entry gates by date of birth*

WOMEN

	Date of birth				
	1901–10	1911–20	1921–30	1931–40	1941–50
1	2	3	8	20	6
2	0	5	9	6	0
3	0	0	3	5	10
4	2	8	6	3	0
Totals	4	16	26	34	16

MEN

	Date of birth				
	1901–10	1911–20	1921–30	1931–40	1941–50
1	1	1	4	15	4
2	3	5	9	7	3
3	1	0	1	5	6
4	3	9	15	4	0
Totals	8	15	29	31	13

The main conclusion to be drawn from these figures in conjunction with the overall figures is that the women managers, who are more highly qualified and have taken less time on the whole than the men to achieve management status, are nevertheless concentrated in the most junior levels of management. This is not due to their being younger, because it has been shown that the age distribution of both men and women is very similar. It is clearly nothing to do with paper qualifications or expertise, since the women are better qualified and have greater expertise on entry. It must be assumed that men have more senior management status than women in more cases because they are regarded as possessing characteristics desirable for managers other than qualifications and expertise. One important question needs to be asked. Are the women over-qualified for the work they are doing? If they are, this could account for some of the frustration shown in some of the interviews in this report, and it could mean that Company A is not fully exploiting its potential management resources.

TABLE 6 *Age of achieving management status* (*numbers*)

	Women	Men
20–24	10	5
25–29	17	26
30–34	31	19
35–39	15	20
40–44	14	12
45–49	4	6
50–54	2	5
55–60	0	1
	93[1]	94[2]

[1] The total is 93 because 3 women are still in management training.

[2] The total is 94 because 1 man is still in management training and 1 man had a broken career in which it was impossible to assess the age at which he achieved management status. The other man with a broken career achieved management status on his return to company A.

There is one other point of considerable interest, and that is what is going to happen to the highly qualified management trainee or graduate women who have achieved management status so young—between the ages of 20 and 24. It would appear to be in the interests of Company A to do all it could to keep these women, who could be the top management of the future in view of their strikingly successful start. There are a number of comments on their prospects in this report. It could be that if this type of woman recruit leaves the company there is very little prospect for women managers rising above their relatively lowly status, since it has been shown by the figures in this section that qualifications and expertise alone in no way guarantee a high degree of career success.

4. *Characteristics of women interviewed in Company A*

The women interviewed in Company A were selected to represent the spread of women in the organization as a whole, by age, marital status, experience and qualifications. Twenty women at present working in the organization and 1 former senior woman manager were interviewed. This was a sample of approximately 20 per cent of the women managers in the organization. Three of the 5 women senior managers were interviewed.

Four of the women came from the Advertising Department, 4 from the Market Research Department, 3 from personnel divisions or departments, 4 from service divisions of Head Office and 5 from marketing or operating companies. The woman who left had been a senior manager in personnel.

Seven of the women were under 30, 12 were between 30 and 50, and 1 was over 50.

Five of the women—all under 30—had entered the organization as graduate management trainees. The other 15 had entered in a variety of ways, reflecting the characteristics of the group as a whole. Most of them had joined with specialist qualifications which they had acquired before coming to the company. Three of the women had been recruited as a type of graduate trainee before the management trainee scheme had been opened to women. It would be fair to say that the majority of the women interviewed had come to the company bringing with them a fair degree of expertise, and were not fresh from university. Some further analysis of the extent to which this was true of women managers as a whole has been written up in the section on the general characteristics of the group.

Nine of the women were single, 2 were divorced with children and 1 was divorced without children, 6 were married without children and 2 were married with children.

Of the 7 women under 30, 5 were married (of whom 1 had a child), and 2 were single.

5. *Characteristics of women interviewed in Company B*

All the 14 women interviewed in Company B were graduate scientists. Ten of them were between the ages of 35 and 50, 1 was over 50 and 3 were in their twenties. All except one, who was a personnel officer, were engaged in work of a scientific nature. Two of them had an executive grade, 4 were classed as managers, 5 were Senior Scientific Officers with greater or lesser degrees of managerial responsibility, while the 3 women in their twenties were Junior Scientific Officers.

Of the 11 women over 35, 9 were single, 1 was married without children and 1 was married with children. Of the 3 younger women, 2 were single and 1 was married without children.

6. *Promotion procedure in Company A*

Most management jobs over a certain level have to be notified centrally, and the job description is circulated to all the departments asking for names to be put forward. In addition, all managers have annual interviews and if it is considered that they are ready for promotion their names are put on a list, which is consulted when vacancies arise. From these two sources, a long list of possible candidates is sent to the department concerned which will then decide whom to interview. It is very unusual for a management job to be advertised internally and applications invited. It is not so unusual for management jobs to be advertised externally or for management selection companies to be used, but the general policy of the company has always been promotion from within the organization.

There is ideally some kind of career planning, but this seems to apply only to the really high-fliers who are picked out and sent on specialized courses, and some attempt is made to give them the breadth of experience which Company A, like Company B, regards as desirable in top management. Company A, perhaps because of its greater size and complexity, has proportionately a slightly greater number of women with managerial functions than Company B, and senior women are more evenly spread around the organization; nevertheless, there are still areas which are virtually closed to women. The women interviewed complained that there seemed to be little thought given to their future career prospects and that their promotion often seemed to take place on an ad hoc basis, whereas they saw their male contemporaries being singled out and talent-spotted.

It was interesting to note that, as in Company B, some of the most successful women had carved out a little niche of expertise for themselves as the part of the organization in which they were working expanded. It was the rare woman who had actually reached her present position by directly competing head-on with men at every stage of her career. The women tended to have done well in the most quickly expanding parts of the organization or in little corners where they were the only people with a particular skill or specialized knowledge. As in Company B they tended to do less well in the sales, marketing and commercial areas and in the 'general management' area.

In Company A, women have done well mainly in the more specialized areas—in market research, advertising, personnel and to perhaps a more limited degree as scientists and accountants. In all these areas it is possible for them to be judged first on their expertise and secondly on their managerial ability. However, it is by showing marked ability in their speciality that they are considered for managerial posts.

It is also interesting to note that all these areas of the business are to some extent service areas, in that they are not on the whole regarded as being in the mainstream of profit making. It is still extremely difficult for a woman to be considered suitable for a job above a certain level in the operating companies of the organization, and in fact it is only in recent years that women have been allowed into the main marketing areas of the operating companies in positions of any responsibility.

The common objections to women in management jobs in the marketing areas of the business were discussed with both men and women. The women believed that they were not considered suitable because men thought that they would not make good salesmen. They said that if they had no selling experience they could not be considered for senior marketing jobs, and therefore they could not climb up the promotion ladder in that area of the business. Women also argued about the general acceptance of the marketing areas as 'mainstream'. A number of them thought that marketing was as specialized as market research or advertising.

However, one of the main arguments put forward against the employment of women in 'general management', which many of the women pointed out was in fact 'marketing', was that continuity was essential and that women could not be relied upon to stay. The argument went as follows: young men coming in on the management trainee scheme often went into one of the marketing companies. Only a small number of the marketing companies would take young women trainees, and even if they did, they did not give them the same opportunities for promotion as they gave the young men. The reason for this was that they did not expect them to stay. If the point was made that many young men left the organization too, then the answer was that the young women were more likely to leave than the young men. What about the women who did not leave? What chance did they have for getting on in the marketing field? The answer appeared to be that by the time it seemed clear that they were not going to leave, they did not have the necessary experience to take jobs of higher management in marketing companies.

The women interviewed concluded that the not inconsiderable turnover of young men in the company was regarded as a fact of life, while the turnover of young women was regarded as proof of the hypothesis that most young women were going to leave in any case. They thought that top management felt it worth training and promoting young men in the hope that they would not leave and in the knowledge that they would contribute something to the company while they were there. On the other hand the women thought that top management did not see any point in doing the same for them, since they had no hope that they would stay, in spite of evidence to the contrary, and did not recognize that the contribution made by young women while they were there could be as good as, if not better than that of the young men.

7. *How Company A women viewed their job opportunities and careers*

There was a marked difference in attitude between the senior women, the middle management women, and the women under 30.

The senior women had had to fight hard to get where they were, and had achieved their positions through what appeared to be a mixture of sheer excellence, great staying power, considerable expertise in their jobs, and the fact that certain men in key positions had been prepared to fight for their promotion. They all said that it was much easier to be at the top than to get to the top, and that in fact they enjoyed enormous advantages over their male counterparts. Being in such a minority they were bound to be noticed more, they usually had a special place in any meeting and in a way they were regarded as showpieces. They also felt that resentment of them once they had reached the position they had reached was minimal. 'It is only the men who are inadequate at their jobs who are resentful of you, and will try to prevent you going any further. The men who are secure and good in their jobs will help you. And when you reach my position, most of the men are very good.'

The middle management women were more subject to what they considered to be discrimination against them in the promotion race. Most of them thought that if they had been men they would certainly have moved faster within the organization, if not further. They took it for granted that women would be slower getting off the mark than men. 'They're waiting to see if you're going to stay with them. It's fair in a way, but it does mean that the men overtake you, and you've got a lot of catching up to do.'

The younger women under 30 were much less philosophical about their job prospects. These young women had either come in as management trainees or with an expertise. They saw young men overtaking them and passing them by, and could find no reason for it other than the fact that they were women.

'They simply should not take on women as management trainees if they are not going to give us the same opportunities.' This comment by one girl was typical of the feeling among the young women. They felt that the promises of the selectors had not been kept. They also felt that the purpose of the scheme which was to recruit the future top management of the organization was not being adhered to in the case of women. They very much resented being treated as assistants, or in some way inferior to young men. They were much more confident of their own abilities than the older women; they were much more ambitious and much more determined. Nevertheless, there was a general feeling that the fight to get on in the organization was tougher for women than it ought to be, and that there were a large number of cards stacked against them. They seemed more prepared than the older women to fight their way out of the areas where women had traditionally done well, and to compete directly with the men. In general, they gave the impression of being a lot more competitive than the older women. The importance of these attitudes and the implications for future policy will be examined in greater detail in a further section.

One fairly senior woman looking at the job opportunities for the younger women said this:

> 'I think that success is coming younger to everyone today—if at all. If you're good, you're not stopped. My contemporaries and I were blocked for a good ten years, and then we got on because our field expanded so much. The women before us came in as secretaries. Ours was the first generation of women graduates to come into business from university. We were a pioneer group who had to sell ourselves as businesswomen. There had been a tremendous image of women in business as dragons and bitches. I think we had

to overcome this—get men on our side. It's much easier for young women today.'

This image of women in business was referred to by a number of women. They felt that women were much less readily accepted in the business world than in other traditional women's occupations. However, this lack of acceptance was not only confined to men, in their view. One senior woman said that it permeated the whole of our society, and that the thought that women and business did not go together was one of the myths of British life. She thought that it definitely militated against women's considering a career in business —that business was in some way 'not ladylike'.

> 'I think it dates right back to early conditioning. They feel it's not their world. They come to us diffident and it takes a long time to get rid of this diffidence. I think they don't always make maximum use of their talent because they're all tied up inside—they impose conditions on themselves. Their mothers are very important. Even if they're ambitious for their daughters, they're not ambitious in this kind of way. They say that business is not for their daughters.'

8. *Career patterns in Company B*

The majority of women interviewed had spent most of their working lives with Company B, and a high proportion had never worked elsewhere. This was in marked contrast with Company A.

Company B was often cited as a firm with a record for paternalism and concern for its employees, and it was thought that this bred loyalty for the firm, particularly in the 35-plus age group. This was felt less strongly among the younger age groups, for a number of reasons. First, since there was such stability of employment among the 35-plus age group there were clearly fewer opportunities for promotion. As one woman put it: 'There is just a big wall of people in senior positions, all of whom are in their forties. A young man or woman looks at that and they know they've got to leave if they want to get anywhere.'

Secondly, this big wall of people in their forties is there because of the expansion in scientific research and commercial activities in the years immediately following the war and in the 1950s. This meant that people in their twenties were promoted very quickly as their jobs and projects expanded. One departmental head said 'At 19, I was doing work that no 19-year-old could possibly hope to do today.' This quick promotion also helped women, since if they were in on the ground floor of the expansions and were the only persons with the know-how in a certain field, given that they were scientifically equal to a man, then they too were given the opportunity to rise in the hierarchy. It is paradoxical that the prospects for a bright girl look far dimmer today than the achievements of her predecessors would indicate. To a large extent, career prospects for both men and women depend on the expansion of scientific research. In addition the organization has become bigger and more formally structured. The fluidity of the post-war situation in which empires rose has been placed under stricter control, and the whole promotion procedure has been rationalized.

9. *Promotion procedure in Company B*

A young scientist often comes into Company B as a Junior Scientific Officer, and can expect to remain as one for two or three years. His promotion will generally come when he has reached the top of his grade in terms of salary. Salary is linked fairly closely to age, so that it is possible for a young graduate of 22 to look forward and say 'I will probably be earning £2,000 at age 32.' After being promoted to Scientific Officer, he can expect to stay there for seven or eight years when he could be promoted to Senior Scientific Officer 2 and then to SSO 1. Promotion into posts with some managerial responsibility can take place at certain points along the line—laboratory head, section head, unit head, departmental head and perhaps a directorship. If he or she moves out of the research field, he moves into another similar grading system.

The company realized that it was not perhaps spotting all its potential managers and that the turnover rate in young scientists seemed to be rather high in certain areas. Four years ago, it developed a management development scheme, designed to recognize and encourage the future managers of the company. It has a central staffing panel, and departmental heads are asked to refer potential top managers to this committee, which will then endeavour to ensure that these people are given the breadth of experience within the company and its subsidiaries which would be desirable. Talent-spotting was company policy before the introduction of this scheme, but was much less rationalized.

Most of the present managers have had a wide variety of experience, though not all have scientific qualifications. Some have research experience, but this alone is not regarded as sufficient in a company which exists primarily to make a profit. It is regarded as desirable for a top manager to have had factory management, production or commercial experience. It is important to note that none of the women in senior positions in Company B had had factory management or commercial experience, and that no women had senior production experience.

The women interviewed were all working as scientists, and were mainly involved in scientific research. They tended to be specialists in narrow fields, from which they had not been offered the opportunity to break out. It must be stressed that, with one or two exceptions, they had never wanted to move out of these specialist areas, but when they were asked in connection with this survey about moving they felt that they would never be given the chance. All this means that the chances of promotion for these women is restricted to a relatively small pyramid, if so many areas within the company are closed to them. For a man, the traditional way up to senior management has been a zig-zagging course between different functional or geographical areas within the company and its associated companies. It is also considered desirable for potential top managers to have put in a spell overseas, or certainly to have moved around this country. Only one of the women interviewed had been abroad for the company, and then it had been on the basis of her considerable expertise; she had not played a managerial role. Only one or two of the women had moved around this country at all. Whether the others would have gone or not was irrelevant, since they had never been asked. 'It is always assumed that women won't move, so they never ask us. This means that we're never given opportunities to move out or up', said one senior woman.

As far as promotion in the research field is concerned, it is becoming more and more desirable to have a Ph.D. This clearly activates against women, who are less likely than men to stay on at university for a higher degree, according to Company B. They also felt that women Ph.D.s were less likely to go into industry than men Ph.D.s. They thought that women were thinking less in terms of a life-long career in which the greater the qualifications the higher the prospects, but much more in terms of finding an interesting job and good money before marriage and children. In other parts of the business, it is becoming increasingly desirable to have some kind of professional qualification.

In the areas where there is a growing emphasis on such qualifications as a Ph.D. it seems clear that men with Ph.D.s are likely to be promoted more quickly than men and women without Ph.D.s. Since the assumption appears to be, particularly in research, that the future heads of section units and sections will have Ph.D.s, and women tend not to have Ph.D.s, the prospects for women scientists look less rosy than they have done even up to now, particularly since women cluster in the research areas and opportunities in the other parts of the organization are limited. Even within the research area itself, opportunities for women are greater in some areas than in others. Women have done much better within the biological sciences than in the chemical sciences. This is in part related to the tradition that more women become biologists than chemists, and in part to the refusal by management to contemplate women occupying senior positions which have been held by certain key personnel in the past in areas of the organization predominantly concerned with the chemical sciences.

There is no doubt, in the minds of many of the men and women interviewed, that sheer male prejudice has held back a number of able young women from even being considered for junior management posts, particularly in the areas of the organization where women have in any case been accepted only on sufferance. They also feel that this prejudice has again prevented women from being accepted at all in certain male strongholds—particularly on the sales and commercial side. There seems to be a firm body of evidence to suggest that women are excluded quite deliberately from even the most junior posts in these areas simply because they are women. It is argued that women do not make good salesmen, that the customer or client does not like being sold to by a woman—even if the customer is a woman herself. It is held that women will not be prepared to travel around the country, get their hair wet, or have the necessary stamina to keep up with the job. It is further argued that without sales experience, it is not possible for a woman to gain the necessary experience to get on in the sales or commercial departments. These arguments were also heard in Company A, and perhaps it would be fair to regard them as widespread in industry.

Finally, it is interesting to note that very few women have been recommended for management development in the four years that the scheme has been operating, although a number of women have been on management courses. However, the scheme is still in its infancy.

Chapter II
WOMEN IN SENIOR POSTS

1. *How men see women working in top jobs*

In both companies there were reflections of the very different views held in general by men, ranging from the outright anti-feminist to the more liberally minded who felt that women were not getting a fair deal, and who had done all they could to help able women to gain promotion and recognition in the work they were doing. The older the man the more he was likely to feel that 'a woman's place is in the home', but not all the younger men were as liberal as the women interviewed thought they were, and open-mindedness about senior women seemed in the last resort to depend on the character traits of the men interviewed rather than on their age or their seniority.

In Company A, a senior man with long experience in personnel work summed up the feelings of a lot of men:

> 'A man will accept a woman as his secretary because it helps him to be complete. His secretary is his office wife. If she's wise enough to complement him, they'll make a good working team. She does his office housework for him and she's well down in the hierarchy. He objects to stability in himself because it leads to stagnation, but he needs stability elsewhere. He sees his secretaries come and go and thinks that all women come and go. He therefore thinks that women graduates will come and go and will not be stable. So therefore he thinks that he cannot entrust a job of any responsibility to her.'

He analysed further what men in the company felt about young women graduates:

> 'They don't promote women above the level of brand manager in the marketing companies because they think they're not going to stay. That's the reason they give, anyhow. Market research is a glorious excuse for getting rid of women. It's now regarded as a woman's field because there have been some outstanding women in it. We have tried hard to get a woman in here on a top level other than in market research, but they wouldn't have her.'

What were the reasons for the suspicion of women in senior positions?

> 'Women did themselves a great deal of harm in the inter-war years. They were real martinets—some of them. They subordinated all their womanly instincts and tried to start exactly where men started. It was all wrong.'

In Company A, a young man in a senior position was interviewed about women's prospects in the organization. His analysis of women's performance and prospects was devastating:

> 'A manager in a line management position must be an entrepreneur, and I don't know any woman in this organization who has these entrepreneurial qualities. You find them in little shops sometimes, but the girls who come in here are all too nice. I find that a lot of them lack personality—all a bit faceless. I look for individuals. The men working for me are all very marked individuals.'

He felt that women and business did not really go together:

> 'I reckon business is authoritarian. If you give people responsibility, they must get the job done. A lot of people talk about team spirit and co-operation, and women often get things done by coaxing. I don't think this is the way. I think it's very difficult to take a woman seriously. A man goes into a meeting determined to get something out of it. If I go into a meeting, something has got to happen at the end. Women can give nice little presentations, but they don't turn the knife—they don't leave the impression that they're going to make no concessions and that what they want must be done. I think women lack persistence and a competitive feeling. There are some men I'm scared of, but no women.'

He also felt that women were not sufficiently committed to their work and were not prepared to make sufficient sacrifices to their jobs, either in terms of time or emotion:

> 'Our life is very demanding. It's very difficult to combine marriage and the kind of work I'm doing, for example. How can you knock off at 5 and go home? I don't and very few of my managers do. How can you equate that with running a home? I came in on my holiday, and I called one of my managers back from Wales from his holiday. I wouldn't do that to a woman. I feel that a man is going to get something out of it—improve his career prospects—but it's no good for a woman. I think one strikes a different bargain with a woman. You don't ask for a 100 per cent effort from a girl,

and you don't give her a 100 per cent reward, either in money or in job terms.'

And finally, he talked about women and promotion:

'I wouldn't promote a woman above a certain level, even if she were better than a man, because (a) I wouldn't trust her to stay and (b) I don't think she could set the standards. I'll push for a lot of people in this company, and I'm willing to take risks in appointing people, but not for a girl.'

It is perhaps fortunate for the women in Company A that not many men were prepared to take such a strong line about them. But nevertheless, it is possible that this man was verbalizing some of the stereotyped views held about women. It was not usual to find all the stereotypes together in one person, but individual men certainly agreed with certain aspects of his views.

As far as the men in senior management in Company B were concerned, most women simply lacked 'managerial ability'. They had a high regard for their skill and expertise, but felt that most of them lacked an ability to organize other people:

'It might be irrational, but I think it's difficult to put women in charge of men. As I remember some of the women Ph.D.s we've had, I wouldn't put them in charge of anybody. I think they were not objective enough about people. They were swayed too easily by whether a chap was nice to them or not. They might have been marvellous scientists, but I would shudder to put them in charge of a group. I think it might be changing now, though.'

A senior man in a production department of Company B had this to say when comparing the prospects for men and women:

'When we recruit graduates we look for two qualities—management potential and scientific ability. Perhaps half our male intake are not top-notch scientists, but they've got drive and initiative—future top men perhaps. When I look at the girls we've employed in the last 17 years, there's only been one who's come in with real drive. Why do we pick girls at all? Purely on scientific ability. For certain jobs—a chemist say—we'd pick the man because we'd want him to go on production work—shifts and so on. But then for some other work, we'd pick a girl. If we're looking for people for lab. work and not to work on production then we'd pick a girl if we could, because she introduces some stability. A man is always trying to get on. You have to balance this against whether the girl is likely to stay either.'

Even senior men who were particularly well disposed towards women felt that the ability of women to organize or exercise managerial functions decreased as the size of the unit grew. They felt that women lacked the fundamental ability to organize large units without worrying what was going on at bench level. However, they thought that the company did not encourage or develop women with management potential. They thought that one of the factors which positively discouraged women from even considering the possibilities of moving up the ladder beyond a certain point was the extraordinary versatility that the company expected from its top management. They thought that women might worry about the degree of adaptability required.

In Company B, one senior man concerned with personnel said that his impression was that young men were more self-propelled than the young women. He thought that perhaps the shortage of good scientists meant that the young women were treated with kid gloves to persuade them to come to the company, that everything was done to help them when they joined—for example they were found somewhere to live—and that they did not have to exercise any initiative at all. He thought that this perhaps meant that the girls sat back and waited for the management to develop them, rather than show the initiative themselves. He believed that this applied to the employment of all women in the company. 'The girls are probably better than the existing job opportunities. But if they'd only come and see us, we'd move heaven and earth to do something for them if they were good enough.'

There seems to be the same vicious circle operating in Company B that has been found in other organizations. If the women do not show initiative in actively seeking promotion, they are overlooked, because initiative is a desirable quality in senior management. However, women who have agitated for better prospects or promotion or more equal treatment are branded, only too often it appears, as troublemakers.

One small example of this from Company B illustrates the point. This story was told by almost every interviewee, whether man or woman, and had clearly epitomized to most people the position of women within the organization. In common with many other organizations in Britain, Company B had a number of dining-rooms for staff. The most exclusive of these was the 'Executive Dining Room' which was reserved for members of staff who were on the Executive grade, all of whom were men. The trouble arose when eventually two women were put on the Executive grade, and appeared eligible for invitation to eat in the Executive Dining Room. The situation was further complicated by the fact that they had to be invited—mere membership of the grade was not sufficient qualification. After what seems to have been a great struggle, these two women were invited to eat in the Executive Dining Room. However, there are senior men who still find this breach so distasteful that they have not eaten there since the day a woman first set foot in it.

2. *How women see women in top jobs*

There was a significant difference in attitudes towards women in top jobs between the two companies and the BBC. The BBC women tended to think that women in senior positions were not very different from women further down the ladder, and that, on the whole, as long as they were aware of the dangers, they did not display any unpleasant or unfeminine characteristics. The women in the two companies were not so sure. They had the impression that women in industry had a tougher struggle to get to the top than women in the BBC, and that this perhaps affected them more. This senior woman scientist said:

> 'I don't think women are very good at being powerful. It could come with time and tradition. I think women who become top women don't have the ability to lead other women. I've often thought how glad I am to work with a man. Women can be very irritable, especially at the menopause. I feel sometimes that I am—that I really must take myself in hand. Many women when they've got two jobs—house and shopping as well—get very physically tired. Many men here go home to a lovely atmosphere and the meal cooked. It must be heavenly.'

It is quite clear that characteristics which are acceptable in a man are not so acceptable in a woman, and it is not only the men who dislike what they see as ruthless women displaying unfeminine ambition. This woman scientist was not too keen on them either:

> 'The forceful women in the company have gone far. There are a lot of people here who would rather not cross them. And of course they get what they want—more lab. space or cupboards and so on. Then it's reflected in morale—the youngsters in our lab. don't see why they shouldn't have new cupboards either. I think people should be judged more in scientific ability and not by their ability to make themselves and the issue unpleasant. If they want something, some women can be quite ruthless in getting it—or taking it.'

The characteristics of concern with detail, attention to minutiae, and meticulousness were generally attributed to women by women in both companies. In Company B, where most of the women were working as active scientists, these were felt to be positive characteristics rather than negative, although some women saw the negative side particularly when the woman was promoted to more managerial work:

> 'When a woman has power, I think that her critical faculty tends to make her hard on people under her—more nagging than a man. The feminine concern with detail is not so good then. A man tends to see the overall thing and doesn't see the adjuncts. He sees a large issue large. A woman might make a mountain out of a molehill.'

In common with most of the other women scientists interviewed she felt that women were better at bench level than men, and most of the men interviewed agreed.

One woman scientist had this to say about women's characteristics:

> 'I think that some of the negative characteristics of women can be an advantage in some fields. I feel that most of the women I'm in contact with have a tendency to be more meticulous and more scrupulous about details. Men are less scrupulous because they don't think something is important—but this can get out of hand. I think that the difficulty with being so meticulous is that you pay so much attention to detail that if you're not careful you can't see the wood for the trees.'

She had some interesting things to say about her fellow women scientists in direct contrast to a former speaker:

> 'I think the women here need more personality. Quite a number of my colleagues here are quite retiring people. Perhaps the scientific field is not representative. Perhaps my colleagues have got on in spite of their personalities—because of their experience. They've been here a long time and acquired experience and know-how which is not readily come by. If they came in from outside, perhaps they would have to have powerful personalities.'

In fact, a number of women felt that the women in Company B lacked drive and the necessary aggression to get on, as well as the desire to take responsibility. Most of the women appeared to be dedicated scientists whose work was very important to them. They were so involved in what was going on that some of them were reluctant to relinquish their actual scientific research. It was quite clear that there were many men in the same position, who simply were totally involved in their research and did not wish to have too much managerial responsibility. The women thought that men would be more impelled to seek promotion for financial reasons and because of prompting from their wives.

The modesty and lack of ambition of the women in Company B in comparison with the men was summed up by this woman:

> 'I think scientifically I've gone as far as I can. I realize my limitations. Men who are higher up than I am are in broader fields. A person in that position has to have more personality than I have. They often have the ability to say something even if they don't know the answer—something plausible will come out. Possibly men are better at covering up their weaknesses and inadequacies than women. They rarely admit they're in the wrong. They're very quick to grasp the salient points, and they have the ability to sift them.'

One woman expressed a somewhat uncharitable view of women in senior positions:

> 'I think women tend to whine a bit about their work—and they obviously feel things so personally. I think some of them tend to flap like wet hens when something goes wrong, which doesn't inspire confidence. Men find it irritating, and if they can avoid it, they do. I think the top management feels that there's a lot of the firm's money tied up in a really responsible job and that women just aren't as competent as men at really big jobs.'

One woman who had not come up through the company thought that women in Company B tended to be brow-beaten by the competitive atmosphere at the top, and that they were inclined to be more deferential towards top management than she was. However, it seemed to her that too much was made of the differences between the sexes:

> 'I've seen men whom I would call bitchy and petty, and I've worked with men who were over-concerned with detail. I'm not convinced that there are typical male and female characteristics.'

In general, the women in Company B seemed to divide into two distinct types—the unassuming, modest and essentially rather retiring type, and the rather more outgoing and ambitious type. However, this was also true of the men interviewed. Company B gave a rather gentlemanly impression, and there were clearly patterns of behaviour expected from its staff. There were things which were simply 'not done' and outright ambition in women appeared to be one. As one woman said: 'It's considered a bit off to actually ask what one's career prospects are.'

On the whole the Company B women appeared to be less extrovert and ambitious than the Company A women. It would be very difficult to say whether this was because they were scientists, because they felt that there was no point in being ambitious, or because of the kind of hierarchy in which they found themselves.

Women in both companies stressed that women were much less likely than men to engage in internal politics, especially for their own advancement. Some of the women were critical of what they considered to be unnecessary manœuvring on the part of some men:

> 'So much of our work is spread through so many sections that it is essential for us to cooperate. One very ambitious person can disrupt the whole team, if he's not objective about his work. Some men will employ political manœuvres to get on. Because we work together so much, we have ample opportunities for stabbing each other in the back.'

In Company A, one of the problems of women in authority in industry was clearly to avoid being more masculine than the men. They felt that women had had a harder fight to be accepted in industry than in either the BBC or as scientists, particularly in traditional managerial positions with other people working for them. They agreed that a scientist or a radio or television producer could be judged on individual ability and not so much on how good she was at managing other people: This senior woman saw the pitfalls awaiting women in industry:

> 'I think that people in authority can be either authoritarian or permissive, and the authoritarian line doesn't go very well with women. It *can* be successful, but I think that women should persuade rather than dictate. Men have an easier approach—but authority tends to produce the extremes in women. They find it difficult to be relaxed. Women have had to fight so hard that they tend to be less relaxed, more anxious, more rigid.'

It was striking how many of the women interviewed in Company A stressed the importance for senior women to be feminine, and many of them clearly went to great lengths to emphasize their femininity:

> 'I'm wearing a red dress today—and I usually wear bright colours. It's so miserable just looking at all those grey suits in the dining-room. They like it too—say I cheer the place up. And it means that I'm noticed, which I wouldn't be if I were wearing a grey suit too.'

And a number of women thought that if a woman did not underplay her femininity she probably stood a better chance of being accepted in the man's world of work in which she had to operate:

> 'Because I'm not unattractive, people are more inclined to come and see me and say: "Can you help me out?" Men like working with a woman providing she is feminine and not a masculine type. If I tried to act more like a man it would do more harm than good.'

Several women in both organizations thought that women were often not as successful in their careers as they ought to be because they simply did not know how to treat men: as this woman in Company B thought:

> 'I think that women still think too much about equal rights and not enough about how to handle men. I think the future for women lies in learning how to act as human beings rather than women. I think they must learn not to stand on male vanities. I've thundered at a man in the past—but now I don't. I've learnt that it doesn't pay to battle any more.'

Another senior woman in Company A thought that women often acted before they thought out a strategy:

> 'I think some women do not work out how they can convince people that they should have something they want. Some women go rushing along like a bull in a china shop, and demand their rights. I think that women must learn to treat men as individuals and not as men.'

In general, most of the women thought that it was advisable for a woman who wanted to get on in an organization to avoid direct clashes with men, and that if this meant opting out of certain avenues of self-advancement it was just unfortunate.

3. *Difficulties encountered by women in senior posts*

The difficulties which the women encountered in both companies ranged from meeting downright prejudice and exclusion to much more subtle irritations. All the women interviewed felt, like their BBC counterparts, that women were under much closer scrutiny at all stages in their careers than their male colleagues:

> 'The management look at women a lot more closely. A woman has to do a job better than any man. She has to prove that she can do it. Until they were sure that I could do my job, they watched

me much more carefully than they would have watched any man. I know they've given jobs to men and they haven't been at all sure they could do it.'

These remarks from a woman manager in Company A were echoed almost exactly by a scientist in Company B:

'A chap is all right in a job until he has proved himself unacceptable, but a woman is not all right until she has proved herself acceptable.'

And this type of comment was heard time and again in interviews in both companies.

There were certain difficulties mentioned by women in Company A which were heard far less often in Company B, but this was largely due to the different types of work the women were doing. Company A's women worked far more in departments or divisions where senior people had contact with 'clients' or 'customers' or other outsiders of some kind. Most of the women in Company B did not move in work circles where contact with outsiders was general. Research scientists on the whole do not go to business lunches.

The Company A women resented very much the thought, uppermost in many of their minds, that they had not been promoted to certain positions because they would then have to take people out to lunch and 'the client wouldn't like it'. Again this phrase was heard in numerous interviews in Company A, both by men and women. There seems to be a marked reluctance on the part of certain businessmen to welcome the idea of talking business with women at all, and certainly not over a lunch, drink or other semi-social occasion, according to many of the interviewees.

One woman said:

'As a whole, I think men don't know how to treat women in this kind of situation, and some women don't know how to behave. I think men have built up a kind of means of communication on a social level. Men among men have their own jokes and way of discussing things. If women join in they either sound vulgar or too masculine.'

Some women felt that men can be very rude and unpleasant to them in a way that they would never be to another man, and most of the women interviewed had some story to tell of having been snubbed or slighted:

'There was one meeting, at which I had done a great deal of work.

> The Chairman of the meeting asked all the men to have a drink and ignored me.'

This outright resentment was commented on by another senior woman:

> 'I've found any trouble I've had has been from the inefficient men. Any man who is efficient and confident in his job has no problem with women. As I've gone higher up the ladder my progress has been easier. I find that I'm more readily accepted the higher I go.'

The women in both companies also thought that they were often not considered for jobs which involved any travelling, particularly if the job meant going to a subsidiary in the north of England, which was thought to be much more anti-women in positions of responsibility than the more enlightened south. However, Company B women seemed to come up against this kind of male prejudice less than the Company A women. They thought that this was perhaps because women were more likely to be accepted as scientists and therefore as experts, than as 'managers'. The women in Company A complained that they were thought to be secretaries or certainly in some junior capacity if they were accompanied by a man.

It was pointed out that there were often no facilities for women managers in certain subsidiaries, particularly in factories, and some women spoke of the difficulties they met when they had to eat with the managers they had gone to see, since they were not allowed in the exclusively male 'mess'.

However, one senior woman in Company A had reached the somewhat bizarre situation of having been sent abroad more or less continuously for a year or so. The organization was at first reluctant to let her go to the East End of London on her own, but within a few months, she was travelling all over the world representing the company. She usually travelled with a man, but not always. She found that in the end, she had to ask for some time at home, since she found that her private life was disappearing.

The traditional areas in which women were not accepted also caused some difficulties to women, if they happened to stray into this territory. One woman scientist said:

> 'I had to go to a sales conference, and on one evening of the week-end, they have a big dinner. I was astonished when the Sales Manager asked me what I was going to do that evening, because I couldn't come to the dinner. So I had to go off and have dinner on my own, while all the men went to their big dinner. I lecture

these people on my subject, and we shall continue to send a woman, and it will just have to change.'

There was, in fact, a general feeling by both men and women in the two organizations that it was a man's world, and that the women who had really achieved something had come to terms with this man's world. The main difficulty for the women seemed to be how to get a good foothold in the man's world, because it seemed that once they had done this, and proved their ability, they were then treated as something special. But for most women the difficulty seemed to be to get above a certain level. Money was not considered a handicap. In fact, in both companies equal pay has operated for some time, and job for job the women did not appear to be lagging behind the men. None of the women complained about their salaries and in fact, those who spoke in any detail about their earnings considered them to be good.

There was one other rather curious difficulty that some women came up against, and this was that they were perhaps too good at their jobs. This meant that their superiors were very reluctant to part with them, and that their promotion would be blocked in this way. This case was cited in Company A:

> 'There was a job going—a very senior job—and there was a woman who was uniquely qualified. The Director said that they really couldn't spare her from the job she was in. I went off the deep end and said that he would never say that about a young man—no one's indispensable. Within a few weeks that woman was offered the job. I'm afraid that a man will hang on to a good woman rather longer than he would be allowed to hang on to a man.'

4. *Advantages of being a woman in senior posts*

Once a woman achieved promotion above a certain level, she frequently found that there were certain great advantages in being a woman. 'Once they've seen you they don't forget who you are.' This was a typical remark made by women in both companies, but more particularly in Company A, possibly because it was so much larger an organization. There were other advantages for senior women:

> 'I think women have the tremendous advantage that they can be honest. Very often I have been very conscious that I am being sounded out for the simple reason that I could say what I think. A man would think: "What does the old devil want me to say", but I have nothing to lose. I don't want to get on the Board. I

think women have quite a lot of power, because they have nothing to lose—no responsibilities. At worst, if I say the wrong thing, I stay where I am, but if I were a man with a wife and children, I'd have to keep thinking whether I was scoring a black or not.'

Another woman thought that perhaps the very fact that most women are not as ambitious as the most ambitious men could work in women's favour:

'I have an entrée to all the directors' offices. It would be much more difficult for a man on my level. There are one or two men around my age at about my level who have far less entrée than I have. Most men feel that I am not a threat. I've deliberately opted for a different role from them.'

A number of very senior women thought that perhaps the fact that they had opted for different roles—or had been pushed into certain specializations—in fact made their position easier. In other words, if they had removed themselves, or been removed from direct competition with the most ambitious men, they found themselves playing a unique, almost complementary role as trusted confidantes:

'People tell me all sorts of things because I'm safe. They'll talk to me about their domestic problems—ask me to see their daughters and talk to them. I think that women can afford to be more honest. I'm not in the rat-race. Nobody could do my job, and they think I couldn't do theirs.'

There are undoubtedly advantages in being a senior woman, particularly, it appears, if she is in a job which does not compete too directly with men. Perhaps this is one of the reasons why the most successful women in the two companies were in specialized areas.

5. *Women and families*

Out of the 35 women interviewed in the two organizations, only 5 had children, and 1 of these was born shortly after the interview took place, so that the interviewee had no experience of actually working with the responsibility of a child. It was thought by all the women interviewed that it was very difficult to work in a business organization as a married woman with a child, and in fact, 2 of the 5 women were divorced, and 1 of these had not started working in any position of responsibility until after her divorce.

Therefore the evidence of women with children working in top jobs was very limited indeed from these two organizations. It was quite clear that no encouragement was given to women even to think of continuing to work after having a baby in either company, and this particular problem was particularly pertinent to the younger women interviewed, most of whom were married.

On an ad hoc basis, the situation was rather different. A number of men and women in positions of responsibility said that they would look very kindly on the idea of a woman who was experienced and good at her job who wanted to return to work. This was especially true in Company B, which was altogether a much more closely knit company in any case. However, it was stated quite categorically time and again that a scientist could not really expect to be out of scientific work for more than a year or two if she wanted to remain up to date on her reading and general scientific knowledge, because of the rate at which research was developing. This meant that it would be difficult for a woman to expect to come back into the organization even on the level at which she left, particularly if it had been a post of any responsibility.

In fact, in Company B, a number of cases were cited of former women employees who had left to have a baby, and had then returned as holiday reliefs. All this was done on an ad hoc basis and it was not official policy to encourage this. Several of the women interviewed spoke of certain of the women working for them whom they would willingly have back again after a year or two out, but their general feeling was that once a woman had left, even for such a short period, she could certainly forget any thought she might have had of promotion. The general feeling was that a woman with a baby should not have thoughts of promotion in any case.

A very definite impression was given in most of the interviews in Company B that, although individual married women were very good and highly responsible, married women on the whole were not as reliable and dedicated as their single counterparts, and that therefore they were less suited to be research scientists. It was stressed in many interviews that scientific research was a full-time job, and one in which one could not down tools at 5 o'clock and go home. It was most certainly not a job in which one could work shorter hours, since most experiments were designed to last a certain length of time and continuity of observation was essential. This seemed quite reasonable; 'If I'm growing a culture and I leave at 4 o'clock, it's very difficult for someone else to comment on the rate of growth after that.' However, there seemed to be no willingness on the part of most of the scientists interviewed even to consider that jobs could be redesigned to accommodate other timings, particularly in the sacrosanct field of scientific research. There was very much the feeling that this was the way it was done and this was the way it should be done. This feeling was not limited to scientific research only, by some people interviewed. As far as redesigning jobs was concerned, there was a general belief in both companies that they could do without married women so why should they think in terms of redesigning jobs for them. There were always enough young men and single women coming up who could quite easily take their places.

In both companies, it was accepted that most of the young women employed were going to leave and not come back and, particularly in Company B, this led to the tendency for the young women graduates to be used in some areas as 'a pair of hands'. The women complained that skilled technicians—without graduate qualifications—were becoming increasingly difficult to find, and that they were being used as rather superior technicians. They felt that this was being justified by the management by saying that they would leave in a couple of years in any case.

This allocation of jobs according to the length of stay expected could have some bearing on the actual length of stay. It is possible that if people feel frustrated or under-employed in their jobs they will not wish to remain in them. In Company A, some comparison was made between the length of stay of men and women graduates in the market research organization and in the scientific departments. It was found that the men and women in the market research department stayed for more or less the same length of time—an average of about five years—and that, perhaps even more interestingly, they left for the same types of reasons—for better jobs, money or prospects. On the other hand, the scientists stayed for a much shorter period of time—an average of about eighteen months—and more women left to get married or have babies. There are probably a number of reasons for these differences—some of which may be imponderable—but one of the explanations put forward by the market research department was that the women there were treated exactly the same as the men—their job opportunities were the same, they were given early responsibility if they were suitable, and it was made clear that they were wanted. Another explanation was that scientific laboratories are often situated in geographically inaccessible places, and that it is much more likely that a girl will marry someone who does not live or work near one of these places than that she will marry someone who does. On the other hand, market research departments or companies are usually in the centre of London, and the likelihood of a girl's future husband working in or near London is much greater.

One interesting sidelight on this emerged in the interviews. A few years ago there was the possibility of a whole department of Company A being moved from central London to the north of England. This was resisted by many employees for a number of reasons, but perhaps the most interesting reason was given by some of the young male managers who said that their wives would find it impossible to find work which suited their qualifications.

The comparison between the market research and scientific research departments has some moral for Company B, and in fact all companies which do not fully exploit the potential of young women. It seems unlikely that it is only women scientists who feel frustrated or who are not making full use of their capacities or training. There was evidence from Company A that in other, less enlightened, parts of the organization young women graduates were also regarded as useful information-finders or superior clerks who would leave as soon as the right man came along. And indeed, the point would be proved, since many did, simply because they felt that they would get no further in their jobs. It was pointed out by a number of young women interviewed that it was often assumed that a young woman was going to leave to get married and that was the only reason. They pointed to instances of young women who had indeed left on marriage, only to take their expensive training and acquired expertise and market value to another smaller firm which had no inbuilt prejudice against married women working and were prepared to 'give them a break'. Most of the younger women interviewed in both companies, apart from those lucky few working in the market research department of Company A, thought that management was only waiting to be proved right in not promoting them, when they left on marriage or to have a baby.

The degree of responsibility given and the responsibility felt by a person towards his or her job clearly have a lot to do with one another. A frequent complaint about married women, both by men and women in senior positions, was that they were late in the morning, did their shopping in the lunch hour and came back late, stayed away if their children were ill, possibly stayed away if their husband was ill, and generally did not show enough dedication to their jobs. However, on closer scrutiny it became clear that none of these married women was in a position of any responsibility, and the interviewees did not think that those few married women who held jobs of responsibility displayed these characteristics.

The married women interviewed in both companies felt that they were under even more scrutiny than the unmarried women. They thought in many cases that they were more scrupulous about the hours they kept and the time and energy they devoted to their jobs than any of their colleagues: 'I simply can't take any time off to take my daughter to the dentist, unless I take a holiday. But a man has much more freedom.'

The whole problem of whether or not a woman was going to stay with a firm is clearly one which militates against the promotion or even recruitment of women at all. One senior woman said this:

> 'My own view is that I would rather have a very good girl for five years than a mediocre man for ten years. I would feel that those five years had not been wasted. The point is that we can't make them all chairman of the company, and we're fortunate if marriage or children take some of them away from you. If you have a number of first class girls who have been with you for five years, one of them has to be promoted, and if some leave it's easier. If a girl wants to stay on after having a baby, I say that she can do what she likes as long as her work doesn't suffer, as long as she's a valuable person to us. But I really mean it—if a girl wants to be in the line for promotion she has to do all the things that may mean—courses at which she might have to stay a couple of weeks, staying away overnight.'

The young women interviewed were particularly bitter at the fact that young men shot ahead faster than they did, and seemed to be clearly being groomed for stardom. In Company A, they thought that the organization had not worked out what it wanted from its women management trainees.

> 'They say that they're going to treat us the same as the men, but half of the departments won't have women anyhow. Women tend to get pushed into one or two places which like having women and there they stay. They all seem to forget that you can't treat an intelligent woman like a moron and hope she won't notice. I say to people that I'm not going to have a baby for at least three years, and they say that I can't really be too sure of that. You'd think they'd never heard of the pill. I think an intelligent woman can be expected to work out her own life.'

They thought that the organization could only think in terms of their male trainees. In other words, if a young man left, it was extremely unlikely that he would ever be considered for a post in the organization again. The young women pointed out that this should not be applied to a young woman who left to have a baby. The organization tended to write off the girls who left in the same way that they wrote off the men trainees who left. However, some of the girls thought that this should not be so if the organization could bring itself to reconsider reemployment of women graduate trainees, perhaps after a certain time away from the organization.

The whole question of leaving and coming back, or working in a part-time or freelance capacity, was discussed with men and women in both companies. In Company A, it was generally felt that it was very difficult for anyone—whether a man or a woman—to leave a line management job, and expect to come back to it or a similar job even a year later. It was felt that no post could be held open for this length of time, and that, in any case, there were too many good people coming up behind who could not be frustrated. In a hierarchical structure, as is found in so many industrial organizations, there simply could not be gaps in the line of command.

One of the interesting aspects of this study was that apparently very few women had ever left either organization with a view to coming back, and very few had ever come back. It was simply not a thing that was 'done', and, with very few exceptions, it was not discussed, let alone encouraged. Most of the women interviewed, with the vocal exception of the young graduates, had never even considered it as a problem for women.

However, there was one area in Company A where the possibility of part-time or freelance work was a reality. This was in the market research department. There were a number of explanations put forward for this. First of all, the nature of the work makes it possible for it to be carried out on a 'package-deal' basis, in that one person can take a project away and work on it from beginning to end, without too much need for constant consultation and close collaboration with other people. Secondly, there is a shortage of really good people in this field, so that there is a need to exploit all resources fully. Thirdly, the management of this department facilitates and even encourages this type of working.

It was often pointed out in both companies that management was not always as far-thinking as it might be in considering how a job could be designed to fit in with an individual, and how this could be of benefit to the organization. Senior men and women in both companies agreed that it was not only in market research that jobs could be parcelled up and taken away, or that some jobs could be done by two part-timers. However, it was stressed that once a women left a company, even if she kept in touch by doing freelance or part-time work, she would find it exceedingly difficult to be considered for promotion. Even in the unusually flexible market research department, it was thought that it would be the exceptional woman who could make a 'come-back' into the promotion line once she had left. This was partly thought to be due to the technical nature of some of the work—the continually developing research techniques which had to be kept up with—but also due to the fact that organizations cannot keep jobs open while their incumbents go away for a while. In both companies, as in the BBC, it was pointed out that only the really good men were sent overseas, because of the difficulty of fitting the mediocre men back into the organization. Perhaps it would be in the organizations' interests to think in the same terms of their really good women.

6. *Reasons for women's lack of success*

Probably the main reason for the lack of success by women as a whole in both firms is the very fact that there are fewer of them. Fewer are recruited, fewer stay after their late twenties, there are fewer women graduates than men, and so on. Nevertheless, everyone interviewed, whether man or woman, agreed that there were other factors operating which made it more difficult for women to reach senior posts.

On the recruitment level, Company A has an elaborate management trainee recruitment scheme, for which far fewer girls apply than men, and relatively fewer of these girls are selected than men. The scheme has only been open to girls since 1962, and applying for management traineeships in industry is by no means the ritual with girls that it is with young men, who, even at 21, see the potential benefit of having a big industrial traineeship under their belts, even if they have no wish to stay in a large industrial enterprise. There is still the feeling, which is referred to in another section of this report, that big business—or even little business for that matter—is not ladylike, and that nice girls will not thrive in the competitive, cut-throat atmosphere of the commercial market-place. It is interesting, however, that certain areas of big business have gained respectability in the eyes of young women, and that advertising or market research are thought to be suitable areas for them to work, which is perhaps one of the reasons why there were relatively more of them to be found in these areas than others. It is a chicken and egg situation, since they are more readily accepted in these areas, and therefore find it easier to get jobs in these areas. This means that more of them go to work there, making these areas more attractive to other young women. This can have the effect, undesirable to most of the women already there, of creating female enclaves. Senior women found this undesirable, since they feared that it would cause an imbalance of sexes in the other direction, that it could devalue the department—both financially and in terms of influence in the organization as a whole—and that it could mean that the department might find it difficult to attract the best possible people, whether male or female.

However, this situation is limited to one or two areas. In most others, young women have a fight to get themselves in, and then a fight at every level to get themselves up. An interesting phenomenon, noted especially in Company A, is that women have found it relatively easy to progress in fields where an exceptional woman has paved the way. In one particular male stronghold, where a very talented woman has made her way to top management, she has kept her eye on recruitment:

> 'They used to send me lists of people for consideration for jobs, and the names of the girls were always very firmly scored through. I asked why. Now I know they will at least consider a girl on her qualifications, because they're scared of what I might say.'

An important reason for women's lack of success is, of course, traditional attitudes: women have never done this job, so women can't do it. It is significant that in both organizations women have done well in those areas which are relatively newly developed, such as market research or advertising and public relations, or in areas where there are relatively more women graduates than men, such as biological research, or in an area where only women would be considered, such as industrial nursing. It appears that women who have achieved something have not only come to terms with a man's world, they have also side-stepped the confrontation, and have opted for roles complementary to those of senior men. It is the rare woman who has made her mark in an essentially male-dominated field, and if these women's jobs were to be analysed in some detail, it would probably be found that they have carved out a special type of expertise which does not impinge on or compete directly with that of their male colleagues or superiors. This of course contributes to women's lack of success, since it severely restricts the number of openings to the top available to them.

Perhaps another reason for women's lack of success is to be found in women themselves, and the extent to which they bow out of a man's world. One senior man had this to say:

> 'I think women don't get any further than they do because they're not thinking right. They're not thinking in terms of a career. They're not thinking of the job after next. I'm a politician—not of the back-stabbing sort. I consciously foster things which will do me some good in my career. I think women ought to do this sort of thing a bit more. I really feel that women ought to learn to market themselves a bit better. First of all they ought to get the

product right. This means that they shouldn't wear mini-skirts or look too much like pretty dollies, because nobody will take them seriously. On the other hand, they mustn't look masculine. Then, once they've got the product right, they've got to learn to advertise it. They've got to project what they've got. I'm very conscious of my image. When I started I was appalling. I was very much a grafter—not a chatter. Now I'm a chatter—very good in meetings. I used to be very diffident. You've got to grab yourself by the bootlaces and pull yourself up. And then there's the public relations aspect. You have to develop relations—you've got to be seen in the right places. If you're capable, it's a good idea to get into the right situation, and then be seen to be talking good sense. I just don't think women go about all these things in the right way.'

The question of educating girls to be less diffident about themselves and their abilities was raised frequently in both companies. Both men and women concerned with selection said that it showed at recruitment stage:

'The girls are terribly diffident, even if they have fought their way through as far as a Board. How can you get them to come out and show their talents? You see very shy girls, who when they do say something are very good. I've been accused of being hard on them, but what should I do? They're going to be pitchforked into situations and they've got to be able to cope. It's far better to fail them at the Selection Board stage than for them to be failures at their jobs. The judgments which will be made about them will be applied to all women, so they've got to be really good.'

This was a woman talking, but a man concerned with selection felt very much the same:

'How can women be educated over time to demonstrate that they have equal potential to men? It is probably true that a lot of women are only equipped to handle information-giving jobs, because they simply lack a man's authority. They've never been brought up to feel that they ought to have authority or to exercise it.'

And yet another woman concerned with selection:

'A lot of women are not properly trained to take responsibility, If they have just been to an ordinary girls' grammar school, it just doesn't fit them for responsibility. Women teachers don't discuss things, it seems, and they don't seem to know what the outside world is all about. A lot of women here have been much too sheltered, I think.'

Another reason for some women doing less well than they might otherwise have done is that they have found themselves in a hostile atmosphere, or stuck in a backwater where it was very difficult to show their capabilities. On the other hand, a number of women said that they owed at least part of their success to the great help given them by certain key men who have fought for their promotion. These men seem to have performed the same function as the fathers or husbands of the women company directors. They have given real support and help to very able women, and have helped them to plan strategy, get on to the right launching-pad and generally offered advice on how to get on in a man's world. One woman described these men as 'office uncles', and there is no doubt that the path to the top for certain women would have been a lot more difficult if office uncles had not existed.

And finally, another main reason for women not going further than they do is that many women do not want to leave the job they're doing, or at least the field they are in. This was particularly true of the older women, possibly because they had found a niche for themselves, and were reluctant to compete in other areas where they could not rely on their expertise to establish their right to be in a position of some authority. However, another important factor emerged from the interviews with women in the BBC, which was that women liked to be involved in actually producing or making something. In the BBC, this was shown by the fact that so many of the women were reluctant to be promoted away from close contact with the studio or camera. In Company B, the women scientists were reluctant to relinquish responsibility for the work being conducted at bench level, even if they were not actually involved in what was going on, and similarly, although to a lesser extent, the women in Company A retained a great interest in day-to-day matters of detail, and were usually fascinated by their specialization. It is interesting, however, that it was not only women who were unhappy at the thought of leaving their particular field. Many men too, according to personnel managers, were difficult to move. The difference was that pressure was put on the men to move in the interests of their careers, while it was very rare for any pressure to be put on a woman to move. If the woman wanted to move out or up, the pressure had to come from her, and this was true in both companies.

7. *Advice from the men and women interviewed*

Both men and women were asked for the kind of advice they would give a girl coming into the organizations. Some of this advice was conflicting, particularly between the older and younger women, but there were certain areas where everyone was agreed.

The main recommendation to any girl who wanted to get on was to be very good at her job, preferably by displaying a particular talent, and to work hard. This advice held true for young men too, but it was felt that a girl had to be better than a young man, since so many things were against her success. It was then thought that a girl should show confidence in herself and her ability, even in the face of apparent rebuffs. If anyone wanted to get on, they had to be seen to want to get on. This meant that a brilliant girl should not hide her light under a bushel, and should not be discouraged if her excellence did not appear to be immediately recognized. A number of people in senior management positions thought that not enough young men and women realized how closely they were being watched for signs of potential top management, and that confidence and expertise were two prerequisites for top management. Many of the younger women interviewed doubted very much whether such a close scrutiny of their potential was in fact taking place. They thought there were many more elements of chance operating than senior management would like to think.

Several senior women in Company A advised young women not to come into a large organization as secretaries and then hope to work up the ladder from there. They thought the days in which a brilliant girl graduate could gain promotion in this way were over. They thought that it would in fact be a handicap, partly because the first vital years in a company would be wasted, and young men would have gone past the first watershed in the promotion race by the time a young woman had emerged from being a secretary. One or two of the older women thought that this was untrue, particularly if they themselves had come in as secretaries, but in fact, as the analysis of entry gates of women managers shows, the statistics prove them wrong. In Company B, the specialized nature of the company meant that the question of coming in as secretaries and rising to the top was not relevant.

An interesting piece of advice given by women in Company A was that of using Company A as a training-ground and then using the training received as a useful lever to getting a much more responsible job in a smaller company. Although it was not thought that salaries were poor in Company A—on the contrary, they were held to be good—nevertheless it was thought that the degree of responsibility given in Company A was not always as high as it might be and that other firms were much more willing to give responsibility to young women, particularly if they were out of the Company A stable. It was pointed out that young men had been doing this for years, and that there was no reason to suppose that young women were so different from young men. In addition, of course, because the degree of responsibility offered to the young women was sometimes much higher than they had had at Company A, the salary was often much higher too.

The question of money was frequently misunderstood by senior management in both companies, particularly with regard to the younger women. Women kept a very close eye on their market values, and were very much aware of how they related to men. Even if they agreed that they were earning good money, which most of them did, nevertheless they did not feel that they ought to be paid any less than men doing equivalent work. They thought that the equal pay slogan was sometimes stretched a bit, and that it was difficult to compare responsibilities. Women who had been a long time in either of the companies frequently stressed that their replacement value was much higher than their salary. They thought that their devotion to their jobs was sometimes exploited. The younger women were much more vocal on this point, and kept a very sharp watch on their market values outside the companies

A recommendation from the older women follows logically from the evidence presented in this report, and this was that young women should not compete in predominantly masculine fields, but should find themselves an expertise and make themselves very good in it, proving their indispensability. Some women, particularly the younger ones, were less sure. The younger women saw no reason why they should not compete with the men on equal terms, particularly since they said that they did better than men at university, only to see these same men pass them by for promotion in industry. Some of the older women saw the dangers of predominantly female enclaves which could form if too many women moved into the same specialization.

The whole question of attitudes towards promotion and the desirability of treating men in the right way have been discussed at some length in this report. In general, the women interviewed stressed that women should not try and behave like men, either in being too masculine in their manner, or even in trying to do a job in the same way. One or two of them said that this was sometimes difficult since women were usually trained by men. They thought that both management and the women themselves needed to recognize that different people did jobs in different ways, and that women needed the confidence to recognize that their way of doing a job was not necessarily worse because they were women.

Another broad area of advice to women who wanted to be successful concerned what are generally accepted to be female characteristics. It was thought by both men and women that girls ought to learn to become less concerned with detail and to try and develop the capacity to see the problem as a whole. In both companies, there appeared to be a great difficulty for women here. If a woman is judged on her expertise, it is not surprising that if she is ambitious, she tries to develop this expertise and to show how good she is. If this means that she is considered an expert, and a person to be consulted on detail, it is not surprising that she finds it hard to shake off the image of being concerned with detail and unable to 'see a large issue large'. It can then become increasingly difficult for her to be considered for potential top management, since her very skill in her expertise militates against it. The difference for the very bright young men is that they are not so frequently encouraged to develop an expertise, that they appear to be considered more often as potential top managers and therefore moved around the organization more, thus shaking off the image of being good at only one thing, and that in any case the stereotype of 'being concerned with detail' is not held as far as they are concerned.

In general, it was thought that a girl who wanted to get on ought to proceed in a way not so different from that of a young man who wanted to get on. She ought to be good at her job, hard-working, confident but not aggressive, pleasant to be with, capable of delegating and taking responsibility, of seeing a problem as a whole and not to take things too personally. If she managed to combine all these qualities it was thought that, in fact, she had an advantage over her male counterparts, since she was likely to be fairly unique and would not be overlooked. It was also considered very desirable for her, either by luck or design, to attach herself to the department of a man who would be prepared to recognize her qualities, give her responsibility and would fight for her promotion.

8. *Future prospects*

It was perhaps surprising that the most realistic appraisal of the future prospects for women in industry came from the senior men scientists interviewed. They were very much aware of the question of supply and demand affecting what was going to happen to women graduates, and were realistic about how a shortage of good qualified men would make any firm, however reluctantly, look around for potential substitutes. Not only would the firm have to look around for potential substitutes, however, it would also have to bend a lot of its rules, redesign jobs, rethink its reemployment policies and, in general, fall over backwards to employ qualified women graduates—on their terms. It was pointed out that the factories in each organization employed large numbers of female workers, and that numerous facilities were offered to married women with children, who wanted to return to work. Special 'school' shifts were offered and even school holidays were catered for. It was thought that the shortage of labour in the factories could easily soon be reflected by a shortage of skilled and highly qualified labour on the management and scientific side.

This senior scientist summed up the thoughts of many of his colleagues:

> 'I think that in this company administrative changes tend to be forced upon them by external pressures rather than by any deliberate policy. I can't imagine any sweeping procedural changes coming about with regard to the employment of women. I think they will need to promote women because the men are not available. Then the old prejudices will have to go.'

Another senior scientist thought that the situation in which women did better would be forced upon firms for another reason—the sheer economic necessity felt by women graduates to go on working, even after having children. He thought that there would be an increasing tendency for young women with a young family to try to go on working, simply because they and their husbands felt that they could not allow their standard of living to drop:

> 'I think that at the moment very few young women go off to have their families and then come back, but it is going to happen. In my generation it never happened, but with youngsters today—if they both work they can easily have a joint income of over £4,000. When they come to have a baby, I've seen girls near tears because of the drastic cut in the family income. I think we've got to think in terms of sabbatical years for having babies—breeding years. I suppose a girl could expect two to three breeding years in her life. But we've got to see that the income is maintained.'

He thought that attitudes towards married women were changing all the time, and that younger men had quite a different attitude towards their wives working than his generation, which would have an enormous effect on future prospects for women:

> 'Men of my generation don't like to see a pregnant women around the office or lab, but the youngsters don't mind. I think that the wives of the older generation don't like it either. They don't like the thought of their husbands working for a woman. I think

attitudes in science are going to change too. At the moment they don't like women who agitate to get on, but they don't like men who agitate either. Among reputable scientists there is a distaste for the 'go–go' type of person. But this is going to have to change. Young scientists aren't going to go into scientific research, and young men aren't going to be too interested in becoming scientists. There are no perks, no cars, it's a hard grind. You've got to be really good to get beyond £2,000–£3,000 a year. And so I think that here is the opening for women. I think you have seen what women can do in the computer industry, and I think that science is going the same way.'

This general lowering of standards as the demand for scientists grew was referred to by a number of senior men. It was also thought by a number of them that if the turnover in young men science graduates continued at the same rate then more might be done to encourage young women to stay by giving them promotion and responsibility. However, here the essential problem of Company B reappeared—the limited promotion prospects available to either men or women while the senior positions were filled with relatively young people who showed no signs of retiring or moving on for several years.

It was thought by both men and women interviewed in Company B that there was no good reason why so many areas in the company should remain closed to women, and that in time women would break into hitherto all-male sections. It was quite clear to the scientists that certain prejudices against women were held in some areas of the company, and that these prejudices would have to go, as the demand for skilled personnel increased.

In Company B, there was surprisingly little recognition by the women themselves of the role which married women with children might play in the future. Perhaps one of the reasons for this was that most of the women interviewed were single. However, some of them recognized, like most of the men, that more women would demand to go on working or return to work, and that there would be an increasing need for their services. They thought that the firm could think now in terms of which jobs could be redesigned for part-time or 'package-deal' work. They thought that there were a number of jobs which could be done by scientists which did not demand the presence of one person eight hours a day five days a week. They also thought that there were jobs which did not demand the keeping-up-to-date of the research scientist, but which nevertheless demanded a scientific background, which would be suitable for women who had taken a few years off to have children and wanted to come back to work when they had gone to school. They thought that the pool of graduate women scientists who had not worked for some years could perhaps be tapped.

Certain problems with regard to bringing back women into an organization some years after they had left were mentioned. It was thought that an older women might find it difficult to fit into an organization where the people on a level with her were much younger and those of her own age held much more responsible positions. It was also thought that a woman who had been used to being responsible only to herself and running her own household might resent taking orders from people in authority. However, on the other hand it was recognized that women of this age and experience could possibly bring a stability to their jobs which younger women might not. One senior man remarked that young women's minds were only 50 per cent on their jobs, in his view, and the other 50 per cent was thinking about whether or not they were going to get married and what they were doing that evening.

In Company A, there was perhaps more awareness of the problem of married women, probably because more of the women interviewed were or had been married, and perhaps because more younger women were interviewed in Company A. It was, not surprisingly, among the younger women that the greatest interest in the problem was shown. The older women were either not directly affected or had worked out some kind of compromise situation for themselves. Yet again, the senior men interviewed were aware of the problem as a whole, but felt, as in Company B, 'let the other chap be the first to start redesigning jobs for married women'. In Company A, they stated that the demand for managerial staff was expanding at a certain percentage every year and that, at the present recruitment rates of men graduates, they could not hope to get staff of a high enough calibre. Therefore, they knew that they would have either to lower their standards or tap another source. The other source was, of course, highly qualified women. It was, in fact, the recognition of the problem which led Company A to open its management trainee scheme to women in the first place.

It was being recognized that it was not necessary to rule out completely the possibility of reemploying staff—either men or women. As it became more common for young men to move around after they had left, it was thought by some managers that it would become acceptable or even desirable to train graduates, allow them to leave and go to another company and then have them back into Company A, complete with increased experience. Some managers in Company

A thought that its policy of promotion from within, and its reluctance to reemploy former staff, could lead to an inbred type of management, which could have its advantages and disadvantages. It was thought that a rethinking of the organization's attitude towards reemployment could lead them to thinking of actively encouraging young women who had gone through their management trainee scheme to come back after having had a family. This man thought that the system ought to be rationalized:

> 'I think there ought to be a planned re-recruitment of women. If they leave for family reasons we ought to send them a card every year seeing how they're getting on and if they want to come back. Up until now it hasn't been accepted that it could happen—and a lot of women leave never thinking that they could come back. I think the company ought to tell them how they *could* come back if they wanted to. I think the company could start changing their attitudes.'

The young women interviewed thought that their attitudes were very different from those of the generation of women older than themselves. Most of them were torn between the jobs which they enjoyed so much and the wish to have a family. They felt resentful that the choice was apparently so clear-cut—work or nothing. They thought that even if they could not redesign their own jobs to be done on a part-time basis, they certainly knew of jobs which could be done by them in this way. Only one of the young women interviewed had ever spoken to a superior about the possible dilemma. The others all thought that the moment they mentioned the possibility of having a baby their superiors would assume that they were about to do so, and that that would put paid to their chances of promotion. The girl who had spoken to her superior said that he had told her he would have her back, in some unspecified capacity, but that he would only consider it for someone of her experience, who had been in the company for several years and had reached a position of some seniority. There was clearly an enormous breakdown in communications between these young women and their superiors over a very important issue—important not only to the young women themselves, but also to the company. The young women thought they were not being given a chance, and that if they did leave with no possibility of coming back or working freelance or part-time, this would only confirm the worst suspicions of management who did not want women managers on the grounds that they were bound to leave, and would therefore be a waste of resources.

It appears that in Company A, as in the BBC, the importance of personal contacts with superiors can make it much easier for a woman to do freelance or part-time work or to be considered for reemployment.

'Better the devil you know' is still an enormous advantage, and a girl who has built up a good work reputation and can build a little niche for herself could find employment. However, the very fluid nature of the organization, with fairly rapid management changes, was pointed out as a disadvantage. 'The boss with whom one got on well might easily have moved right out of that field two years later.'

One senior man concerned with selection and recruitment thought that Company A could set an example:

> 'I think we could help establish a climate of opinion towards the recruitment of girls and in particular the re-recruitment of highly qualified women. We could let men managers know that part of the assessment of them as complete managers is how they solve this "problem". I think enlightened management could play a big part in changing attitudes. At the moment, particularly in some parts of the business, if a girl leaves, there is a big sigh of relief and an entrenching of the traditional viewpoint.'

Chapter III
CONCLUSIONS

The main conclusion from the report must be that a great deal more attention needs to be paid, both by the women themselves and the management of big firms, to the question of how women present themselves and are regarded. This comes up in the report in a variety of forms from personal appearance to the art of becoming visible for promotion, of managing office uncles, of avoiding being type-cast as a specialist and of toughening up the nice mice. There is considerable reference in interviews to the need to get the product and the package right so that the rest will become much easier.

Women clearly need to be encouraged from a very early stage in their education to regard themselves as capable of doing jobs which are not traditionally women's occupations, and to 'think big' and not be put off from applying for promotion or change simply by lack of encouragement from above. In some way, the problem of showing initiative without being thought aggressive and unfeminine needs to be solved, and there is no reason to suppose that intelligent women cannot solve it. Clearly, schools and perhaps universities could do more to help girls become less diffident about themselves and their potential, so that they could present themselves in a way which would make it more likely for them to be considered for selection and promotion. Ability in a job situation is very difficult to measure before a person has actually done a job, and it has been shown quite conclusively in this report and others that employers are far less willing to take a risk with women than with men.

It is here, perhaps, that the attitude of the employers is important. There is evidence from a number of studies that women perform very well in jobs into which they have been pitchforked, although, left to their own devices, they might never have considered themselves capable of doing them. Employers could consider the possibility that it might be worth their while to give women opportunities which hitherto they have not been given. They could perhaps take a very close look at some of the women whom they have considered diffident, and see whether in fact these women are diffident and whether they have been developed by the firm to their full potential. If so many of the women interviewed, particularly the younger women, feel that their potential has not been fully exploited, it could well be in the interests of management to examine their development policy with special reference to women. They are willing to take risks with young men, who may leave them or fall down on the job, but appear to be extremely unwilling to take any risks whatsoever with women. The report shows quite clearly that women in the market research department of Company A, who do get pitched in with equal responsibility and opportunity, perform their jobs very successfully and profitably from the firm's point of view, whereas women in other branches of the firm may end up by living down to the low expectations held of them. This is also true of Company B, where women have done very well in the biological sciences departments, and have been unsuccessful in other departments. It certainly seems true for both companies that women do well where they are allowed to do well, and it has been said in justification that these are areas where women have either a special aptitude or training. In fact, there is no real evidence to support this view, since women can clearly not do well in departments where they are either not allowed in or are deliberately kept below a certain level.

If management recruits first-class people, whether men or women, it has everything to gain from seeing that these people learn to act in ways which are most conducive to their own promotion and so to the welfare of the firm. If companies recruit women who are as good as, if not better than, young men straight from university, who then do not appear to perform as successfully in jobs as the young men, could it not usefully turn its management development attention to the particular problems of these young women? It appears that this is not done in many cases, simply because it is commonly felt that it is not worth developing these young women since they will leave in any case. The point made in the last paragraph, about living down to expectations, is clearly relevant here again.

The point about young women leaving leads on to the biggest problem of all—that of what to do about the small-child break in women's careers. It is obviously unrealistic to assume that women and men will have similar career patterns and, if full use is to be made of first-class women, some systematic appraisal of their special problems needs to be made. There is also the problem of the strongly motivated attitude to careers of pre-marriage girls as compared to men, which is shown very clearly in the surveys of graduates carried out in conjunction with this study.

First of all, there is the question of how long a job can be protected in the case of maternity. In both companies, it was felt that a woman could not expect her job to be protected for her if she took more than the shortest possible time away from work, and the women themselves were very much aware of this. There were a number of reasons put forward—that a line management job could not remain empty, that a woman would lose touch with her specialization if she were out of it for more than a minimum period, that people further down the ladder could not be held back, and so on. However, in Eastern Europe, where far less stress is laid on the sanctity of family life, women's jobs are held open for up to a year after birth, and there appear to be no insuperable difficulties. Perhaps there is a real case for examining the possibility put forward by one of the men senior scientists of recognizing that women should have 'breeding years' and that their jobs should be held open and their income maintained. The economics of retraining an already trained person who can offer stability and loyalty as compared to training someone of unproved ability and suitability have never been properly examined in either of the companies, and it appears probable that they are by no means unique in this. However, they cannot make any valid pronouncements on the subject until they have analysed the situation. It is impossible to say that women would not want to return after having a family if they have never asked them whether they would want to or not. A great many assumptions on the wishes of highly qualified women have been made without consulting the women concerned.

There is clearly some change in the attitude of young women towards their work. The women interviewed in Company A showed a strong desire to return to, or to continue in, work after they had had a family, and they were quite prepared to go to a smaller firm if Company A would not reemploy them. Their pattern of moving around appears to be becoming similar to that of young men who drop out of Company A after two or three years and go somewhere else. This pattern is very common among young men graduates in large companies. These companies justify their attitude towards the young men by saying that if they lose one today they will gain another from somewhere else tomorrow. In future, the same could be said of women.

Secondly, both firms are in a position, in view of their size and flexibility of operation, to look closely at the question of women working less than full-time. The phrase 'part-time' has been used in this report, but a recent study has suggested that this is often a misnomer, and that in fact a lot of so-called part-timers are almost, but not quite, full-timers. It often may simply mean that they are unable to commit themselves to unlimited overtime although they are not working less than normal weekly hours, or it may mean that they do not put in a full working week at a desk in an office, but do quite a lot of work at home. It is important to note that this latter method of working was used by some women employed by the market research department of Company A. It was suggested in the body of the report that it might be worth while for firms to consider the possibility of retaining their first-class women by parcelling up jobs to be done by the women at home or partly in an office. It was frequently argued that there were not many of these jobs around, but there can be no doubt that if companies really wanted to keep someone employed they could redesign jobs so that they could be done in a more flexible way.

There are perhaps two types of women who want to work less than full-time. First, there are the women who want to opt out of full-time work only while their children are small, but to come back into the promotion line in full-time work when their children are older. Secondly, there are the women who want to stay in less than full-time work. It is the first category which is more important when looking at the prospects for women in top jobs. These are the women who may be potential top managers, and it would often be in the interests of firms to create career opportunities for them.

It was frequently argued both by men and women in Company B that scientific work could not be parcelled up and given out in this way. It is not suggested that women could grow cultures in their kitchen sinks but that there are many fringe scientific jobs which could easily be done competently by a highly qualified woman scientist working less than full-time. It could be in the interests of the company to look for more work of this kind. There is, in fact, a highly paid woman scientist working less than full-time in Company B, and her employment appears to have been a complete success.

Thirdly, there is the question of recruiting older women who have had their families, and giving them the chance not only to enter as qualified and experienced professionals, if that is what they happen to be, but to start at the bottom as trainees and accelerate up if their merits justify this. There is a lot to be said for the stability and maturity of women who have gone through the hurdles of marriage and family. There is evidence to show that ambition and aspiration perk up after a woman has had a family, only to collapse again when it is realized that there are very few openings. The alleged problem of only 50 per cent concentration on the job because of thoughts of marriage is overcome, and there is no real evidence to show that married women with families who are working in responsible positions are likely to spend 50 per cent of their working day thinking about their families. In fact the evidence collected in this report and other occupational studies shows that married women with children are perhaps harder on themselves in this respect than married men with children.

This leads on to the point that many of the stereotypes held about married women working are based on experience by employers with women of a much lower level and much slighter degree of job commitment. In other words, employers tend to judge highly qualified and highly paid women not by their actual performance and behaviour but by the behaviour of clerical and factory staff. There is general international evidence to show that highly qualified and highly paid women show a much higher degree of career commitment than those lower down the scale, and in fact are likely to be in the work force during most of the years of a normal working life. There is also the probability that occasional absences may have quite a different significance for women at this level, who may simply be using their time more flexibly and getting the job done just the same, from what is found at lower levels where absence from work during working hours means that production actually gets lost. The absenteeism rate for married women administrators and managers in this country is considerably lower than that for women further down the occupational scale.

There is an important and interesting conclusion which has special significance to the question of specialization. Throughout this report both men and women interviewees implied or specifically stated that the specialist areas in which highly qualified women tended to work were on the whole outside the mainstream of the business, and that this was one of the reasons why women did not rise to the most senior positions in the companies, since they did not have the breadth of experience necessary for the highest management positions. The evidence shows, however, that some of the specialist areas are well within the mainstream of the business, and that 'mainstream' is often loosely applied to mean the sales and marketing areas of a company. For example, accountancy, scientific research and market research are specialist areas, but are not ancillary areas. There is also ample evidence to show that men who work in these areas are not regarded as outside the mainstream for consideration for promotion, and do not regard themselves as specialists who could not be considered for promotion.

The policies of large companies towards inbred management and the reference made to it in this report could have some implications for the employment of highly qualified women. There is a good case today for saying that traditional policies of promotion from within and a lifetime career need to be dropped in the interests both of fresh talent within each firm, and of recognizing that many professional and managerial jobs cannot be regarded as secure in middle age. This means that many able and well qualified people are bound to be on the move. This increased flexibility of employment may well lead to the rethinking of jobs, which could smooth the path for the highly qualified woman who wishes to return to work, but is unable to find an opening in the rather rigid structure of no reemployment which operates in so many firms today.

There is also the fact that large, nationally known firms like these have perhaps a special responsibility for looking out not only for the best human material for themselves, but for conservation and full use of the nation's manpower resources.

One point which was raised in the report has special significance for this study. This was the impression held by the young women in Company A that smaller companies were more likely to be happier hunting grounds for them than large, formally structured companies. It is not possible to prove this statistically in this report, but it is interesting that they thought it true and could point to friends or former colleagues who had found it true. They thought that the smaller organizations were more likely to recognize their qualities, to give them more responsibility, to pay them more money, and to offer greater promotion possibilities. They thought that in a smaller organization a woman had more chance to shine and to be judged specifically on her individual contribution rather than be regarded as a junior member of a team. Perhaps it is true that women operate in a more relaxed way in the more intimate atmosphere of a small organization, but if this is so, it is not necessarily the fault of the women, but possibly of the large organizations for not creating the opportunities for women to be accepted in the formal structure of a highly organized hierarchy.

There is a strong case for removing all discrimination which is laid down in rules or tacitly accepted, for example in accommodation which would normally be open to all members of a firm's staff, or in attendance at functions. It is quite clear that as the number of women increases many of these problems disappear, but the very fact that they are still present means that there is still room for progress. The more senior women there are around, the easier it becomes to accept women in senior posts in general.

There is the possibility that science has its own special problems which affect the employment and promotion of women to a greater or lesser extent depending on the firm. There is some evidence that a research scientist might be past his or her best as a research scientist, although not necessarily as an administrator, at the age of forty. This has implications not only for women scientists, of course, but also for men. It has particular relevance for Company B, which has the particular problem of having a large number of scientists in their early and mid-forties. If it cannot find suitable administrative posts for all its men, it is highly unlikely to pitchfork women into administrative posts, even if they were capable of being successful in them. It is equally unlikely to promote young women when so many highly qualified young men are clamouring for promotion. The outlook for young women in Company B does not look any brighter than it did for their predecessors, and this is not very encouraging for them, considering the social and economic changes of the past twenty years. Some senior managers in Company B made the point that there has been some progress, however. They are continually trying to persuade certain areas of the company, like the Sales Department, to have women, whereas ten years ago, no-one was trying to give women the breadth of experience needed for top management.

There is another problem which requires closer examination, which is the question of how true it is that a scientist who drops out for two or three years—or even longer—cannot get back within a measurable time. The evidence found in the occupational study on architects shows that someone who returns after a long gap may indeed need to start relatively low down and to work pretty hard to rebuild the necessary network of communication and knowledge, but is nevertheless a better prospect for the employer, in that in a junior job she can earn her money more quickly than a raw graduate, and can also learn and relearn faster.

And finally, perhaps the most important factor in this argument is the demand for managers. It is generally accepted that there will be a continually increasing demand for managers, and some specific forecasts were made in the Unilever Quarterly Review, *Progress*, in January 1964:

> 'We have found on the Continent that for the next five years we shall have to provide for a total increase in senior management of about 10 per cent, and in junior and middle management of about 25 per cent. The overall increase will be 23 per cent.'

This increase, of course, relates only to Unilever, but gives some kind of indication of the necessary increase in management required by a large organization over the period in question. The writer goes on:

> 'The limits to Unilever's expansion will largely be set by its managerial resources. Sometimes we have had to postpone a proposal for a new venture because the necessary management to put the plan into effect could not be deployed. In spite of hopes

that management would become less scarce as time went on and the fruits of post-war management planning became ripe for picking, we are still having to search for the right man in the right place. . . . *The scarcity of management talent has introduced a further responsibility, which is that no talent is overlooked by the organization wherever and at whatever level it is to be found.*'

Perhaps companies like Unilever and Companies A and B could find that they are overlooking talent in the shape of the highly qualified young women they have within their organizations. Companies of this size and stature spend vast sums of money on management development, and still succeed in having discontented and under-employed young women on their staff, who have not been given the opportunities to test whether or not they have management potential or not.

The writer in *Progress* goes on to say:

' "Nobody knows what it is that makes a good manager good", according to J. A. C. Brown in his recently published book, *Techniques of Persuasion.* How then should we appraise the potential of our managers, for it is their potential in which we are vitally interested? We have gone by experience and possibly by intuition in the past but we do not really know enough and we have therefore decided to do more research into the subject in order to find out more about the criteria, the attributes of a good manager. If our research should yield results we would in future be able to be more objective in selecting people for promotion and we would thus do more justice to the individual, thereby avoiding a sense of frustration in the case of the good man who is not stretched to the maximum of his capabilities.'

Experience and intuition are clearly not enough to appraise the potential of managers, but then neither is the implication that it is only men who may be frustrated and not stretched to the maximum of their capabilities. Perhaps a complete rethinking of the role of women in management and a new look at their potential would go some way towards solving the problem of finding top quality managers.

Part Two

THE WOMAN DIRECTOR

Chapter I
THE WOMAN DIRECTOR AT LARGE

1. *Introduction: background to the report*

Unlike the other groups studied in this volume, where the selection of samples is facilitated by precise knowledge of the total populations in the records of the organizations concerned, there is no such record of the population of women in business in general or of women directors in particular (or businessmen either for that matter). In fact this study was deemed more than usually worth while since little systematic information was available about the career histories and strategies of businesswomen.

Whilst business in itself is not classed as a profession, though in its managerial aspects and specialized techniques it appears to be rapidly developing in that direction, the director can join a directors' organization, in the form of the Institute of Directors. The Institute aims to present a corporate view of its members' interests and, in this as well as other respects, it can be regarded as contributing to a process which will make its members into a profession. Its numbers and influence have certainly grown impressively in the years since the war, from a few hundred to over 36,000 (excluding members resident overseas) today.[1] Apart from its library and information services it has also amassed, through its Medical Centre, a great deal of material concerning the medical and vocational records of its members.

Such extensive and detailed records of directors certainly do not exist elsewhere in this country in a form which would permit relatively easy access for the purpose of research. We were therefore fortunate that the Institute agreed to a joint venture which would have the twofold object of obtaining revised data for an enquiry that the Institute itself made ten years earlier, for example age, family development, qualifications and career development; and from this

[1] It is interesting to note that although only 962 (or less than 3 per cent) of the Institute's members are women, as long ago as 1926 the second Viscountess Rhondda was its President. In her long and distinguished career she was, among other things, a director of John Lysaght & Co. Ltd. as well as of many other companies, a Governor of the London School of Economics and Political Science, and Editor of *Time and Tide*.

material to select a sample of women who would be approached for interviewing on aspects that could not satisfactorily be treated by a written questionnaire, for example the interplay between family and career factors

The written questionnaire, which was sent out in 1968, was constructed to take account of the Institute's three main categories of membership:

(1) Housewives/nominal directors
(2) Retired working directors
(3) Working directors

and it was agreed to devote most of the questions to the last group. In order to maintain a record of those who had returned their questionnaires, all the women members were asked to complete a separate card giving their name and address. Only the names and addresses of the respondents provisionally selected for personal interviews were made known to the author. With the Institute's cooperation, however, we were able to compile a table of the regional distribution of women members by reference to the city or county that they were living in.

The Institute had surveyed male members in 1966, and there had been a considerably higher response rate than was obtained from the women. Nearly 50 per cent of the men had returned their forms within a week of receiving them whereas in the 1968 survey less than 30 per cent of the women had returned their questionnaires within three months of receiving them in mid-July. Scarcely more than half the sample of non-respondents who were followed up in mid-November had returned their second brief questionnaires by the end of the year. Over 40 per cent of these had not completed the original questionnaire because of 'pressure of business' and 28 per cent 'because of holidays'.

The intensive personal interviews account for 9 per cent of the respondents, who in turn represent 29 per cent (or 279) of all women members of the Institute. A random sample of 8 per cent of the non-respondents eventually yielded rather more than half the number of those circulated or over 4 per cent of the total. The sample of men referred to for purposes of comparison relates to the 8 per cent of the membership (only 15 per cent of whom were sent a questionnaire) who had responded to the survey in time for preliminary results to appear in the April and May issues of *The Director* for 1966.[1]

[1] Since the samples vary considerably in size we have referred to *Standard Errors for Percentages* compiled by Alan Stuart of the Research Techniques Division, London School of Economics, and published in the Applied Statistics Series by the Royal Statistical Society.

2. *The average woman director*

Age and marital status. Well over half the Institute's members, male and female, are over 50 years of age and less than one sixth are under 40. One quarter of the women have never married. One fifth are widowed and 10 per cent are divorced or separated.

Education. One third of the women directors had been to grammar school, another third to private school and the remaining third were divided equally between public school and either elementary, secondary modern or an unclassified establishment.

The men's education, if we allow for ambiguity of classification, tended more to the extremes, nearly half going to public schools (compared with 17 per cent among the women) and over one eighth to secondary schools against only 4 per cent of the women who had attended secondary modern schools. The women, therefore, tend to be more homogeneous in their origins.

From the career point of view, the educational background is of interest primarily to assess how far it has been carried over into their after-school training. By this criterion, there is a sharp falling off in the status of the establishments in which the women pursue their education and training. Not that we are passing judgement on the quality and suitability of the education or training received, for however unexalted these institutes may be academically, such training or qualifications may have been more relevant or useful to those who entered business.

Nevertheless, the fact that nearly half the women received training in secretarial colleges not only appears to match the stereotypes associated with many women who have risen in business, it also indicates the low expectations of women who work and the corresponding valuation placed upon them by society in general. More than half the directors had no formal qualifications at all. As it happens, less than a third of the women directors are now engaged on work for which they had been trained.

Social origins. The solid middle-class background of the woman director, already indicated by the nature of her education, is confirmed by the figures relating to the occupations of their fathers, about two thirds being the daughters of professional men or businessmen. A considerable number, or 12 per cent, of the women failed to give their father's occupation. Comparison with the information on the social origins of men directors cannot be exact because the breakdown of occupations in the results so far available is less refined, so that some of the comparative figures had to be deduced. However, it is reasonably clear that the men are more heterogeneous in origin than the women, with 40 per cent of their fathers being skilled workers and 10 per cent semi-skilled or manual workers against 10 per cent skilled fathers among the women and 3 per cent semi-skilled. However many manual workers there may be among the women's fathers is concealed among the 18 per cent who placed themselves in the residual category.

The point of entry. More than half the women directors left school between 16 and 18 years of age compared with one quarter leaving between 14 and 16 and one fifth between 18 and 21. Only two thirds of men directors were at school after 16 against three quarters of the women. A breakdown in this age group is not available for the former although we do know that whereas a third of men over 65 were educated only to primary school stage, no less than 82 per cent of the 30–39 age group attended grammar or public schools. The educational differential between the sexes, therefore, is diminishing.

Scarcely more than a quarter of the women intended to follow their present career when they left school. Nearly 40 per cent obtained their first job by personal contact and rather less than one third through advertisements. With men, family and social contacts accounted for more than half the number of first jobs but strict comparisons with the women are difficult to draw owing to variations in the descriptions of categories. School or university appointments boards accounted for less than 10 per cent of such entries among both men and women, while few of them entered employment through the Employment Exchanges.

Reaching the board. Among the women directors, promotion as a means of getting on the board of directors accounted for 40 per cent of the sample, about one quarter had founded their own companies, and one sixth did so in conjunction with their husbands. More than a fifth owed their board appointments to family connections or inheritance. Nearly one quarter thought they owed their success to no one but themselves. Less than one third and one fifth respectively acknowledged the help of their husbands and fathers.

All but 7 per cent of the women respondents worked for the companies of which they were directors and again very nearly 90 per cent were executive directors. Rather over one quarter were chairmen, a slightly smaller proportion were company secretaries and over 40 per cent were managing directors. Among the men, who worked for larger companies on the whole, there were relatively fewer chairmen and there was less 'doubling up' of posts than among the women.

Size of company. It is perfectly consistent with the preceding statistics that only 10 per cent of the women directors sat on the boards of public companies. In terms of company size, moreover, only 7 per cent, against one third of the men, were on the boards of companies with issued capital of £500,000 or over, and 77 per cent, compared with only 41 per cent of the men, were directors of companies employing under £100,000 in issued capital. Furthermore, in respect of the number of employees, over 70 per cent of the women were directors in firms employing under 100 people whereas only 5 per cent directed firms with 1,000 employees or more. Similarly just over half exercised a controlling interest, while of the nearly 60 per cent in family firms, almost half were through the respondent's family and about a third through the husband's. About half the husbands were or had been directors of the same companies as their wives, about one quarter were professional men and 15 per cent were managers or executives of other companies.

Earnings and income. Nowhere are the advantages of being a man in business demonstrated more convincingly than in the statistics relating to earned income before tax. Nearly half the respondents, compared with only 11 per cent of the men, earned less than £3,000. Between £3,000 and £5,000 there is relatively no difference between the sexes, one third of each earning sums like these. Among salaries and other earnings over £5,000 the percentages for men and women directors were 56 per cent and 17 per cent respectively.

Domestic help. Of the 80 per cent of women with domestic help, more than half used the services of a daily, with the great bulk of the remainder divided equally between occasional and resident domestic help. Rather more than half of the average women directors spent less than £5 a week on domestic help.

Leisure. Although all but one sixth of the respondents thought of themselves primarily as businesswomen, and 82 per cent of the latter were in full-time salaried employment, two out of every five considered they had enough leisure. Lacking any standard or conventional definition, leisure is a term open to individual and subjective evaluation. Does it include the time available to be with the family or devoted to voluntary work or is it that portion of the week that may remain for exclusive personal use?

About five in every six women respondents belong to clubs or associations and 40 per cent of them to their professional association compared with 50 per cent of the men.

Membership of the Institute of Directors. Duration of membership is very largely a function of age. More than half had been members for over six years, and, as we have seen, a similar proportion are over 50 years of age. Only 14 per cent used the Institute's facilities regularly, although 42 per cent had business or residence in the area administered by the Greater London Council. About one quarter lived in South-east England and 10 per cent in the Midlands.

3. *The top woman director*

As previously indicated the women selected for interview, from the total of 279 questionnaires returned completed and on time, represented a qualitative sample based on age, marital status and income. These criteria virtually excluded from the start any detailed consideration of that not inconsiderable proportion of the Institute's members who are either retired or regard themselves primarily as housewives. A similar proportion of the 'businesswomen' were for selection purposes virtually disregarded as they are part-time or unpaid. In addition, since two thirds of the women directors live and work in London and the South-east and the older retired members tend to live further afield, particularly in East Anglia and south-west England, the regional distribution was bound to favour the country's most populous and constantly growing region, with the balance of interviews coming from among the scattering of suitable candidates that could be detected in the Midlands and North.

Despite this deliberate descrimination or, which may be more to the point, because of it, it is worth while to consider just how far those selected for intensive interviewing differ from their less distinctive sisters.

Age and marital status. On average they are about half the age of the average women director, nearly one third of them being under 40. Two thirds of those interviewed were married compared with less than half the women directors in general. Whilst widows accounted for only 4 per cent of the interviews they comprise nearly one fifth of the respondents and nearly one quarter of the non-respondents. The divorce rate among the interviewees tended to be higher but the statistical significance is only fractional in this category. This may be a reflection of the relatively larger number who were married whilst still in their teens.

Although the age differential is clearly reflected in the distribution of children's ages, about two thirds being under 16 and three quarters either at school, university or undergoing training, this only serves to underline the success these women have achieved despite their domestic responsibilities.

Education. Their educational background was generally less 'private' than the conventional women director's and more geared to the grammar school or even secondary modern school. One fifth, however, had been to public school so that, bearing in mind the difficulties of comparison, the overall educational profile is somewhere between that of the man director on the one side and average women directors on the other. They were also somewhat more disposed to continue their education and training, particularly through evening classes and also university where they appear to have the academic edge over women directors in general.

The entry gate. Almost half the number of women interviewed obtained their first job through advertisements and hence, initially at least, were more exposed to competitive conditions than other women directors who owed more to personal contacts. Their greater self-reliance is indicated by their method of reaching the board which, compared with women directors as a whole, tended to be more frequently, by means of starting a company on their own than by starting with their husbands or obtaining it by inheritance or family connections.

Although the women interviewed appeared to have progressed to the top more through their own efforts alone than the generality of respondents, they were rather more aware of and willing to acknowledge the assistance they had received from their fathers, probably in the early stages of setting up their businesses, and their husbands from whom they received moral support if nothing more tangible.

There may be grounds for believing, therefore, that the type of help received by the women in business has shifted from direct participation by the husband or other members of the family, to background support by the husband for the wife's dual roles, and early training in the family business by fathers who rely on their daughters to see that the company's affairs are competently managed in the future.

The trend for the career environment, therefore, seems to be stiffer competition all the way up the ladder, but accompanied by increasing self-reliance. This two-fold development is not inconsistent; it is only to be expected where the pioneering phase of mutual aid with like-minded friends or the support of husbands and relatives gives way to individual effort.

With basic skill and motivation becoming the determinants of success, women now appear to be reaching the board earlier at a higher rate than their predecessors. Nearly half the select sample were directors before they were 30 against considerably less than a third of all women directors.

Size of company. Nearly one quarter of the women interviewed sat on the boards of public companies compared with only one eighth of all women directors. Their midway position between men and women directors is confirmed by the figures of company size.

They tend to be associated more than the latter with larger concerns but cannot match the men in their relative distribution among the highly capitalized concerns.

Differences in the relative proportions of the size of companies in the sample affect the statistics pertaining to ownership. Only 40 per cent of the select sample exercise a controlling interest compared with 51 per cent of all women directors and the ratio for family firms is similar though the proportions are higher in both samples. Among the latter firms, the connection is more likely to be through the interviewed women's own family and much less through the husband than among women directors in general.

Earnings. The income differential between the women interviewed and other women directors is startling. Whereas 80 per cent of the former earned over £4,000 per annum this was true of only one third of all women directors. On the other hand, there were relatively twice as many men directors earning £5,000 per annum or more than among even these high-fliers. Put another way, women directors are doing rather well if they earn more than £3,000; men, by contrast, are scarcely making the grade if their income is below £5,000.

Domestic circumstances. As with other women directors, about half the women interviewed used the services of a daily domestic help but over a third employed a resident domestic. Moreover, two out of three spent more than £5 per week on domestic help. These figures reflect both their more demanding family and professional needs and their higher disposable income to afford such assistance. It also includes their greater willingness to delegate the conventional responsibilities of the housewife and mother.

Despite their greater orientation to London, the select sample were no more conspicuous in their membership of metropolitan clubs than women directors as a whole. They are considerably less inclined to join social, sporting, religious, civic and benevolent bodies and show more reluctance or have less time to serve on committees although this appears to be a regular feature in the off-duty responsibilities of the majority of men directors.

It would seem, therefore, that the more dedicated younger, ambitious businesswomen is less able or prepared to be distracted by extra-professional pursuits, even well deserving causes, nor does society or her local community seem to expect or even desire it. It is improbable that communal expectations or the professional woman's consciousness of the responsibilities and privileges her role bequeaths will remain in this mould indefinitely but the considerable cross pressures on her will have to be relieved first. We shall be examining the precise nature of these pressures in Chapter II.

Chapter II

SOME INTERESTING CASES

1. *Introduction: overall characteristics*

In the intensive case studies the relationship of half the respondents to their companies could be described as either in the nature of a rescue operation or being associated with its development into an expansionist phase. A slightly smaller proportion were entrepreneurs, in the sense that they set the company up, either alone or with their husbands or a partner; and the remainder, no more than a handful, can be described as following a public service career.

Again, half of them had part of their career associated with wartime conditions, nearly one quarter of them being secretary/personal assistants, and a sixth involved in voluntary service. For most of these the wartime experience proved fruitful to their subsequent careers. A small number had grown up with the company and, by being involved closely with the head of the company and a small number of colleagues, had remained with the organization until it had outgrown its origins.

An interesting feature of the group is the large number of overseas connections. More than one third were immigrants, the children of immigrants or had lived some period abroad; in fact more than half of the women interviewed had some strong overseas connections either through their parents or their husbands.

More than half the women indicated that their major role in the business was selling but only a handful were engaged in buying. In terms of industries or economic activities the women were divided between seven major groups: engineering, food, clothing, manufacturing, finance, research and servicing.

2. *Supply and demand for women 1939–64*

The environmental conditions that appear to be crucial in determining successful progression up the path which these women have chosen, or been guided or propelled along, are the general economic circumstances, particularly the labour market, at the outset or during the early decisive part of their career, the nature of the occupation or economic activity to which they were committed, and the personalities, whether through heredity, environment or contact later in life, who have influenced their lives, or at least the public aspects of them.

If this sounds somewhat deterministic, it is not meant to belittle the achievements and efforts of these gifted people who were both willing and able to exploit to the fullest advantage the situation that confronted, beckoned or challenged them. But most of them fully realize that future prospects will depend on how social and economic circumstances evolve, and that it is unwise to make a projection based on the particular set of circumstances that have obtained in the past.

a. *Wartime initiates and protégées.* The most decisive event affecting the careers of more than a third of the women interviewed was the Second World War. One of them now approaching retirement was before the war in a fairly sheltered junior capacity as secretary to the sales director. He was a close relative of the chairman and subsequently succeeded to the top position, expanding the firm rapidly through takeovers and the development of branches in other parts of the country. In her early days with the company it employed only a few men three days a week. As the company was still on the small side, she was unofficially, in her own words, the assistant to the sales director, her duties obviously extending beyond the purely secretarial functions of attending to correspondence and filing.

The process of becoming involved in sales, her 'life blood' as she put it, was one of 'slow and painful adjustments', as she had previously no desire to enter industry. In the event she has found it a satisfying business in which she has been substantially better off than she would have been had she continued with her classical education.

The war not only wrought a revolution in the fortunes of the company and its employees, who were by now working seven days a week on overtime, it provided her with the experience and responsibility necessary eventually to place her on the board, 25 years after joining the company. A conjunction of other factors occurred at the same time, though as she herself admitted 'the war was entirely instrumental' in developing her career, and she regards herself as 'very fortunate'. The chairman died and her superior, who took over the managing directorship, saw that she would be more involved on the sales side, which in fact entailed processing orders to the works, seeing the work through and helping the manager to deal with orders. The increase in the volume of work lay in the fact that the company provided a key specific item to industry in general.

After the war when she became sales manager herself, the wartime conditions were perpetuated, if not intensified, with the keen demand from abroad, especially rehabilitated Europe, a situation which continued for 12 or 13 years. In this period, as she readily agreed, she became a 'highly competent rationer' to sort out genuine as opposed to purely speculative enquiries. For the next ten years or so, her career developed in a highly successful way, including travelling, which she likes—half the company's activities being overseas—and meeting people.

The last phase of her career, in which she feels she has been rather spoilt, having always had the 'red carpet treatment' began two years ago with the geographical expansion and structural change in the company. Her 'empire' (a phrase which would undoubtedly infuriate her as she deals roughly with 'imperialists' if internal politics come to her notice, although this has not averted the good-humoured taunts of her male colleagues who allege she got to the boardroom by 'stamping on everyone's face') has now been divided and she deals exclusively with the UK.

She seems a trifle rueful at the limited amount and scope of travelling she does now, but she is not the brooding type, being a cheerful, sporting and abundantly healthy person. She has no intention of retiring yet and has remained on good and sociable terms with the new chairman whom she has served devotedly and who was, for his part, 'always in the background if a problem became excessively difficult'.

We have dealt with this case, although the terms of reference of the study concerned mainly younger, middle-aged married women, as it is not only interesting in itself, but is illustrative of circumstances highlighting the career path of many of her younger counterparts.

Primarily, of course, there is the classical wartime 'take off' entailing as it does an abrupt reversal of the ratio between supply and demand, not only for the product but, what is more important in this context, for labour as well. Such a situation provides a stimulus for the movement of women forwards and upwards in two ways: it raises the demand for labour in general and reduces the supply of male labour available for civilian employment. Any remaining reluctance on the part of young, able-bodied women is reduced by the call of duty and the direction and drafting of labour by the central government.

A group of women in the engineering field, married with children, and all in their forties, followed a strikingly similar career pattern. They began work in the early war years, foregoing higher college education in the process and starting in small companies that subsequently mushroomed and changed drastically in form or ownership. They were thus placed close to the head of the company and his successors or likely heirs. In every instance their companies had substantial growth prospects as they occupied key positions in the industry, a factor due in no small measure to the inventive and business acumen of their respective founders.

Within ten years, by the end of the war or the early post-war period, that is, these women had managed to make themselves indispensable, owing their subsequent survival to, variously, the need to preserve continuity in a period of change of ownership, special relationships built up with the owners, and by sheer dogged persistence, hard work, loyalty and close personal relationships with colleagues on the board.

Again, all of them in the last three or four years have experienced changes in their working or personal environment, the full consequences of which have yet to work themselves out, *viz.* a succession of changes of ownership, changes foreshadowed on the board or in five cases by domestic upheavals. Most of them thought they were fortunate; the remainder, who had struggled the most and furthest, were considered 'determined and obstinate'.

The other women who held positions of responsibility during the war and later made substantial progress as the result of it are in a rather different category. They are characterized either by work with voluntary societies and charities, or considerable involvement with or commitment to their children or dependants. Clearly the choice of a public career in these circumstances makes this wartime group a much more complex one than those involved in a secretarial or personal assistant capacity in a small manufacturing company. In fact there is more conflict at work between career and family, of the need to push their career in the interests of their dependants and, in some cases at least, the reverse, the women feeling compelled to take up a career through the breakdown of marital relationships. Even this elaboration may tend to blue the distinctions between the case histories of what is in fact a fairly heterogeneous group who are linked less by unifying themes common to all than by certain experience or features shared by two or more of them.

Nevertheless, apart from their services in wartime, they do share other characteristics justifying common treatment in this context. They are all around 50 years old and in recent years have entered a new phase of their careers, the final outcome or success of which it is impossible at this stage to foresee. All have led or are leading full lives with considerable personal commitment or dedication but because of, rather than in spite of, this, there is a considerable degree of preoccupation with their duties and responsibilities outside. Only one has never married, two of them have remarried and three have been divorced; one has a husband unable to work and two of them have elderly parents or relatives as dependants. The two women who had remarried were also the only members of this group with children, both of them had had considerable breaks in their career whilst bringing up their children and both of them had managed freelance or part-time work at home in writing or publishing, and both had been engaged in political organizations.

One of these still thought of herself as a housewife able to undertake part-time work for her husband's company at home. For this work she was able to draw upon her experience 25 years before when she had been employed to conduct aptitude and intelligence tests in the Services as part of the screening process for recruits. This work was directed by a distinguished psychologist who later in the war was to be instrumental in finding her a civilian job when changes in her personal circumstances demanded it.

Another woman with an altogether contrasting career had, before moving to the business world, spent 18 years in the public service, being concerned during this period with a wide range of administrative work such as preparation of legislation, allocation of scarce resources, manpower budgeting, consideration of schemes put forward by local authorities and other bodies, and advice to Ministers on quasi-judicial matters.

In her change of career some years ago she was anxious not to become typecast but to continue to be regarded as being capable of a variety of functions; and during her 14 years in business (during 13 of which she has been a director) her posts have included responsibility for personnel policy and critical appraisal of trading enterprises, although most of her time has been spent on financial policy matters such as budgeting control, long-term revenue and capital forecasting, advice to the board on proposed acquisitions and disposals, assessment of the profitability of the individual undertakings in the group, advice on allocation of profits between distribution and reserves, making arrangements for capital raising, maintaining and overhauling a pension scheme and investing its funds.

At the outset of her postgraduate life she had intended to read for a higher degree by evening study but the intensification of work in the public service as war approached put an end to that. She had also thought that after about the age of 35 she might enter politics but she found by then that the habit of serving both parties equally as a public servant had unfitted her for party politics.

She feels that she was lucky in her career, partly because the war accelerated promotion and responsibility and partly because she had senior colleagues who were particularly unprejudiced about the employment of women. She has never regretted her career. Indeed she was brought up to the view that, having accepted the then unusual privilege of a university education, she was morally committed to putting her talents and experience to maximum use; and not to have continued with a career would have been unthinkable, although obligations to elderly parents and to other relatives have sometimes caused conflicting loyalties. She is a trustee of a charitable trust and governor of a university college.

Her career 'sister', as it were, in this group began somewhat lower down the social, educational and administrative scale but became almost a household name in her political career, a record of ups and downs which, in terms of electoral fortunes, mirrored the destiny of her party. She readily agreed that publicity for her trenchant attack on the Government helped her in securing the nomination for a seat, as she felt the scales were rather loaded against a woman. In this respect, reform of constituency nomination procedures which removed the advantages previously held by well-connected candidates opened the door for her, but it was her fierce advocacy when the party was low in morale that enabled the threshold to be crossed. Good timing also marked the ending of her ministerial career and her entry into business just after the peak of her party's fortunes had been passed.

She herself believes that luck is tremendously important in a woman's career both in politics and industry, where marriage presents an obstacle to progress, and she expressed surprise at how few women there were in high positions, apart from women who started their own businesses, even in the textile trade which has occupied much of her attention in recent years.

Her decision to enter business, although prompted by financial considerations—at her age she had to ponder the fact that she had no pension and an elderly aunt to consider—was not quite the leap in the dark that it would appear to be, since she was by now well connected. She had also worked in the private sector on two earlier occasions.

After grammar school and secretarial college, she worked as a private secretary for some years before the war and as personal assistant to various directors of several companies in the post-war years. Her apprenticeship, as it were, in public life began when she became secretary to a Cabinet Minister during the war. A highly critical moment in her career occurred when his Principal Private Secretary went to the United States. The Minister wanted her to succeed but the Treasury tried to block her appointment, as being without precedent for a woman. Her Minister took the issue to the

Head of the Civil Service, whose decision was that as it was a temporary department with temporary staff they would make an exception in her case. Therefore she was allowed to become Principal Private Secretary to a Minister (the first woman at her level to have such a chance). She met with some antagonism from the other PPS's, who at first refused to believe it.

This incident seems worth recording in its entirety as it clearly marked a decisive point in her career. Moreover, an important precedent had been established, however unusual the circumstances, and another breach in the wall of male prerogative had been effected. Increasingly, of course, the pre-war Civil Service was to become swamped by, in the words of someone who witnessed the process, 'an inrush of businessmen' and later on by the 'so-called professional Civil Servants'.

Nevertheless, the woman in question received 'every consideration from the Treasury and the Cabinet Private Office' in contrast to lesser departments, which attitude and experience prepared her for her return to administration as a Junior Minister after the war. As for the future, her two careers may conjoin in 1970 when she has an excellent chance of returning to Parliament.

b. *Entrepreneurial opportunists and planners.* We turn now to discuss the circumstances governing the entry of a new generation of talented young women into entirely new or highly specialized fields, into areas hitherto monopolized by men and into 'traditional' women's occupations to which they were able to contribute original and revolutionary twists.

For this was the period of the consumer 'revolution' in domestic appliances associated with the rise of commercial television when women entered employment in numbers unknown in peacetime, particularly married women, itself a response to the sustained demand that had accumulated and been restrained by six years of war and a similar period of post-war austerity and restrictions.

This period witnessed an enormous expansion in advertising, marketing, market research and public relations. It also heralded the ascendancy of the computer, an increase in the scale of business, an acceleration in amalgamations, mergers and takeovers, the application of modern techniques to business, the advent of the consultant and the establishment of business schools and colleges of management.

The end of this period saw a great increase in government planning and intervention, as well as much greater economic uncertainty and upheaval both at home and abroad, as a result of which economic experimentation has been overlain by economic restriction. This presents a challenge to the women now approaching middle age who started their careers in the favourable conditions of abundance in contrast to their immediate predecessors who had known only, but had benefited by, scarcity.

If we again examine some cases in detail, this should enable us to throw more light on the processes at work in forming a career and to determine the factors that have wider significance. First, a woman in her thirties, married with children all under 12 years of age, with a university degree and several years' 'always pushing and fighting' for her chosen career. This takes us back to the early 1950s and the start of her career in a very large confectionery company, a conjunction of events she regards as fortunate as it also marked the end of sugar rationing. 'The 1950s were wide open, you couldn't go wrong.' She was in, therefore, at the beginning and well equipped mentally and educationally to cope with the work in experimental psychology involving interviewing people and questionnaire design.

The job had been brought to her notice by her college principal, her feelings towards whom are ambivalent though she admits her admiration for a brilliant 'ideas man' who exercised considerable influence over his pupils—who indeed appears to have combined the attributes of the perfect father in leaving them to themselves but at the same time allowing it to be known he was always there if needed. Two years later she joined a well-known organization as Research Manager. Four years later still, at the very peak of the affluent society, she became a director with a seat on the board. She was still under 30 and it was about this time that she discovered her latent managerial qualities, notably the ability to select people, a talent that was to prove of inestimable value some years later in her continued battle with authority, and in the further development of her career.

Meanwhile, she had found her research company, 'staffed by good brains', to be 'a wonderfully stimulating environment' in which she gained a lot of confidence to reinforce her already considerable powers of perseverance, energy and strong motivation. This was a climatic year for her in other ways in that it also marked her marriage to a man in a competitive organization who has since moved on to manage the marketing side of a manufacturing firm.

Professionally, a period of intense mobility afterwards ensued; she moved jobs twice in a year with a selected entourage, to go eventually into partnership with a man who originated overseas but had been long resident in the UK. It was then the mid-1960s with business becoming more difficult, and her choice of business partner was dictated by considerations of security; in other words, he had more capital to draw upon, she had the contacts and highly qualified workers.

Having reached the top, her current feeling of uncertainty at being a woman in a man's world, now becoming a good deal harder to accommodate to than when she entered it, is intensified by the feeling that she is at a crossroads in her career. She could enter administration completely and not as she has done in the past, partially or intermittently, dictated by the needs of the moment and her own suspicions of administration undertaken by someone else. She is attracted to the idea of entering management full-time and largely giving up a research role but this is more of a challenge and she sees her future in terms of mergers and amalgamations and therefore must attempt to gain managerial expertise. She summed up the position by saying 'I used to be very optimistic, but it doesn't work now. Conditions in recent years have entailed a certain loss of confidence but this is a function of maturity.'

The economic situation in 1960 provided tempting conditions for another woman now just turned 40, and she too is at a crossroads in her career. When she started her own specialist trading company after many impatient years as secretary in a company in the same trade, she was the 'first woman to start a firm in this field from scratch'. People at first were very sceptical although the idea of women in this trade is widely accepted, if they do not actually dominate it, in France (she was born on the French border) where women in business are very powerful. As it happens, in this country, she feels now that part of her business stems from the sheer novelty of her being there at all, such incredulity being not inconsistent with a conservative, naive and even ignorant strain she has discovered in the trade and has turned to her own advantage. Her particular strength, however, derives from specializing, in this instance, in fragile goods which she sells to wholesalers.

Her firm is a small organization employing a handful of people and flexible enough to cope with trading conditions that are a 'terrific gamble, requiring split-second decisions based on confidence between buyer and seller'. Her organization in fact represents for the trade an early exercise in systems analysis. Her then husband, an Organization and Methods expert, helped to set up the company and designed a method of running an office with a very small staff but able to handle a large turnover. She certainly needed moral assistance at the time as the man she had proposed to partner proved to be a confidence trickster who stole half her capital and was later prosecuted and jailed for forgery. In retrospect she feels that this was the best thing that could have happened to her as she had not previously had the courage to start alone. As for the future, she feels that business is becoming increasingly difficult.

The choices confronting her are either to associate with other businesses of like character to absorb costs, though so far her sex has proved an obstacle here, in that a prospective partner's family is opposed to women in the trade; or to expand to such an extent that she would have to confine her work entirely to administration and no longer do her own buying and selling—but this would restrict her freedom, would not be demanding enough and would deprive her of direct contact with the trade which she is able to assess so swiftly and accurately. Alternatively she would have to join a large firm and run their import department. Either way, she would be reluctant to sacrifice her independence by becoming part of a big unit as she values personal contacts and is not happy tied to a desk. But the risks she takes will be calculated ones, not gambles. In her own words, she is 'a plodder who will never make a great scoop, but who will not become bankrupt either'.

There appears to be some consensus among the women who move in the more exalted social circles that it is the professions associated with the City of London where the male prerogative is most strongly entrenched, notably banking, insurance and stockbroking. As one women who had been initially passed over for the top financial post put it, 'the really hard core are the merchant bankers where men are brought up through inheritance to exercise terrifying responsibilities needing quick decision and judgement, alleged to be attributes women are less likely to possess; in public service, on the other hand, money is public and buttressed about by advice of one kind and another'.

We have in fact encountered two women who have been allowed to observe and advise on but not actually to participate in the mysterious male rites still practised in the City, but before considering their experiences, let us first look at a young woman who has 'been running the whole show' in her firm for a number of years without owning any of it and is sometimes in need of advice herself.

Now in her thirties, this woman feels that she could not have achieved her position if she were married. She was strongly attracted to fashion, but on leaving university in the 1950s she found her degree of little commercial value so she took a secretarial course in order to enter on the ground floor.

Her first job was as a secretary in the correspondence department of a women's magazine. She had a very low opinion of her female colleagues, whom she regarded as ill-educated and lazy and, after six months, feeling she could do more, asked the editor to be transferred to an editorial department. For this combination of audacity and keenness she was rewarded with the job of Assistant Fashion Editor, the jealousy of her superior, and ostracism by the rest of the senior members of the staff. On the strength of her work her new superior was moved to another post. Her rise in this firm came to an abrupt end when she was sacked for an error made by another member of the staff. But although she was offered her job back 48 hours later, she had meanwhile found another job. The incident proved to be a blessing in disguise since, through the agency of a friend, in 1961 she joined the staff of an old-established cosmetics firm on a part-time basis, her income supplemented by freelance work.

The crucial point in her career came when a director left and she volunteered to organize a mobile exhibition. This was her first chance to exert her administrative ability since her active life in student societies and by now she was both working full-time and had many ideas she wished to put into practice. One of the latter provided an important breakthrough for her and the company. Since then she has 'fallen in love with marketing and product development'. But today she is confronted with the fact that she has no shares in the firm, which are all held by its ageing founder, who was previously helpful to her but who will not discuss the succession, and there is the presence on the board of the Chairman's relatives to increase her doubts on this matter. She is at a loss as to the right course of action, glad she is nearer 30 than 40, and regrets the fact that amongst women there is no substitute for those masculine pub lunches where new openings can be discussed, or for the 'old boy' network.

A self-assured 40-year old, who is proud of her Slav background and willing to give advice in the export credit field, has been a partner in a firm which specialized in the development of business in Eastern Europe. As in the previous case, there is the kindling of interest at university and an abrupt change in career three years out from college. Her husband was formerly prominent in politics, but her most valuable connections have been a family friend in a government department and her partner.

Although she feels that women are better than men in terms of performance in new occupations, she did not foresee them being admitted to some institutions, for example as full members of Lloyds, in her lifetime. But male supremacy does not concern her professionally where she is treated as a specialist, her function being advice, problem solving and to obtain credit cover. As it is she is very much at home in a small company and, not surprisingly, finds that, numerically at least, men, the traditionalists in business, are more prone to empire-building and tend to become too single-minded and therefore the poorer for it.

Her nearest counterpart began her career at 19 as a sales representative. It was through one of the company's distributors that she met her second husband, 30 years older than herself, who was to prove the medium, by force of personality and teaching ability, through which the foundations of her successful career were laid. He taught her 'not only to think and to find the right answers, but how to run small businesses and get people to work enthusiastically and well for me'.

After three years her husband, a pioneer management consultant, sold out to a large holding company, and she stayed on to become director of one of the group's subsidiaries. Characteristically, she declined the managing directorship as she enjoys selling, getting out of the office and travelling, advantages that would otherwise have been denied to her along with the higher authority to which she likes to resort. Although she prefers to sell to and negotiate with larger organizations, as the people she has to deal with in these bodies are in her opinion more intelligent, she herself would find the routine life of such organizations rather restricting.

As it is she has only recently gone freelance to become managing director of her own company specializing in the management of clients' funds in the UK and abroad, as well as interests in acquisitions and sales, marketing of patents and new products. The contacts she gained whilst travelling, particularly in North and South America, as well as the numerous unpaid business chores she undertook on behalf of them and her friends, provided both the instrument and the incentive, as she now has agents in New York, Paris and Geneva. Her partner in New York heads the Investment Company and is the majority shareholder, and the real head of the business.

On the whole, her opinion of other women in business is rather unfavourable, as she regards them as amateurish, irresponsible, and unable or unwilling to adjust themselves to a man's world. Short of being content with secondary positions the only way for women to succeed is in flexible occupations.

An even younger woman, on the other hand, with a baby daughter, who nine years ago began her career as a representative in the field of educational aids, derives a successful livelihood in the company of, and in the market for, trained women.

For her it is a positive advantage that women do not seek 'the few jobs at the top'. She finds that with employers who are looking for integrity and complete loyalty to the boss this is a good selling point. On this assumption she has successfully exploited the market for female executives with a good education, and a professional approach to the job which often involves periods of travel. Surprisingly, for those who believe that single women are preferred by employers, she is more often than not looking for married women in their thirties with the kind of balanced character which reconciles them to absence from home on business.

A keen champion of her sex who feels that women are becoming increasingly accepted as candidates for responsible business appointments, her triumphal progress in executive recruitment for the US received a jolt when the incoming Johnson administration bowed to domestic pressure and she was forced out of the lucrative US market which she did much to pioneer and develop. Nevertheless, with half her clients coming from the US she remains optimistic about women's chances, particularly in the next generation, which she sees as an age of specialization, particularly in fields involving personal contacts, such as personnel work, public relations, selling and marketing.

She feels an even greater satisfaction and some exhilaration on leaving behind what she calls the protégée period two years ago. During that period she was helped by a succession of advisers: her father, a family friend, the director of her former company (from whom she received encouragement and valuable contacts) and her husband.

For at least one of the women interviewed, competition between men and women and the relative virtues of each is, if not irrelevant now, likely to become so. Her attitude of mind is conditioned by, and no doubt of benefit to, a business where 'half my customers are homosexuals'. Her business centring around display modelling is closely associated with the fashion industry, her models acting as 'interpreters of fashion at a particular time in order to push the sales of clothing', particularly to young people where she sees the greatest narrowing of the difference between men and women, bisexuality being both conditioned by behaviour and appearance and a reflection of the more profound changes, though in another sense modifications, that she implies are occurring between or within the sexes.

In more mundane fashion, she was 'lucky' when she started, arriving in the UK from the Commonwealth in 1953, modelling first in her home, a studio, a whole house and finally moving to the West End in 1964. From 1960, when her first collection was presented, the business began to expand. In this respect she was fortunate in her choice of husband shortly after arriving in this country. He is an Industrial Designer, 'a source of ideas and talent who knew everything', and guided her. She, on the other hand, is aware of the significance of chance in her career, describes herself as merely a 'worker', and is proud of her Jewish heredity and conditioning which gives her an instinct for running small businesses.

Her present uncertainty over her precise identity, the future of her company and taxation problems could perhaps be linked with her background, as her parents were exiles from Russia. The small-business instinct is also now being put very much to the test in a world dominated by big business in which the 'individual is less important'. It would doubtless help to reduce her sense of isolation if she knew that her experience and feelings are not untypical of those of her own generation and sex who have climbed a long way up the career ladder in a manner and fashion not thought entirely appropriate for a woman.

3. *Career milestones and motives*

In terms of reaching the top the women selected for interview fall into three broad groups: first, those who inherited their positions in a family business; secondly, those who grew up in the lee of a director, beginning in a fairly humble capacity as a secretary and ending either as a sales director or chairman—sometimes taking the company even further than their sponsor; and finally, those who either from the outset, or more commonly through a combination of personal or domestic circumstances, felt compelled to have a career. For convenience we may label these 'Inheritance', 'Sponsorship' and 'Entrepreneurship', though in fact the various case studies contain elements of each.

Thus the relationship between, say, father and daughter in the family business is not dissimilar in its characteristics from that between a director and his secretary who subsequently joins the board, and sometimes even succeeds to his position. Similarly, in the Entrepreneurship cases it is difficult if not impossible to find instances of pure entrepreneurship in the sense of starting or reaching their position entirely unaided. Either initially or somewhere along the line, there is someone who has provided these women with the jumping-off point or, in the case of established organizations, been the instrument of take-off into an expansionist phase. Likewise, in the Inheritance and Sponsorship categories, the individual concerned often displayed qualities of originality and leadership which would put them on a par with the genuine Entrepreneurship cases.

Closely involved with a choice of career is the question of the motive for entering a particular career and the incentives needed or received in the actual job. Once again it is possible to classify the in-depth interviews, this time into five groups, although in some cases they contain elements of each.

Not necessarily in order of numerical importance or implying any hierarchy of values, we find idealism, closely linked with duty and the idea of service, to be prevalent among the women and a prime motivation with some. Secondly, there are the rebels against society and those who must have freedom and independence in their business life. Thirdly, we have the more conventionally ambitious and those inspired by the challenge of success. Next there are the victims of circumstances—they did not choose a career but life forced them into it. The remaining category had chosen their career primarily because of family reasons.

Whatever their motives and however they arrived at their managerial positions, it would be difficult to say that the women interviewed, with one or two exceptions, could be said to have started their careers in a positive manner. Very often they took the career path through entirely fortuitous circumstances: the war, the illness of a parent, even the break-up of a marriage, have been among the factors that impelled them to follow a career. Of the half-dozen or so cases where positive factors contributed to the selection of a career, the choice had been determined quite young, even before adolescence. Very often these people were not only the more impressive figures but had also progressed further in their careers, and had the greatest prospects ahead of them. As one women who had made good in the clothing industry put it, she finds women who are really intent on careers very efficient.

An almost universal characteristic of the case studies is that at some stage the educational phase is abruptly terminated, in some through the opposition of parents, the intervention of the war, or similar factors, and in others voluntarily by the woman herself, deciding that the outside world has greater attractions than the academic life. The factors influencing these women to take the career road are worth analysing in some detail.

Among the idealists we find the woman who, having made a successful career in public administration, transferred in middle life to senior administration in business. The motivation here was strongly influenced by heredity and environment; her parents were both professional people with progressive views and she had been educated at Oxford in the 1930s. Her new role she feels gives scope to her experience, judgment and imagination.

A much younger woman who started her own company specifically to meet the needs and exploit the potential among talented women in her own profession had come over to this country as a refugee. Of

Jewish origin, she felt guilt over her good fortune in not being one of those who died in the concentration camps, gratitude towards the country of her adoption and the need to give something back. This has been translated into the cause of female emancipation by providing a specific employment opportunity. In this way she felt she was carrying a torch, working against the odds and meeting a challenge.

Two women in the engineering field, of Celtic origin, had clearly both been affected by their experience as school girls during the Depression. One had been brought up in the North-west where the Depression was particularly acute; the other's father had been obliged to leave Wales for work in the Home Counties. Both felt an obligation as employers to maintain continuity of employment.

Another idealist of a different kind, a political one this time, to some extent had retreated into business from a dislike of English academic life for which she was well qualified, having pioneered a faculty of East European history in a Commonwealth university, and her disenchantment with left-wing politics. Displaying a strong aptitude for business she had taken an interest in finance during her university vacations and was offered a partnership by someone she met at a party. She now has a very specialized job providing scope for individuality, originality, tangible results and a sense of doing good, apart from high job satisfaction which involves advice and problem solving. There is also the incentive of freedom and travel.

Of those motivated mainly by a sense of duty, all were daughters or widows involved with or succeeding their fathers or husbands in the same business. Two of them knew they would inherit the business anyway and received a commercial education. In their cases the respect for and influence of the father was sufficient to override any other wishes they may have had, and they eventually became so immersed in the business and its expansion and development that any alternative career was finally ruled out.

Again there is the same interest in people, the strong personal contacts in the trade and the reverence for their father or husband as well as family tradition.

An immigrant from the Commonwealth with an ex-refugee husband had found herself in middle life plunged into the business world. The succession problem had never been discussed with her husband and at his death, her son not being interested in the firm, she felt compelled to take over, carried along on a wave of sentiment and staff loyalty until such time as she felt able, with the knowledge she had acquired through reading and the support of the other directors, to stand on her own feet.

Among the rebels, three were immigrants to this country. One of them had a constant pattern in her career of a fight with authority in masculine form, overlain, rather paradoxically, by a respect for male dominance. Being a strong character herself her response to this authority was to push against it with all her strength until it yielded. In her case work provides short-term outside goals, excitement and a good income 'as a sign of your worth'.

A Continental woman from a similar bourgeois background was brought up by a Victorian aunt who impressed upon her her complete uselessness. When she came of age, inspired by her English contacts which included her first husband, she came to the UK and after a succession of jobs, including a period as a secretary, she decided to branch out on her own in the same trade, with help initially from her second husband. To her, as to a great many of her contemporaries, money seems secondary, a great deal of what she earns is given away. Until this time she had never had a job which gave her enough responsibility, or satisfied her craving for independence and personal contacts. She has found fulfilment in the very demanding food markets of London as well as variety, interesting personalities and challenge.

The woman from the Commonwealth likewise depended heavily on her husband. Her parents were Russian Jewish refugees with a Victorian outlook, opposed to higher education for girls, and the only alternative for her seemed to be as a secretary. It was a great relief to her, therefore, when at the age of 11 she met someone in the fashion field and she realized that here lay a creative alternative. As it was, what had begun as a hobby as a child now employed all her talents.

A middle-aged London woman, now a company secretary, was the daughter of a labourer, often out of work with an attitude towards his many children that they should leave school as soon as possible to support him. Her mother missed her chance of higher education by not being allowed to take up a scholarship to a grammar school. The woman herself had been to grammar school but her humble circumstances precluded her from studying for the profession at which she had aimed. As it was she joined a firm not far from her home and has been with them ever since.

The last of the rebels, a very English 'little woman' character, and a member of an old-established firm with origins in the steel industry, had a constant battle with her father who regarded her as completely useless. Her earlier intention to go to university led to a clash with her father and she had taken a temporary job in an importing firm during the war, thus gaining the experience and responsibility she needed when later on, as her brother was still at school and her sister not interested, she stepped in and made a success of her father's firm when he became ill.

She felt that the family firm was ideal for women in business as it is not so easy in such an environment to create the antagonism which often arises in large organizations where the chances of advancement are remote. In her job she also found variety and scope for writing.

The ambitious women motivated by the need to succeed were, with one exception, very young. Although self-motivated from an early age, all were strongly influenced by family circumstances, either modelling themselves on, or inspired by, their fathers, or, by contrast, reacting strongly to the frustration they sensed as girls on the part of their mothers and their mothers' female friends. The sense of injustice obviously still rankled with some, and they identified themselves strongly with feminine advance.

One of the youngest among the former group had always wanted to be a success. An early training in drama school equipped her to deal with contingencies which constantly occur in business. She was inspired by the example of her parents, particularly her father and her grandfather. Hence the sense of challenge and the desire to serve people.

One of the most impressive of those interviewed, she had built up a thriving business in partnership with an American in the domestic appliances field. She had a background of business in the family and had helped her father in his hotel. A period of living abroad, when she managed a secretarial college, proved of great benefit to her in an administrative capacity. She admits she has no flair for her present calling but likes the challenge of hectic work.

Another girl strongly influenced by her father, a successful short-story writer, had wanted to follow him by being a journalist, a difficult calling to enter, even for a woman of proven ability. She had received her first pay packet as a result of working as a nurse in a mental hospital in the university long vacation, and realized then that success is to be judged by the objective criterion of money. Like many of her equals she found it stimulating to work with men and regarded work as her fulfilment.

The oldest in this group, a child of German Jewish refugees, found working with women brings understanding. Audacity, she felt, was her outstanding characteristic, and wanting to do a job with the challenge of taking up something new. Job satisfaction is derived from the fact that she can do what she likes.

Among the victims of circumstance, we have a 50-year-old woman who had set out to demonstrate, on the break-up of her marriage, that she could do a job well, and was not motivated as she thought many businesswomen were, by the need to show they could do the job better than a man. She was also carried along by the desire not to let people down and pride in doing a good job. She had spent part of the war lecturing on technical subjects which she had learned entirely from books.

At the top end of the social scale, the daughter of a man of independent means and a socialite mother needed a career for financial reasons when she found that the fortune she had expected to inherit no longer existed. From being a debutante her first job was selling cooking oil to fish and chip shops. The social gap proved too much, but with the help of her husband she began a successful career in his company until starting her own.

She derived satisfaction from the feeling of building something of capital value, the absence of routine inseparable from large organizations, intrigue, excitement, plotting and planning. In her own words, her business mirrors her social life; she is constantly attracted to people who want looking after and who cannot manage their business affairs.

Another case concerns a woman whose entry into the family business arose by chance. She had occasion to visit London whilst on holiday when her father asked her to collect the mail from his London office. She found chaos, the agent was ill and subsequently died, and her father asked her to stay. That was 30 years ago. Apart from early familiarity with the industry (she had played in the family works as a child) she was fortunate in having been trained as a designer in several leading firms in the same industry. Another woman who had made her career in sales owed it to a chance circumstance of a personal contact of her father's and the demands of war. For technical reasons she had to wait a year before entering college, so she took a temporary job in a local firm at the instigation of her father who knew the managing director. Like many of her kind she found her ideals of service could be satisfied as much by working for the war effort as through her chosen field of psychology. She felt the attraction of positive action which her job increasingly gave her.

Her counterpart was found in the clothing industry. In her case entry to university had been prevented by the onset of myopia. On the advice of her headmistress she took a secretarial course in London followed by a job as secretary to a director of a local firm.

The remaining cases are all women with several children whose orientation to their families is so complete that their business exploits take on more the flavour of desperation and anguish rather than the rewards, albeit mingled with conflict and preoccupations, associated with the strong personal motives of the career woman.

Indeed some of these women had actually made their families the object of their careers—setting them apart from the stereotyped picture of the ambitious or talented woman torn between domestic and family responsibilities and her professional duties. One woman, married to an officer in the armed forces, had discovered her flair for sales by acting as a stand-in at an antiques exhibition in her local town, her motive being financial as she was determined to give her children the benefit of boarding school education. Another woman had very little previous experience except voluntary work during the war and a boring secretarial course prior to her marriage. Her husband, an outstanding administrator, had an exceptionally well-paid post in the canned foods industry, which he sacrificed some years ago on the insistence of his wife who was afraid that his prolonged absences as a buyer for the company would wreck their marriage. They eventually set up a company to manufacture and market a product inspired by her children.

4. *The woman director at work*

Having discussed the general and particular circumstances and events that guided these women along the career path and the personal factors that governed their entry, there are a number of important aspects to consider relating to their work performance, their working environment and their relations with their colleagues.

What qualities do they bring to bear in accomplishing their work; how in fact do they manage; what governs their attitude and actions in dealing with people, customers and staff, fellow executives, seniors and juniors; and how important are these qualities, working methods and patterns of behaviour? Are they specifically feminine? To some extent the answer depends upon their position in the firm and the nature of the activity in which they are engaged.

To begin with they bring to their work the benefit and breadth of mind of good education either in terms of attainment, or, with a small minority, fairly convincing evidence that they could have reached the same levels if only by the determination and industry they have exerted and expended in pursuing their goals. Secondly, they are endowed with higher than average intelligence, though this judgment is based on brief personal assessments during the interview and detailed analysis of their career resulting from these encounters, together with their answers to the questionnaires.

Undoubtedly, innate intelligence and quickness of judgment have been instrumental not only at critical points in their career paths but in day-to-day business life. Closely involved with this is the capacity for making rapid decisions based on further qualities of knowledge and experience, the ability to communicate this clearly across the board and down the line, coupled with a talent for persuasion and the ability to win the co-operation, loyalty and trust of colleagues, employees and clients.

It is obvious that however strong the motivation, however favourable the circumstances, it is the ability to see and to seize an opportunity when it presents itself, to estimate the consequences of alternative courses, to have the self-confidence to take a calculated risk that form the prerequisites necessary to success.

> 'The occasion for my making the change was the advertising of a post but I already knew much about the group of companies concerned [an Oxford woman contemporary had worked there] and I liked their aim of providing a way of life and not merely a means of earning a living—in this respect attempts at nationalization up till then had seemed to me disappointing. This was something in which I thought I had a part to play and also there was still more "pathfinding" work for women in business than in the public service, where we were by then accepted. It was hard to break away from familiar and congenial work where my prospects seemed assured and launch into a field where I would have to make my mark all over again. But I felt that at 40 I could just do it and, if I left it later, I wouldn't. So I decided for the leap in the dark.'

> 'I was the laughing stock of the . . . world when I began in 1962 with £6 share capital and £6 working capital and a portable typewriter. But I felt there was a pool of women, who could be employed, usually graduates or of graduate status with a bias towards maths. I had no business background before, couldn't read a balance sheet. But I learned a great deal about profitability. I went along to a local productivity meeting at . . . where I discussed my problems with a lecturer on the staff of the Business Studies Dept. and he sent someone along to help me for two or three months. Work started to flow in.'

> 'I had never done anything like this before and didn't know a thing about the trade, but if you believe in anything enough you can get it across. We had conferences and arrived at a formula. I did the blurb and the packaging. I saw an advert in the local paper by a local firm. I spoke to the buyer but realized I couldn't go into

production until I got sufficient orders. He gave me a provisional order for 250 provided I got the balance of the order from someone else. He gave me the name of the buyer of . . . in Oxford Street from whom I got the rest of the order. Not long after we were invited to appear on television at the start of . . . TV. At the same time we advertised and the thing snowballed'.

A parade of insouciance in the face of adverse or even hostile forces is matched in some cases by more positive or aggressive action. A display of boldness or audacity is often called for.

'My first job was in their Training Department. I applied for an assistant's job when I was only 19. They refused point blank, so I went to one of their competitors who gave me a job previously held by a woman of 45. The London Director was a brilliant man, but then the company was taken over and he left. I had previously wanted to make a demonstration film of the company's equipment to show at a Schools Board meeting in Leicester where they were using it. I obtained no support and my London Director suggested I should form my own firm. He pointed out that there is a ceiling in large companies for women and consequently it would be better to start my own providing I had the good nerves necessary at the top, was very sure of myself and had a sense of timing. . . .'

'The company was in serious financial straits when I took over and I was advised to close it by both my Accountant and the . . . Bank who regarded me as merely a woman. So I sacked the Accountant and went to my own Bank where . . ., who is now a director of the Bank but was then the general manager, gave me a loan on the basis of a five-year plan to work off the loan and death duties on the former chairman's estates. I duly paid back the loan of £38,000, an overdraft of £29,000 and Death Duties of £57,000, Later I learned that the Bank had decided to give me the loan for my impudence in requesting them not to call it in in the event of a credit squeeze.'

Once having reached the top, what are the prevailing characteristics of their major business activities? Again to the forefront there is the imperative need for decision and the process of decision making.

'Before a decision do your homework, the rest is a calculated risk. A bad decision is better than no decision at all. In making a decision I would first look at the product to see whether it is marketable, then at capital outlay and cost. I would ask for all the figures to determine its profitability and the space and work needed. Then a long board discussion plus separate thinking. A solution is then hammered out, the final decision depending on what is good for the company.'

As the comparatively new head of the company, this woman has learned to ask the right questions, to get the right answers and occasionally to strike a balance between technical enthusiasm on the one side and financial caution on the other. Although inexperienced at first, she had the advantages of working with her predecessor as well as considerable wealth of her own and the security derived from the knowledge that most of the company's shares were held by a trust thereby relieving the company of ordinary debts.

A young woman who worked her way up more tortuously from a secondary modern school laid most emphasis on being an efficient personality and the willingness to accept responsibility. Not sparing of herself she is very demanding of her staff since, proud of her example and conscious of the need to bring the company up to her own standards of service, she is able and willing, if necessary, to undertake any job in the organization, including operating the switchboard and wrapping parcels.

This concern with standards is a fairly common theme with the women interviewed and is consistent with the perfectionist temperament that so many of them evince and admit. If genius is a capacity for taking pains and a concern with details this would go a long way to establishing the factors underlying their success, were it not for the fact that the business environment also requires the exercise of powers we have been describing and illustrating, the paramount importance of which is undisputed. How then is this conflict, real or potential, resolved? The degree to which they have found satisfactory operational modes will underline the strength of their current positions and future prospects.

To a large extent, and this may be the key to the conundrum, their exercise of the principal managerial functions, the special talents they may bring to their calling and the personality factors that enter into their business lives, are facilitated by, and at the same time underline the reasons for, their gravitating towards some sectors of economic activity rather than others, the nature of the activity they are engaged in, the size of organization, the degree of specialization and their position relative to that of the head of the company.

In other words, as we have discovered from their career histories, their position allows or obliges them to exercise considerable flexibility in dealing with administrative matters, staff relations and customers. Within this specialized framework, either of the small business or in a more advisory capacity, whether owner, entrepreneur, *aide-de-camp* or troubleshooter, they learn, if they are to prosper, not only how to operate to maximum advantage but to live with their limitations.

A group of young women at the top of their class perform their tasks in fairly sharply contrasting manner. One of these has had to reconcile her self-confessed perfectionism with an anti-authoritarian streak that could have prejudiced her career with any one of lesser stature or capabilities. As it is her colleagues have either given way to her, learned to handle it or sheltered her from its consequences. It is significant in her case that some of her best work has been done when this tension has been absorbed by a superior in circumstances outside her control. At its worst on the other hand, when her suspicions are aroused by action on the part of others, she becomes anxious and rigid.

She has considerable powers of self-analysis and this has been supplemented in recent years by the optimism that comes with success and self-confidence. As it is she is realistic enough to appreciate that a sense of conflict is part of the challenge inseparable from achievement and her emotionalism can now be siphoned off when she arrives home to her husband.

This sense of challenge occurred to another woman only after she had entered business, although she too had rebellious undertones, derived from her 'browbeaten' schooldays. A self-sufficient personality, who derives fulfilment through her work, she has moved up 'because I have not sat down and expected work to come to me'. This single-mindedness, combined with a flair for sensing the possibilities of even chance encounters, as well as seizing obvious business opportunities, has been rewarded by increased responsibility, board appointments and corresponding emoluments, the latter to her being a symbol of success.

Despite these achievements, she refuses to delegate. This she attributes to her own over-conscientiousness, and the general tendency of businesswomen, whom she feels tend to be worried and harassed by pressures upon them, to try to justify themselves by throwing themselves into work. Very busy and by conscious choice out in front and on her own, with no professional or other reliable counsel forthcoming (she does not belong to a trade union on principle) she sublimates her emotional needs, when not working, in challenging recreational activities.

The youngest high-powered woman to be interviewed derives solace as well as motive power from the example set by her family. Paradoxically very modern in style and mode of living, she identifies herself with the nineteenth-century values of self-help, hard work and personal responsibility associated with the middle classes. Now she feels the older working classes are being contaminated by the indifference, apathy and complacency (which she, along with others, describes as a *laissez-faire* attitude) widespread among the younger workers, attitudes derived from the impersonality of large companies, and the inefficient and unimaginative management to which this structure of industry gives rise (lack of improvement among which she attributes to lack of managerial incentives).

To overcome the generally poor quality of labour available to her, and the general shortage of labour in an area of exceptionally high employment, she pays well above union rates, and attracts married women who, in her experience, work harder because of the inducement of part-time work. Once there (and she selects all of them as well as male staff), she gets the most out of them by example, by establishing standards of service, by delegating, by working through them and seeing that instructions are executed by deploying them to match their aptitudes and abilities to the jobs available and by being immediately accessible.

An altogether contrasting range of qualities and attitudes may be found among somewhat older women, working in male oriented environments where they are not the front runners, such as engineering and finance, and other fields where 'a woman has to be one step ahead of a man'.

This description of her efforts was put forward by a woman who was forced into business by pressure of events. Nevertheless, she feels she has been lucky in the people she has met, from whom she has learned much about the business world. Despite intermittent ill-health, which has obliged her to live in the country, she has overcome this by her energy and organizing ability. Moreover, her liking for people has been rewarded by remarkable loyalty from her workers who, although paid at union rates, are in a non-unionized company surrounded by large establishments with militant employees in the same field.

Fortunately for her, the company produces highly specialized goods requiring great flexibility to meet specific demands of its clients and for which there is little competition. This has advantages for her personally as an upper-class, somewhat retiring woman alone in a local industrial community (her board appointment was kept concealed from the industry and the fact that she is a woman is not apparent from the firm's stationery), since her sheltered strategic position in the industry allows her not only to retain her identity and dignity as a woman in a sphere dominated by sceptical males but, as head of the firm described as 'the Rolls-Royce of the . . . world', to keep one step ahead of them.

A woman of the same age, head of a company described as the 'Rolls-Royce of the . . . industry', attributed their advantage over other companies in the industry to the firm's being entirely non-unionized which obliged them to keep well ahead of the unions. The loyalty of the employees was further strengthened by the immediate access all of them had to her room. She, too, had had to learn the industry with little or no previous experience and laid great emphasis, as with so many of her equals, on the importance of communications, both internally and externally, and on the human aspects of industry. A good listener by nature, she found this of benefit when attempting to enter business with a mind unencumbered by precedents but open to the ideas and knowledge of her more experienced colleagues.

Realism and a willingness to face the facts of the situation have been the hallmarks of another 'lucky' woman. From being in a fairly sheltered position as 'second lieutenant' in a small company the indispensable position she occupied there has been maintained by her willingness to accept new ideas (as well as new managing directors); she 'sees the logic of the situation and lets that prevail'. By keeping her emotions under control she is able to exercise charm and persuasion in board discussions, a method of handling people to which she attaches considerable importance, not to be undervalued in a company employing mostly men and where loyalty counts for a great deal.

A woman in the same age range who, for anyone with less than her considerable intelligence, would be in a dangerously exposed position in an almost totally male environment, owes her position less to her qualities as a woman than to her skill as a technical adviser. When, from time to time, her calling takes her into ground hallowed by centuries of exclusive male usage, she has to 'manœuvre and circumvent'. Ironically, although her expertise lies in the taking of calculated risks, it is a profession where the margin of error for a woman is almost automatically considered too great to be underwritten.

5. *The feminine role in business mythology*

It is now logical to examine the work interests of women as distinct from those of men.

First, however, we may be begging a fundamental question if it is assumed that the innate differences between men and women are such that it would be natural to find women in some occupations rather than others. Even in the performance of the most demanding physical tasks, at least some women, measure for measure, have been equal to them. The argument does not carry us much further if the basis for discussion is shifted to masculine as contrasted with feminine characteristics. A consensus view would be that for convenience, or by habit and tradition, certain traits are associated more with the male or described as masculine behaviour and some with the activities or reactions of the female, that is to say feminine behaviour. It is then possible to talk in terms of individual men and women who represent varying aggregates of the attributes of both sexes. We should then need to describe the optimum balance of attributes necessary to succeed in the business environment.

Although qualities are individual, however, sexual differences are not immaterial, if only because of the rather extreme differences in male and female conditioning. At least in the society with which we are dealing, the male has been conditioned for work in the outside world where his success is held to require the exercise of reason, while women are associated with feminine qualities such as intuition (feminine because women have lived more natural lives closer to the heart of things where feelings predominate). By force of habit and in terms of numbers, therefore, men are predominant in business. It follows that the women who have surmounted these obstacles have done so by a combination of superior intellect, education, will (including both the motivation and the qualities needed on the way), the acquisition of specialist skills where they are not directly competing with men, a protected quasi-family relationship with their superiors and colleagues, or by being female substitutes to males who would have otherwise been in their position.

To put it another way, we are describing the activities of an unusual group of women who have in many ways assumed the roles of men in the outside world, but taken along with them habits of mind and patterns of behaviour suited for the role for which society has traditionally cast them.

With regard to some of these points, the women interviewed expressed roughly similar observations, in some cases there were direct contradictions, while other qualities were associated sometimes with the male, sometimes with the female.

Only women were interviewed and it is interesting but scarcely surprising that many of them believed that men were more given to posturing, to pompous displays, to expressing themselves in stilted phrases, not to be themselves, and to be unwilling to face the facts. This was held to be entirely consistent with the upbringing of the male preparatory to his appearance in the outside world which, as it is deemed to be competitive, requires the exercise of 'brave fronts and stiff upper lips'. For the most part, since it is a man's world, the women recognized such behaviour for what it is, and accepted it as an accustomed if not indispensable feature of business transactions.

In this context, 'empire-building', which can after all be a creative, and is arguably a male, activity, seems a logical and familiar feature of a fantasy world in which women, normally associated with more down-to-earth situations, feel the need to tread warily, as we have seen from those who have entered the City in the guise of specialists. Only one (and a very short-lived) instance of identifiable empire-building was quoted to us in the interviews in respect of women, whose characteristics relate more to the search for and the building of shelters. In the engineering sector, the interview material showed that women have been able to assert themselves by virtue of the strength of their position in relation to the head of the company (which may of course be themselves). It is surely significant that one woman who had become less securely placed than hitherto in personal terms felt obliged to exercise the softer female qualities and work on the sidelines if necessary.

The converse of empire-building, or an alternative way of making oneself visible, is to try to limit an organization's growth. As one senior woman expressed it, internal politics did not matter when the company was small and the principals were in a face-to-face relationship where cornering the market is a practical impossibility, but arises with its growth where communications become more complex and secretive behaviour, intrigue, conspiracy and so forth are symptomatic of the whole process.

One woman admitted that the question of empire-building was the very aspect of business that fascinated her and she felt that women were deceiving themselves if they thought that this necessary, but no doubt less attractive, aspect of business life had not been practised by almost every director in some form at one stage or another. The exceptions might be either those highly specialized functions where knowledge or advice is called for or those cases where the person is at the top and feels secure enough to be above it all.

There was similarly a minority view that men and not women are the realists. The woman who expressed it had spent all her working life in close proximity to a man who had a remarkable flair for business, a quality she described as being the ability to make judgments and one which is always with you. This she felt is closely related to instinct, or the store of knowledge and experience of other people's reactions and therefore continuous, but sometimes to hunch, which is inspirational and not linked with logic. His degree of realism may also be judged by the fact that she owed her position in the firm in the first place to a traumatic experience many years ago which resulted in the owner's completely losing faith in male administrative ability.

There is adequate evidence from these women that they also owe a great deal to the realms of instinct or intuition, of actions based on hunch and achievements based on flair. They have buttressed this with hard work, organization and knowledge, and where their self-confidence and inexperience has led them to rely on 'natural' gifts alone, with nearly disastrous consequences, they subsequently quickly realized the very real benefits to be gained by applying logic, common sense, and the views and wisdom of others.

Where serious mistakes have occurred they freely admit them. They have not allowed the experience to overwhelm them but rather have turned the situation to their advantage by drawing appropriate lessons from it. It is a necessary part, they feel, of growing up in business, and the more cautious approach accompanying it is a reflection of their own entry into middle age. Their attitude reflects the optimism they have brought into, and which has sustained, their careers so far, the self-confidence they have needed to continue, and the generally high principles expected of themselves and of the people they are dealing with.

There is no denying, however, that the business environment at present has done little to discourage them from becoming rather inward-looking and to induce in them a tendency to undervalue their own considerable achievements. Indeed it is, perhaps surprisingly, their underlying humility that in the main is their common and most memorable characteristic.

A highly contentious area of discussion is entered when such terms as emotionalism, dedication and application to detail are raised.

In considering the last quality we can, in practice, draw only on specific cases where the women concerned worked their way up to a senior position requiring a considerable degree of delegation but where habit, and their strategic position, has allowed them to maintain a residual hold on matters and duties which, in career terms, they would appear to have long outgrown. This is a necessary accompaniment to the comforting, if sometimes illusory, feeling of indispensability.

Thus one director, whose appetite for interfering in everything has been fostered by the nature of her responsibilities, or, to be more accurate, her interpretation of them, and who is reluctant to surrender them despite a reallocation of functions and duties on the board, justifies this zealousness by the universality of interests that ownership bestows on the holder. Although she does not regard herself as hard-working (in the usual sense of personally undertaking specific tasks), she sees her chief merit as her gift for setting other people to work for her and hence for the company. Despite the guilt she feels about this and the exact balance she should strike between her duties as a wife and as a senior executive, any doubts she entertained about her value to the company were set to rest by the deterioration she found among the staff on her return from holidaying abroad.

A director who had also spent her working life in a family business had found that women were better than men in 'implementing the details of a broad decision, men are better at formulating policy, more impatient with detail and fiddling'. Men and women were therefore not equal, and hence, not competitive but complementary. With her departmental autonomy almost complete, apart from decisions needing higher authority from her chairman, she has to delegate though she feels she could do the work better. As it is she still sees all the mail for the factory apart from that of the works manager and the purchasing department. This view of men at work was echoed almost exactly by a financial specialist among our sample.

It is a well-established phenomenon that observations by even disinterested spectators are not entirely independent of the vantage point they occupy; they are coloured by a range of factors peculiar to them: personality, experience, circumstances and so on. In other words, views concerning qualities pertaining to particular types of work and the sex better equipped to perform them incorporate rationalizations based on people's own lives and attitudes.

Hence from a woman dividing her time and thought between her home and the remarkable man she had served all her adult life we have the view that:

> 'Men are more dedicated to the extent that their lives suffer. Women are able to see how unnecessary exclusive dedication is and how it is not good for the business.'

Contrast this with the comments of an entrepreneur running a service for women:

> 'A man looks at life just as a job, he plays with it, but his personal life is more important to him. The job is only a means to an end. Men won't bother about the surroundings of their job, women do.'

Against this there is the more detached viewpoint of a director whose function includes trying to harmonize the views of spokesmen (male) from different departments in a company where most of the clerical and shop floor staff are female:

> 'Men are more status conscious. Women are less proud and make less fuss about the surroundings of their job.'

She was surprised how sentimental men could be.

An even less flattering view of her competitors came from a woman (twice divorced) who is responsible not only for day-to-day business in a particular wholesale trade but also for policy:

> 'Some men are very petty. I was surprised to what lengths they would go to get business. Some are intelligent but there are a lot of self-made men who feel inferior through lack of education. On the other hand, younger men try to create the impression of being important, therefore a woman who can do as well as a man is striking at something fundamental to themselves.'

A number of the women interviewed, then, endorsed the popularly accepted view that dedication to their career takes some men to the top, whereas women in business tend to get caught up in excessive detail. It was, however, pointed out that the woman entrepreneur, even where she may be rather emotional, is not precluded from succeeding, particularly if she is engaged in flexible, specialized, newer-type activities (especially those dealing with people), because emotionalism in business, though sometimes bad, is not fatal so long as it is 'accompanied by 100 per cent dedication'.

'Emotionalism' is the male retort to 'empire-building' and is rooted equally in the type of conditioning associated with the upbringing of women. It is scarcely surprising, therefore, that whilst the women interviewed did not consciously identify their actions with 'traditional' male tactics, emotionalism was generally and freely admitted to enter their personal and business lives.

Among the older women who had been largely sheltered from the need to battle for their positions, the importance of controlling this force was generally acknowledged and accepted, but particularly among the younger women, displays of warmth, sympathy, sentiment and the recognition of people as individuals, if not carried to extremes, were felt to benefit business in terms of improved labour, customer and public relations. In some instances, the emotional and other needs of the family have provided the driving force as well as the *raison d'être* of successful personal sales campaigns.

At the other extreme, women in positions or occupations requiring coolness and quickness of judgment, skill in negotiating, and the provision of technical advice, are hardly likely to allow themselves the privilege, luxury or embarrassment of emotional display (unless tactical reasons dictate the use of unorthodox weapons), any more than men in equivalent positions.

This whole area was neatly summed up by two widely contrasting women. First, a woman who has managed to pursue a career, even if it was broken by freelance or part-time work in order to bring up several children:

> 'If women are engaged in non-emotional work they are no more emotional than men, but otherwise, for example, matrons in schools, they get emotionally involved with children, or with male members of the staff. On the other hand, the men I worked with during the war were very emotional.'

Secondly, from a woman half her age:

> 'Men are more emotional at home, i.e. with situations unfamiliar to them. Women, therefore, are bound to be more emotional in business until they have established themselves.'

Meanwhile, a lonely minority in a world dominated by men, conscious they are on trial and trying to keep one step ahead, the women evince a maternal streak in their dealings with staff and in their fierce desire neither to part with something they have laboured to create nor to sacrifice their employees by accepting proposals in the form of takeovers.

So far we have made few explicit references to prejudice. Indeed, the women interviewed referred to it, in explicit and general terms, surprisingly little. In a general sense, however, women in business clearly have been fighting prejudice almost from the start. Unless they were the only children of men who had a family business and were brought up, sometimes literally like a boy, to man's estate, they usually had to overcome prejudice or discrimination in the type and content of their education and the conditioning deemed suitable for a girl. Very often they had to fight against one or both parents, to ignore the scepticism of bank managers, colleagues and competitors, to overcome the hostility or misgivings caused by their promotion won with assistance from superior, husband or friends, to work through cooperative and understanding colleagues if a customer likely to be embarrassed (such as a Moslem or Japanese businessman) needs to be served, to walk stealthily through notoriously male preserves, and, when at the top, to continue the fight on behalf of their sex among the lower ranks of employees.

For the rest it is a story of well-entrenched positions dug by the women themselves whilst being protected from on high, or of dealing with women, for women, and working in new and highly technical fields. The more general worlds of finance and administrative or line management functions in large-scale industry remain generally closed to them by choice and accessibility.

In general, however, apart from the older women whose main advances on this front were gained during the armistice (not always observed) between the sexes during the war, the role of prejudice is played down in interviews and its absence used to abjure the attitude, apathy and inactivity of the general, particularly the British, female population.

The attitudes held towards other women and the advice the women directors would give them again reflect mainly the age, experience and special interests of the women concerned and the preferences they display for either sex.

There is a tendency for the older sheltered women to be more tender-minded towards their own sex, a reflection of the fortuitous circumstances that helped them in the past and the deeper sense of conflict they undoubtedly feel between family responsibilities and their career, unless they have made the latter the means of underpinning it. The entrepreneurial aggressive younger women, on the other hand, show considerably less sympathy for their sex, but this is sometimes combined, because the nature of their activities necessitates the employment of large numbers of women or is flexible enough to cope with married women's difficult timetables, with a degree of permissiveness in allowing home or part-time work, arranging working hours to coincide with school times, and even the provision of creches.

The views of each group can be summarized crudely: on the one side, that but for unusual, unforeseen circumstances, their natural place, along with all other married women, is in the home where female fulfilment really lies; and on the other side a majority view that if women are still leading a dilatory, pointless, domestic life consumed by boredom and frustration, it is the result of their own lack of initiative, poor organizing ability, laziness, and the misconceptions, often sedulously fostered by men, that they hold of the business world.

6. *The woman director and her dependants*

The problem of accommodating married women with children in the developing structure of the labour market, in terms of part-time work, flexibility over hours, work at home, relaunching after a broken career, and the possibility of starting another career after the children have reached school age, or are in other ways less physically or emotionally dependent on her, is one we now discuss: in short, the domestic side of the women director's life, in so far as it impinges on her career.

First, however, it is necessary to consider the women who do not fall into this category and whose very real domestic problems can be overlooked. In doing so it becomes immediately apparent that, in terms of their actual domestic responsibilities, many of the distinctions drawn between single and married women on the one side and between men and women in business on the other are misleading if not meaningless.

These conform closely to the stereotypes to which society still clings. In other words, the responsibilities of the married man are financed outside the home by regular employment; the mother finds fulfilment inside the home by domestic chores for which she is not even allowed the consolation of a notional income; the bachelor, young and old, enjoys very considerable freedom, comparative financial security and independence; the single girl is a lightweight in business, a shorthand typist or filing clerk who will eventually disappear through the portals of marriage.

By contrast, the spinster not only invariably has to work but, as an unmarried daughter (a role sometimes voluntarily adopted), is expected to care for and provide for ageing parents. She is, therefore, in this context, midway between the married man who is obliged to work but not expected actually to look after his dependants and the working mother who has somehow to achieve a *modus vivendi* in her divided world.

For some women this conventional responsibility for parents (or close relatives) does not disappear with the assumption of the married state; moreover, the husband may either be or become physically incapacitated. There may be no children of the marriage but the wife is obliged to take the career, and hence financial, lead in the partnership. Again, the divorcees and widows in business correspond either to single people without responsibility for dependants or to single people with dependants, if they are still responsible for any children resulting from the marriage.

People in employment (including, of course, the self-employed) consist of first, those (excluding young people for the moment) who must work for financial reasons or feel obliged to do so through the weight of convention; this includes mostly men, spinsters, unmarried mothers, and those women whose marital state has disintegrated or whose circumstances impel them to take the career lead; and secondly, mainly married women with fairly strong motivations for outside employment, to supplement the family income, to occupy themselves as their children grow up and become independent, or to satisfy their compelling desires to follow a successful career. It is obviously the last group who are of most interest in the context of the survey but none of the categories, as we have seen from a detailed consideration of their case histories, is really exclusive.

If we consider first the women with dependants, of whatever kind, the problem essentially is the same, viz., their care and maintenance while the mother or female breadwinner is away at the office. It is, therefore, almost entirely a practical question of the type of help best suited to the individual circumstances of those comprising the household and a financial one of what the household's income will support, given the tax and other reliefs available to them.

In some respects, elderly people are more difficult to accommodate than young children who have more resilience than some mothers would credit. As one very perceptive witness said, based on her experiences with her two children aged 7 and 8;

> 'If anything goes wrong one is inclined to think it is because you aren't there. This is irrational as children are often very much better with nannie. Children take their cue from their parents.'

Older people on the other hand are often a byword for obstinacy among social workers, doctors and housing managers alike. For someone used to the tranquil pattern of domestic life over many years with, first, his wife and then his devoted single daughter, it is not likely that he will take kindly at first to, say, the matter-of-fact briskness of the home help, or the pertinent enquiries of the health visitor. At the level with which we are presently concerned, the shortcomings of the old may do no more than compound the difficulty of finding suitable domestic help on a continuing regular basis, a recurring theme throughout the enquiry, not of course confined to those with only parents to consider.

The woman whom we have just quoted is the head of a family business and is at liberty, within the confines of her own conscience and her judgment of the needs of the business, to make her own arrangements on the balance of time she devotes to career and family. When the children were young, she felt her task was easier since, provided the mother substitute attended to their requirements regularly and was 'naturally domesticated', their immediate practical wants, as well as their respect and liking for discipline and craving for affection, were satisfied. Now they are at school, however, one at a local private school, her belief that children need their parents more as they grow up has oblighed her to work, if not quite part-time, at least modified hours, i.e. leaving at 4 o'clock rather than 6.

At the office she has a very reliable 'front runner' in the shape of a manageress who has never married and has been with the firm 35 years. At home her younger boy is collected from school in the evening by a woman who then makes the tea and stays with him until his mother arrives home from the office. As it is permanency that young children mainly need she has on occasions been obliged to stay at home until another satisfactory nannie could be found.

A further difficulty with the temporary nature of a greater part of domestic service today is that once the children have been trained to follow a particular pattern, it then becomes more difficult for a successor to make them conform to her own ideas of acceptable child behaviour.

There is more than a hint here that looking after young children, as well as other forms of domestic service, need the professional approach with appropriate rewards, as much as a career in business does. This is echoed, if not carried to extremes, by a woman twice divorced and without children. She herself had been brought up very happily by a woman who had been nannie to her father. As a person entrusted with the upbringing of children her own mother would have been 'dreadful' and she finds that some of her friends also make dreadful mothers, success or failure depending on the personality.

In a sense there is a very real difference of opinion between the women interviewed on the best person to look after children and it is the very crux of the argument on whether married women with young children should go out to work. The majority view, heavily supported by traditionalist males, is that, even if satisfactory practical substitutes can be found, the only satisfactory mother is the person who gave the children birth.

The clearest expression of this came not unnaturally from a woman who has time only for freelance work apart from the interest she has in an old-established family firm. She believes that women would suffer most if husband and family were second to a career. She would meet the problem of the frustrated, intelligent non-domesticated woman by educating her emotionally for the inevitable breaks in her career since 'ploughing back talents into the lives of children who need an emotional supply from their mother would remove the feeling of wastage'. This leads to her conclusion that 'women are a good deal less selfish than men and they have to be'. Rather less flatteringly, she thought also that mothers feel jealous of any woman who takes her place as a mother.

These sentiments were inverted by a woman running a family

business which employs mostly women who amazed her by their 'resenting anyone working in their place' and their idea that 'no one can do a job as well as they can'. It might be more accurate to say, therefore, that women are a good deal more selfish than men and it is possibly a good thing for society, but not necessarily for the economy, that they are. Qualities are in fact closely allied to the individuals concerned and housewives, mothers and domestic servants can find fulfilment and hence dignity in their demanding but unspectacular roles.

But it is the in-between women, the half-emancipated generation, the less than wholly committed, who feel obliged to follow, and therefore find the most difficulty in fulfilling, two roles.

Inevitably, this has entailed considerable sacrifices, not necessarily always on the women's part. The most critical moment confronting the married woman at the beginning of her career, or when she is well established in it, is the decision whether or not to have a family. It is difficult, if not impossible, to decide who is placed in the most agonizing position, whether it is the woman who has taken over the family firm who feels she may be on probation until such time as her performance in her father's office justifies her clients' confidence in her, the young entrepreneur who is probably risking a good deal of her capital by branching out on her own, or the faithful, indispensable protegée of the head of the company. A great deal depends on the business circumstances at the time and the husband's attitude.

The position or attitude of the husband appears to be a critical factor in the development of the career and the family. From the evidence available, it is possible to make a further threefold classification, tentative and arbitrary since the evidence is inevitably one-sided though not necessarily biased, into situations where husband and wife are in equilibrium, situations where the wife is the *de facto* though not necessarily admitted or acknowledged leader, and situations where relations between husband and wife have become intolerable. Excluding the housewives and single women, they fall into roughly equal groups.

The first consists of partnerships, either where husband and wife are working as joint sponsors of the enterprise, are working at similar levels in closely related fields or branches of the same undertaking, or are working in widely different fields but are sufficiently well established and of great enough seniority to command each others' support and respect. It is among the latter that some overlap occurs with the next group where the husband tacitly accepts his wife's initiative or career lead, has become resigned to it, or attempts, with varying degrees of success, to adjust to it. Again, it is among the latter where symptoms of disintegration in the marital relationship can occur, one of which we later describe in detail. The third group, consisting of divorcees, are mostly derivatives of leadership situations that became uncontrollable, but contain also the survivors of once-successful situations of partnership or sponsorship.

A number of protégées in the same field had remarkably similar pressures to contend with, but the eventual outcome in each case varied. All the husbands at one time or another worked with the same company for a shorter period than their wives. Each husband applied pressure on his wife in favour of the firm by encouraging her to stay on or by being reluctant to have children at that time or unenthusiastic about the prospect of more children. Encouragement or pressure, real or indefinable, though nonetheless effective, came from the board.

One woman was over 30 when she married after more than ten years' close working relationship with the chairman. She considered leaving at this time but both he and her husband prevailed on her not to, a situation that was repeated a few years later at the birth of their child. Before their marriage her husband had been in a family business but joined her firm for some years until leaving to take up freelance work. In that time she had joined the board, the company was reorganized and her doubts about the wisdom of having more children in these uncertain circumstances were put to rest for medical reasons. She has some regrets but her husband would not have liked a larger family. She does not look back although she feels she could have found another outlet for her talents outside the firm. As it is the only 'break' she has experienced were the few weeks' absence from work after childbirth.

Another woman in an import/export business is thankful that her children were born under easier business conditions than those prevailing in recent years. Married 25 year ago to an employee of the same firm, their first child was born when she was over 30, a second four years later. Soon after their marriage the husband had left the firm to set up his own business. In the year this failed, his wife became general manager of the firm, he joined another firm and was later offered yet another job by a friend. His wife was by now earning more than he, and was firmly committed to continuing her career with the firm.

Had there been children in the early years of the marriage she would have retired, but as it is, circumstances have conspired to make her into a career woman. Her husband was opposed on material grounds (the need for a home and a car) to the idea of a family, and then his own period of job instability, followed by the arrival of their children, made her continuance in the firm more necessary than ever.

She remains much concerned about the care of her children. The younger is collected from school by an employee and waits in her office until she is ready to go home. In the children's infancy she was able to improvise by working three days a week, coming in late and leaving early, taking work home and making greater use of the telephone.

In her absences she was able to rely on an efficient book-keeper/secretary at work and the children's godmother at home. Subsequently, she ran the gamut of various types of domestic assistance, trained children's nurses and au-pair girls following one another in rapid and disturbing succession. She would prefer English girls, who are unobtainable, as she considers that foreign girls require too much leisure time, and au-pairs in general demand the same rate of pay as an ordinary domestic but without the willingness to work as hard. Improvising as she does she has found that, for example, an important meeting at work can upset all these arrangements. Looking back she feels she should probably have retired some years ago although conditions are improving now that the children are growing up.

The influence of childhood events, especially those derived from workingclass habits of thought, is often found among men who have moved a long way up socially by promotion in their chosen profession. One woman, acknowledging her own heavy dependence on such a man, was relieved that she had at last overcome his ingrained opposition to the idea of a living-in help. Clearly, with a joint income running into five figures, a large house to maintain in a good residential area and the very demanding work that the nature of their calling imposes on its practitioners, to say nothing of their young children, occasional domestic help would hardly suffice to meet their particular circumstances.

The robust good health she enjoys is shared by nearly all the women interviewed. Two women engaged in different sectors of a very competitive and demanding trade have applied their good health, energy and industriousness to their multiple roles as housewives, mothers and entrepreneurs. The woman who would be miserable as just a housewife took her first job when her daughter, now at university, was aged 4. Since then she has pioneered her own business almost single-handedly but still finds time to cook meals and clean her husband's clothes with help only once a week from a domestic. She sees no incompatibility in performing these chores, a traditional feature in the lives of Continental womenfolk, and is positively averse to the trend in this country towards the husband helping in the home or taking the children out, a feeling reinforced by her belief that British women are lazy and only too willing to cherish the myth of the downtrodden housewife. Nevertheless, she finds her own particular business a difficult one to combine with raising a family and she would not advise her daughter to go into it.

Like many of her kind, she finds, or at any rate prefers to believe, that her daughter is not only extremely glad she did work, as it would have been difficult to live with a bored mother, but that it also forced her to become independent. She regards her daughter as very balanced and with a sense of responsibility. It was her second husband who became a casualty of her career when he tried to take too close an interest in it but she was resigned to the fact that this marriage 'was doomed anyway'.

The other woman is very pro-British, a combination of sentiment and self-interest, most of the business with which she has been personally identified for over 30 years being in England. Starting in the family firm at 17, she was married at 20. Her son was born two years later, the same year that her father, under whom she was learning the business, died after a long and painful illness. In the circumstances, therefore, she was obliged to work longer hours than usual and 'worked up to the last minute of pregnancy'. Their home was across the road from the business and ten days after the birth she was back at work. She was away three weeks after the birth of her daughter three years later when she was 25. The children were brought up by nannies under her supervision or by herself personally if they were absent. During the war when the family was divided they were looked after by foster parents as she herself had been after the divorce of her parents when she was 8 years old. When she is not commuting regularly to the Continent to attend to family business matters in the charge of her husband and son, she lives in Hampstead where her remaining link with domestic responsibilities consists of cooking the main meal on Sundays.

A group of women whose experiences will be considered together are linked by their childlessness and the strong orientation of their career interests towards fashionable West End activities catering mainly for women. Half are in their thirties, half in their fifties and, apart from age, the possibility of children was precluded for two of them for medical reasons. One is in any case single.

The married women would have liked a family but in each case the husband's position or attitude obviated the need for further deliberation on the matter. One is the sole source of earned income in the household, one partners her husband in the business they founded and a third leads a quite separate business life from her husband, a leading medical figure whose opposition to children was probably based on the sensitive realization that 'I would have felt rather restless at home'.

Where the single or married childless woman is not wholly absorbed in her career she devotes a great deal of her energies, time and money to benevolent societies, religion, politics, sport and travel.

The youngest women interviewed were all married women entrepreneurs who became directors six or seven years ago and are wholly committed professionals with a background of training and experience gained from their own mobility of labour.

The oldest of these has been married for some years and has one child born the year after she started the company which employs almost exclusively professional mothers who would otherwise be unable to work. At least they would be unable to work if they supported her own refusal to delegate a mother's responsibility. The months in which the company was in its infancy corresponded fairly closely to the 8½ months of her pregnancy which she devoted to building the business up. At that time there was little client work coming in and she was able to take three months off after the birth of the baby though she was desperate to get back to work. Five years later the company is well established and 'would run without me if I were pregnant again'.

She has a daily help and part-time nannie and on her two afternoon sales visits she has a babysitter. Her daytime problem will soon be eased as the child will be old enough for school. Meanwhile she works at home where her office is, and also in the evenings when the child is asleep. She never works at weekends as she has few other opportunities to see her husband who is a scientist. Like many of her kind she is indifferent to the appearance of her home and fears that too long exposure to children is not only taxing but carries with it the risk of mental inertia.

In another case, a woman under 30, so far without children, met her husband, a civil engineer, ten years ago and they were married seven years later. An extremely hardworking dedicated personality who takes work home she feels herself devoid of any maternal instinct. The prospect does not bother her, however, as her husband is very tolerant and this, together with good organization, removes the last obstacles there may be to raising a family in harness with a career for the wife. Strongly individualist, she feels that the question of how family arrangements should be managed is a decision between the married partners. As an individual she believes that she could have achieved comparable success in any generation and the equality that must come in careers is held up less by men's attitudes, which will change anyway, than by women who 'think of themselves as child-bearers with an undistinguished role'.

The most advanced view is taken by a woman who regards herself as in the vanguard of her generation and identifies herself with the values of the next. In addition to radical changes in the tax laws, when men will not necessarily be regarded as the householder, she can foresee easier divorce laws with more fluid relationships between husbands and wives in which the nannie/housekeeper will become part of the domestic management triangle but children will not suffer very much. She herself has one child looked after by a professional nannie who is a trained teacher.

She actually started her business whilst she was expecting a child, and 'as I grew larger the building took shape'. She was away from work for only a week after the birth of the baby and then reapplied her energies into building up her company. Her husband, who is in broadcasting and whose hours are less regular, looked after the baby for a short period. Although they share the shopping arrangements she does not know whether he shares her views although he strongly approves of her activities.

The last cases we shall examine are the only examples among those interviewed of full-time businesswomen who have had substantial breaks in their careers or, to be more accurate, a series of loosely connected careers interrupted or disrupted by marriage. They are in their forties, of Celtic origin, twice married with more than two children, and affected by the financial and economic conditions of their childhoods.

The first left school just before the war, and despite her interest in English and an ability to write, did not settle down until joining a domestic appliance company where she applied to go over to the technical side. On the strength of this, the first part of Higher National Certificate and crammer courses run by the Air Ministry, she became responsible for inspection and production of small arms ammunition and then an assistant works manager for the rest of the war.

In 1945 she married a Commonwealth politician and lived abroad for six years where she became a political campaign manager for the leader of the Opposition and research worker and reporter for the national broadcasting network. When her marriage failed she went to Africa to work for a Commonwealth government and met her second husband in Kenya. On returning to England, she settled down after a fashion for seven years in the Midlands occasionally writing broadcasting scripts. When her second child was 3 years old (the other child of this marriage died), she undertook part-time work for trade magazines and house journals and at the end of this period, when they moved to London at the dictates of her husband's profession, she went on the staff of a magazine, subsequently forming her own company and being invited to rescue an ailing professional institute.

The move to London has made it not only easier but possible for her to resume a full-time career. She finds that the capital has all sorts of amenities apart from contacts that do not exist in the provinces. She has an office at home as well as at her business and they are connected by direct line. She has every modern domestic appliance (the result of her residence overseas where domestic help and babysitting is much easier to arrange), and takes advantage of an instant meals service ordered by telephone. Otherwise, she is expected to shop and cook and launder the clothes.

In these circumstances she does not feel she could manage if her children were under 5, an age when they are dependent and the mother does not want to waste the opportunity of moulding their personalities. Nevertheless, she believes it is important to recognize that they will become independent and the mother should therefore develop other interests in stages. At present she manages with the support of her colleagues, the cooperation of her husband and by careful organization of time when her daughters, one at public school, the other at university, are at home. In the last three years she has had trouble finding domestic help but her former, now retired, housekeeper helps in school holidays.

Her present career is an amalgam of her past experience and although she has never really lost touch with industry, she no longer pretends she could work on the factory floor owing to the rapid changes that have occurred. Contacts are also important in her field and it is for these reasons that she feels women are more likely to be prominent in say, electronics, a comparatively new field.

Her compatriot joined the Services at the end of the war and married, while overseas, an officer several years her senior. At the end of the war they were posted home, a disenchanting experience which led them into the hotel business for three years, a period terminated by the failure of their marriage. She moved to London to find work—she received only intermittent allowances—in order to keep the only child of their marriage, an 18-month-old daughter who was left in charge of a nannie. After a year or two of mostly clerical work she remarried, this time a naval officer by whom she had three children. Their nannie, to whom they paid a pittance out of their meagre resources, is still with her, though now retired.

The financial stringency which had haunted most of her and her father's life obliged her to take up work again six years later in order to pay for the children's private education. She discovered a latent sales ability of a very high order which at one period necessitated her being on the road hundreds of miles from home, leaving the children with an elderly nannie. She has few social contacts, her private and business life being built round her family. Meanwhile, she has developed two businesses from her own home, one of which will provide an interest for her husband when he retires. His detailed service mind is complementary to her forward-looking outlook which logically sees herself as a businesswoman rather than a career woman and therefore unlikely to work for ever.

Chapter III
CONCLUDING EVIDENCE

1. *The emergence of the professional businesswoman*

The main interest in studying the career records and experience of these women lies in the lessons that can be learned by those who follow after them; what advice, if any, they would proffer; and the implications of this collective experience for future policy by government, education authorities, employers, parents and teachers.

In the strictest sense of the word, no formal educational or professional qualifications are needed to become either a company director or a successful business executive. This is true not only of the general, administrative business world, but, to a lesser extent, of more specialized functionaries and professions such as personnel management and market research. In respect of the latter, people without degrees and/or membership of their respective professional associations (qualification for which, such as seniority, responsibilities, etc., vary), are becoming increasingly rare. In the less well-defined fields such as administration, selling, even finance, the practical arts which have sufficed for so long to produce our most gifted business leaders are increasingly supplemented, by scientific method applied to management, organization and marketing, quite apart from greater specialization in the field of accountancy.

This is all of a piece, of course, with the large expansion of the professions and the professional attitude in the last decade or so. This expansion, combined with the levelling off that has occurred, at least in theory, in job opportunities, the improved education and critical awareness of the current generation of parents, has produced an attitude to vocational and career preparation which has penetrated downwards to cover at least the top to middle layers of secondary education.

The two-fold process now proceeding, therefore, will make it much more difficult for the talented individual either to be denied the chance of formal educational progression or to make a dramatic leap upwards even directly, much less so indirectly, and the possibilities of sideways or unorthodox moves become even more remote. The rigidity inherent in such a system, coupled with the accelerating rate of obsolescent knowledge and techniques, makes the provision of second chances or second careers later in life at once technically and economically more difficult to achieve and yet all the more necessary, politically and socially, to be incorporated within the emerging structure.

On the face of things the prospects for women, particularly, married women, in this masculine concept of the shape of things to come look particularly unpromising if any lengthy breaks occur in their career. Furthermore, it would seem to allow less and less room for the individualist and the small business organization which provides the means for the expression of women's particular creative abilities.

As we have seen the change in economic conditions coupled with the change in government have brought considerable problems in their wake for the small business which recent fiscal concessions have only partially alleviated. Selective employment tax and discrimination in favour of the Development Areas, where few innovators or women directors are located, affect them particularly. The Industrial Reorganization Corporation and the philosophy of mergers and large-scale units upon which it is based present yet another pressure on the small firm.

However, the large firm may still find it convenient to buy a specific item from 'the corner shop'. Even more important than commodities, moreover, will be the increasing scope for the specialist, particularly in services which could be independent or under the umbrella of the parent organization. Most important of all, while the criteria governing the size of large companies are partly technical and economic (the cost of capital equipment and the possibilities for economies of of scale) partly acquisitive and defensive in nature, the remoteness of authority, the depersonalization of work, the routine and monotony of jobs, serve to underline the overriding importance of communications, an aspect of business life to which the women we interviewed attach the greatest importance and which they profitably exploit.

Closely allied to this is the tendency for ownership and decision-making to be concentrated at the centre, but, of necessity, allowing for very large and real measures of devolution and regional authority where the area of discretion and the resources at their disposal are likely greatly to exceed the capital value of the undertakings on which many of the women interviewed are at present engaged.

In another sense, of course, it could be argued that the large corporation, public or private, and the welfare provisions of the modern industrial state not only afford the security that is the overriding feminine characteristic, but they are essentially feminine in concept to begin with. Hence the later twentieth century stands in complete contrast to the masculine, pioneering, competitive environment of the Victorian world in its heyday. If this hypothesis is sound, then the women we have been describing are poles apart from their counterparts in the corporations which differ from the Civil Service only in the degree of formalization attendant upon the promotion structure.

Apart from being actually outnumbered by the number of men always available for posts, however, it is a logical deduction from the evidence and our analysis that women will differ from men primarily by aiming at certain types of posts or being located in certain types of situation, an adviser almost certainly, a power behind the throne very likely but not so likely to be in total command, giving orders with responsibility to no-one but herself.

While, therefore, on the basis of very crude projections and expectations, it is probably unlikely that there will be a great many women coming forward in the next thirty years at the top, particularly in large companies, the prospects for businesswomen and executives in other positions in considerable numbers look very real indeed. These are likely to be staff management or advisory personnel, departmental heads, specialists of various kinds in sales and finance. In the newer scientific and engineering fields there would appear to be no practical obstacles to the recruitment of women on a much greater scale than hitherto. The traditional roads via the family firm, entrepreneurship and secretary/personal assistant to the managing director may still be open but it is doubtful if they will be more rewarding.

If the destinations can be discerned as a vague but growing shape in the distance, what pathways are the new women of tomorrow to follow to be certain of reaching them?

So far as the women in the interviews were concerned, whether they have reached their positions via family connections, promotion or starting their own companies, there can be no substitute for experience and training, which in their case meant training on the job, sometimes in a variety of organizations in the same industry, sometimes by experience in different departments of the same firm, and sometimes by learning all about the firms from the viewpoint of and through the medium of their own department. Very few of them had formal training outside employment and these were mainly short secretarial courses which, if they were helpful at all, bore little relation to the duties they eventually assumed. For the latter, of course, quite often there were no alternative means of entry. Those women who had been to university found that their degrees had little relevance to their subsequent careers.

At the other extreme, the only daughters of fathers who disliked universities and preferred them to have a good commercial education combined with learning all aspects of the family business clearly benefited from this when they took over the business. They were fortunate also in having careers advice, as it were, within, by, and for the family. Rebels and deviants from the family line often found filial devotion, and the prospect of inheritance, too strong to resist.

For the most part, however, careers advice, in this or any other sense, scarcely existed except by casual reference to an opening, an incidental suggestion of a secretarial course, or negatively, either by direct opposition or scorning or casting doubt on their first choice of career. Both parents and teachers clearly felt girls were predestined to become housewives, and if they did display exceptional academic ability and overcame parental opposition, then they would be likely to read arts subjects at university.

Careers advice was described by one witness well qualified to judge and with experience of North American practice, as 'appalling in this country'. Certainly no-one came forward to speak out for Appointments Boards or the Ministry of Labour. Too often these organizations appeared to be serving the needs of employers rather than catering for the particular abilities of the potential 'recruits' (a term that speaks volumes in itself). Such techniques as aptitude testing are confined to very few private organizations and the units already in being at the Department of Employment and Productivity appear to have a similar range.

The problem of matching needs and recruitments to supply and demand is intensified by a deep psychological gap between the expectations and values aroused by education (and the gap deepens or widens at every step of the examination ladder), and the practical realities of everyday business life. This gap could be reduced, or the blow softened, by a less rigid attitude on such often pointless and archaic disciplinary matters as adhering strictly to office hours. Some tasks simply cannot be executed effectively in the time available or within the confines of the office or factory. A shorter working week, longer holidays and, for women particularly, part-time work would all add to the appeal of the business world.

For the most part, however, since it is a world of business and management that we live in, the gap will have to be closed mainly from the educational side. Some bridges of course are already built or under construction, through the business management schools and colleges of technology. But apart from those destined for the universities, who may be thankful to have no contact, and the specialized colleges which cater for those already attracted to industry in any case, more could be done in familiarizing the business world to those who will have to accommodate themselves to it in some form or other.

Business, particularly industry, has a bad image among outsiders which the mystique its practitioners have created round it does much to encourage. As one woman commented who had come to business late in life with a good educational background, business can be as intellectually exciting and stimulating as any other professional activity. To these women making money is either secondary, an incidental or a means to establishing their newly won status in the community.

The fact that so many of the women interviewed dated their rebelliousness from the age of 11 or 12 may be of more than psychological or physiological significance. At least at this age, five or six years before the preliminary hurdles have to be cleared in advance of university entrance, there is time for unhurried consideration of the girls' interests, qualities and personalities. With boys, who enter the rebellious stage with the consciousness of reaching adolescence, at 15 or 16, it may be too late to change the direction along which their parents and teachers have urged them.[1]

Provided their urges are not primarily destructive in nature, young rebels, and their counterparts, the organizing 'bossy' types, may well possess the leadership qualities needed in business as in other fields, where a sense of responsibility and decisiveness are among the hallmarks of the aspiring manager.

2. *Summing up*

1. The woman director is characteristically associated with small companies employing less than 50 people and less than £25,000 capital, and she is likely to be within a few years of retirement. A substantial number are spinsters but almost as many started their companies with their husbands or owe their directorships to inheritance or family connections. They are likely to be earning not much more than £3,000 per annum and at least £2,000 per annum

[1] *The Daily Telegraph* recently quoted Mr E. R. B. Campbell, Director of the Public Schools Appointments Bureau, as saying that 'A school's good academic record did not mean necessarily that its pupils were the most successfully placed in jobs. Some of the most intelligent young men formed a high proportion of those who came back to the bureau for more guidance because their first job was unsuccessful.'

less than most men. It is an even chance that the husband will be a fellow director of the same company.

2. The daughters of professional men or businessmen, they have the education relevant to their social status until the age of 18 when, as likely as not, they will take a secretarial course. Few have professional qualifications and even now a significant proportion do not think of themselves primarily as businesswomen. Most of them have non-resident domestic help and with most of their children grown up they can participate, or if childless sublimate their emotional energies, in various benevolent, cultural, political or sporting activities.

3. The 'front runners' are very much younger, more likely to be married with children, mostly still at school. Their own education took place at grammar schools rather than private schools (as with many older women directors), or public schools (as with a good many men directors); they are more likely to have a degree.

4. More exposed to competitive market conditions for labour at the very beginning of their careers, nearly half of these younger women arrived on the board by promotion and a third by starting companies on their own. Nevertheless, they are more generous in their acknowledgment of the help they have received from the principal men in their lives.

5. The front runners are most numerous in companies employing between 100 and 500 people but compared with men are few and far between in larger companies. Their incomes are in the range of £4,000–5,000, below the average for most men. However, they are more likely than older women to be able to afford, or have need of, a resident domestic; they are less disposed to support charitable interests or to socialize in clubs.

6. When examined closely and critically, even this 'select' group can produce very few career women, as distinct from businesswomen who started or have remained working from a variety of motives or causes, sometimes purely fortuitous.

7. Economic circumstances, the shortage of labour in wartime, the scarcity of raw materials in the post-war years, and the sustained consumer demand in the decade that followed, cushioned their entry into responsible business positions. Additional security was afforded by virtue of either inheritance, sponsorship or specialization in key products or services, many of which were comparatively novel or specially suitable for, or appealing to, women.

8. The last five years have been the first real test most of these women have had to endure. Although this is true of business, especially small businesses, in general, their situation is rendered more acute by their consciousness of being a minority on trial. A significant number of the women interviewed are contemplating a drastic change in the direction of their career.

9. Apart from their abilities in rescuing or expanding businesses, the women directors studied have been responsible for introducing new products, services, and techniques. Some of them have ingeniously exploited the current demand for certain categories of female labour and produced formulae which enable other women to resume or continue their careers. In a period when marketing has been in the ascendant, many of the women have had remarkable success in this field, an achievement which training boards and company recruitment officers should study carefully to determine whether there is even greater scope for women in this direction. An aptitude for mathematics in an age of computers and data processing is also opening the door to preserves which were earlier exclusively male.

10. The ambitious woman director is often an immigrant, the child of immigrants, or has had long contact with people from overseas. These women are unusually free of the conventional restraints that limit the aspirations of most British women and they are able to capitalize more readily on business opportunities. The nature of the education received in girls' schools, the lack of careers advice and the low expectations of teachers and parents concerning the girls' careers, unless they are obviously destined for taking an arts degree, cripples the outlook and prospects of girls even more than boys in an educational system still largely geared to academic prowess.

3. *Statistical tables*

In the following tables the Select Group refers to the women selected for intensive interviewing from among the 279 women who completed the full-length questionnaire issued to them in booklet form in mid-July. Where applicable, figures are also given for a sample of non-respondents who replied to a follow-up enquiry in November, and with a survey of male directors conducted in 1966.

All calculations are based on a 100 per centile basis, i.e. eliminating, where relevant, not-applicable categories such as unmarried women and those not answering the question. Significant omissions are referred to in the text. However, in some cases the figures will not add up to 100 per cent because of: (1) rounding, (2) some cases when a respondent has ticked more than one category, e.g. children in more than one age group.

. . = not available or included in 'others'
— = nil or negligible

TABLE 1 *Age*

	Women	Select Group	Non-Respondents	Men
20–29	4	8	—	2
30–39	10	24	7	13
40–49	27	40	14	29
50+	59	28	79	56

TABLE 2 *Marital status*

	Women	Select Group	Non-Respondents
Never married	26	16	24
Married	34	48	38
Widowed	19	4	24
Divorced/ separated	11	16	7
Remarried	10	16	7

TABLE 3 *Age at first marriage*

	Women	Select Group
Under 20	13	24
20–24	44	29
25–29	28	29
30–34	7	18
35+	8	—

TABLE 4 *Age of children*

	Women	Select Group
Under 5	6	13
5–10	16	33
11–16	20	47
16+	80	53

TABLE 5 *Children's schooling*

	Women	Select Group
Day school	20	40
Boarding school	19	40
University/full time training	22	40
Working	51	20
Married	21	13

TABLE 6 *Final school education*

	Women	Select Group	Men
Elementary	5	—	5(a)
Secondary modern	4	8	13(b)
Grammar	32	44	31
Private	34	16	..
Public	17	20	44
Other	7	12	5

(a) Primary, (b) Secondary.

TABLE 7 *Type of training or further education*

	Women	Select Group
University	20	26
Technical college	8	9
Professional	18	14
Secretarial college	42	36
Evening classes	24	32
Other	16	26

TABLE 8 *Qualifications*

	Women	Select Group	Men
Degree	13	26	18
Diploma	31	32	..
Professional qualification	20	14	40
None	57	48	52

TABLE 9 *Father's occupation*

	Women	Select Group	Men
Director of your company	22	24	32(a) (both rows)
Manager/executive of another company	23	32	
Professional	24	28	18
Clerical	3	—	..
Skilled	10	—	40(a)
Semi-skilled	3	—	10(a)(b)
Other	18	20	..

(a) Approx. figures only, (b) Including manual work.

TABLE 10 *Age of getting first job*

	Women	Select Group
14–16	15	8
16–18	29	36
18–21	33	32
21–25	14	20
25+	9	4

TABLE 11 *Source of first job*

	Women	Select Group	Men
Advertisement	31	44	15
Labour Exchange	4	4	3
Appointments Boards	8	—	9(a)
Parent's firm	12	8	56(b)
Husband's firm	3	4	
Personal contact	38	28	6(c)
Other	4	12	9

(a) Careers Bureau, (b) Family firm and family or social contact, (c) Direct approach by a firm.

TABLE 12 *Means of obtaining board appointment*

	Women	Select Group	Non-Respondents
Promotion	40	44	28
Starting own company	24	32	10
Starting company with husband	17	12	28
Inheritance	7	4	—
Family connections	15	12	28
Other	2	4	17

TABLE 13 *Sources of help in furtherance of career*

	Women	Select Group
Husband	29	40
Father	18	28
Mother	3	4
Relative	4	—
Friend	10	8
Colleague in present firm	17	16
Colleague in previous firm	6	8
Other	4	4
No-one	23	4

TABLE 14 *Executive post held*

	Women	Select Group	Men
Chairman	28	28	21
Vice-chairman	2	4	2
Managing director	42	44	41
Company secretary	25	20	} 34
Other	19	32	

TABLE 15 *Size of company in terms of capital*

	Women	Select Group	Men
Under £25,000	59	56	
£25,000–£50,000	13	4	} 41
£50,000–£100,000	7	8	
£100,000–£250,000	7	16	13
£250,000–£500,000	4	—	10
£500,000+	8	16	33

TABLE 16 *Size of company in terms of number of employees*

	Women	Select Group	Non-Respondents
Under 10	27	12	24
10–50	29	16	43
50–100	17	24	10
100–500	15	32	12
500–1,000	5	8	7
1,000–5,000	3	4	4
5,000+	2	4	—

TABLE 17 *Husband's occupation*

	Women	Select Group
Director of your company	53	50
Employee of your company	1	6
Manager/executive of another company	15	22
Professional man	25	17
Other	17	22

TABLE 18 *Earned income before tax*

<table>
<tr><th></th><th>Women</th><th>Select Group</th><th>Men</th></tr>
<tr><td>Less than £2,000</td><td>26</td><td>4</td><td rowspan="2">11</td></tr>
<tr><td>£2,000–£3,000</td><td>23</td><td>4</td></tr>
<tr><td>£3,000–£4,000</td><td>18</td><td>12</td><td rowspan="2">33</td></tr>
<tr><td>£4,000–£5,000</td><td>15</td><td>52</td></tr>
<tr><td>£5,000–£10,000</td><td>14</td><td>20</td><td>39</td></tr>
<tr><td>£10,000+</td><td>3</td><td>8</td><td>17</td></tr>
</table>

TABLE 19 *Gross income from all sources*

	Women	Select Group
Under £3,000	32	4
£3,000–£4,000	18	16
£4,000–£5,000	18	24
£5,000–£10,000	25	44
£10,000+	7	12

TABLE 20 *Joint total income from all sources*

	Women	Select Group
Under £3,000	10	—
£3,000–£5,000	22	6
£5,000–£7,000	21	18
£7,000–£10,000	20	29
£10,000+	25	47

TABLE 21 *Type of domestic help*

	Women	Select Group
Resident domestic	23	35
Au Pair	3	4
Daily	57	48
Occasional	24	22

TABLE 22 *Expenditure on domestic help per week*

	Women	Select Group
Under £1	7	—
£1–2	15	12
£2–5	34	24
£5–10	31	40
£10+	13	24

TABLE 23 *Self description*

	Women	Select Group	Non-Respondents
Housewife	8	—	10
Retired	5	—	10
Businesswoman	84	88	73
Housewife/Business-woman	3	12	7

TABLE 24 *Outside interests*

Clubs and Societies	Women	Select Group
London	33	28
Social	16	4
Sporting	23	4
Religious	11	4
Political	22	24
Cultural	21	20
Civic	10	4
Benevolent	18	8
Professional/Union	41	40
Other	16	—
None	14	24

TABLE 25 *Regional distribution of women directors*

Region	Women	Select Group	Non-Respondents	Men
London	42	68	24	55 (London and South-east)
South-east	23	24	24	
East	3	—	7	4
South-west	3	—	14	4
Midlands	10	4	10	13
North	8	4	7	16
Wales	2	—	—	2
Scotland	3	—	—	4
Northern Ireland	—	—	—	1
Channel Islands	—	—	—	1
Not stated	6	—	14	—

4. *References*

Women in Top Jobs: An Interim Report, PEP, 1967.
Margaret Cussler, *The Woman Executive*, Harcourt, Brace, 1958.
Women Executives: Their Training and Careers, London Chamber of Commerce, 1966.

'The Director Observed', *The Director*, April–May 1966.
Who's on the Board, Institute of Directors, 1958.
Heinz Hartmann, *Die Unternehmerin*, Westdeutscher Verlag, 1968.
Madame Prunier, *La Maison*, Longmans, Green, 1957.
Women in Business, Conference at the Café Royal, June 13, 1968. College of Marketing and Guardian Business Services.
The Library of the Fawcett Society, 27 Wilfred Street, London S.W.1.

5. *Questionnaire*

(A) PERSONAL DETAILS

1. Which of the following age groups do you come into?
   - 20–24
   - 25–29
   - 30–34
   - 35–39
   - 40–44
   - 45–49
   - 50–54
   - 55 plus

2. Marital status:
   - Never Married
   - Married
   - Widowed
   - Divorced
   - Separated
   - Remarried

3. Age at first marriage:
   - Under 20
   - 20–24
   - 25–29
   - 30–34
   - 35–39
   - 40–44
   - 45 plus

4. Do you have any children?
   - Yes
   - No

5. Are any of your children:
   Under the age of 5
   5–10
   11–16
   Over 16

6. Are any of them attending:
   Nursery school/Play group
   Day school
   Boarding school
   University/Full time training
   Working
   Married and not working

7. Was your final school education:
   Elementary
   Secondary modern
   Grammar
   Private
   Public
   Other

8. Did you have any kind of training or further education after leaving school?
   Yes
   No

9. If so, what kind?
   University
   Technical college
   Professional
   Secretarial college
   Evening classes
   Other

10. Do you have any of the following recognized qualifications?
    A degree
    A diploma
    A professional qualification

(B) PROFESSIONAL AND BUSINESS DETAILS

1. Is the company of which you are a director Public or Private?
   Public
   Private

2. How large is it in terms of:
   (a) Issued capital:
      Less than £25,000
      £25,000–£50,000
      £50,000–£100,000
      £100,000–£250,000
      £250,000–£500,000
      £500,000 plus

3. (b) Approximate number of employees:
      Under 10
      10–50
      50–100
      100–500
      500–1,000
      1,000–5,000
      5,000–10,000
      10,000 plus

4. Is it a 'family firm'?
      Yes
      No

5. Do you and/or your husband hold a controlling interest?
      Yes
      No

6. If it is a family firm is your connection:
   (a) through your family?
      Yes
      No
   (b) through your husband?
      Yes
      No

7. For how long have you been a member of the Institute of Directors?
      Up to 1 year
      1–3 years
      4–6 years
      6–10 years
      Over 10 years

8. If you are married is your husband also a member?
   Yes
   No

9. Do you look through *The Director*?
   Regularly
   Seldom
   Never

10. Do you use the Institute's other facilities?
    Regularly
    Seldom
    Never

11. If yes, which? ....

12. What other facilities would you like to see the Institute offer women members?
    ....

13. Do you regard yourself predominantly as:
    A housewife
    A retired working/businesswoman
    A businesswoman working full or part time

(C) CURRICULUM VITAE

Please give a brief summary of your career since starting work, drawing attention to:

(a) any major changes in level of seniority
(b) any major changes in type of work
(c) any changes from full time to part time work or *vice-versa*
(d) any complete breaks in your career

Position	*Dates*	*Nature of Duties*	*Salary*	*Reason for Change*

(D) FOR BUSINESSWOMEN WORKING FULL OR PART TIME

1. How old were you when you left school?
   14–16
   16–18
   18–21

2. When you left school did you intend to follow your present career?
   Yes
   No

3. How old were you when you got your first full time job?
   14–16
   16–18
   18–21
   21–25
   Over 25

4. Did you get this job:
   By answering an advertisement
   Through a labour exchange
   Through the University Appointment Board
   By joining your parents' firm
   By joining your husband's firm
   By personal contact

5. How did you achieve your board appointment?
   By promotion from within the company
   By starting/founding the company yourself
   By starting/founding the company with your husband
   By inheritance
   By family connections

6. How old were you when you got your first board appointment?

7. Are you at present:
   in full time salaried employment
   in part-time salaried employment
   not in paid employment

8. If you are in less than full time employment what are your working hours per week?
   Less than 10 hours
   10–14
   15–19
   20–24
   25–29
   30 plus

9. Do you work for the company of which you are a director?
   Yes
   No

10. If yes, are you:
    An executive director
    A non-executive director

11. If the former, are you:
    Chairman
    Deputy or vice-chairman
    Managing director
    Company secretary
    Other

12. Is your present position the work for which you were professionally trained?
    Yes
    No

13. Apart from your own efforts, who, if anyone, has been of most help to you in promoting your career?
    Husband
    Father
    Mother
    Relative
    Family friend
    Personal friend
    Colleague in present firm
    Colleague in previous firm
    Other
    None

14. Roughly what is your present earned income (before tax and including allowances)?
    £1,000–£2,000
    £2,000–£3,000
    £3,000–£4,000
    £4,000–£5,000
    £5,000–£10,000
    £10,000 plus

15. What is your present personal total gross income from all sources?

    Under £3,000
    £3,000–£4,000
    £4,000–£5,000
    £5,000–£10,000
    £10,000 plus

16. If married, what is your joint total gross income from all sources?

    Under £3,000
    £3,000–£5,000
    £5,000–£7,000
    £7,000–£10,000
    £10,000 plus

17. If you are married, does your husband work for the same company?

    Yes
    No

18. Is/was your husband:

    A director of your company or one in the same group
    A manager of your company
    An employee of your company
    A manager/executive of another company
    A professional man
    Other

    (Your company = the one of which you are a director)

19. Is his occupation essentially the same now as it was at time of marriage?

    Yes
    No

20. Is/was your father:

    A director of your company or one in the same group
    A manager of your company
    An employee of your company
    A manager/executive of another company
    A professional man

A clerical worker
A skilled worker
A semi-skilled worker
Other

21. DOMESTIC CIRCUMSTANCES

Do you have any domestic help or help with the children?
Yes
No

22. If yes, is this:
Resident domestic
Resident au-pair
Daily
Occasional

23. How much do you spend per week on domestic help?
Under £1
£1–£2
£2–£5
£5–£10
£10 plus

24. Do you feel that you have sufficient leisure time?
Yes
No

25. What associations, clubs, etc. do you belong to?
London clubs
Other social clubs
Sporting clubs
Religious associations
Political associations
Cultural associations
Civic associations
Benevolent associations
Professional association or union
Other

26. Are you a committee member of any of the organizations to which you belong?
Yes
No

27. Do you think that women could play a greater part in business life in this country?
    Yes
    No

28. If 'yes' what prevents them?

29. What advice would you give a woman of 20 starting on a business career?

Part Three

WOMEN IN THE BBC

Chapter I
STRUCTURE AND ORGANIZATION OF THE BBC

1. *Powers and obligations of the* BBC

The BBC began as the British Broadcasting Company in 1922, when the broadcasting service in this country started. It was formed by the principal manufacturers of wireless apparatus at the invitation of the Postmaster General, and was required, under licence, to provide a service 'to the reasonable satisfaction of the Postmaster General'. At this time the Company had no Charter. The General Manager was Mr J. C. W. Reith—now Lord Reith.

In 1925, a Committee under the chairmanship of Lord Crawford recommended that the broadcasting service should in future be conducted by a public corporation 'acting as trustee for the national interest'. On January 1, 1927, the British Broadcasting Corporation was set up by Royal Charter, operating under a Licence from the Postmaster General.

The members of the Corporation are its Governors, who are appointed by the Queen in Council. There are twelve Governors, appointed usually for five years, who work through a permanent executive staff headed by the Director General, who is the chief executive officer of the Corporation.

The BBC is a non-profit-making organization, and, under the terms of its Charter has to apply the whole of its income solely to promoting its objects which are to provide a public service of broadcasting for general reception at home and overseas. Its domestic broadcasting is financed by the revenue from broadcast receiving licences, and its external services are financed by a Grant-in-Aid from the Treasury.

The BBC has complete independence in the day-to-day operations of broadcasting subject to the requirements laid down in its Charter and in the Licence and Agreement.

The charts below give some idea of the structure of the BBC and its organization into divisions and departments. The main divisions, each with a Director or Managing Director on the Board of Management are Radio, Television, External Broadcasting, Engineering, Administration. The Director of Public Affairs is a new appointment

Organization of the BBC

The organization of the BBC is being streamlined at present following some of the recommendations of the team of management consultants called in to examine the workings of the BBC in 1968. However, the broad lines of organization of departments are as follows:

Board of Governors

Chairman
Vice-Chairman
National Governor for Scotland
National Governor for Wales
National Governor for Northern Ireland
Seven other governors

Director-General

Board of Management

Board of Management

Director-General

Managing Director, External Broadcasting	Managing Director, Radio	Managing Director, Television	Director of Administration	Director of Engineering	Director of Public Affairs	Director of Programmes, Television	Editor, News and Current Affairs

The Secretary

The organization of the BBC into divisions and departments is best illustrated by these charts taken from the and has responsibility for the Secretariat, Publications and Overseas and Foreign Relations. The Director of Programmes, Television, and the Editor of News and Current Affairs are also new appointments to the Board. The BBC has been extremely flexible in the speed with which it has adapted to the changing demands of the organization. New departments and posts are created when necessary, and the organizational picture shown above looks very different in detail from that of even ten years ago.[1]

Under the Members of the Board of Management were one Deputy Director, two Assistant Directors, twenty-four Controllers and seven Assistant Controllers in 1969. Of these posts, only one was held by a woman—that of Assistant Controller (Planning) Television. Under these come the senior staff holding group or departmental responsibility.

In the *BBC Handbook, 1969*, details are given of all senior staff with divisional and departmental responsibility, from the Director General down. Of 211 posts listed, 5 were held by women. However, the BBC points out that not all senior staff are listed in the *Handbook*, and that certain posts which do not involve divisional or departmental responsibility but are nevertheless highly paid, responsible positions are not mentioned in the *Handbook*. Almost all the senior posts in the BBC are found in production and planning, operations or administration, and it is with these areas that this report will be concerned.

Production involves the actual putting together of radio or television programmes, from the planning of ideas, scripting, design, casting, directing and so on until the finished product is heard or seen by the viewer or listener. Decisions on what will be transmitted, when it will be transmitted, its length, format, staffing and so on, are taken at divisional or departmental level. The actual production of the programme is usually in the hands of a programme editor or producer who works in close cooperation with the departmental head, who interprets general policy and passes on decisions made at a higher level. The planning departments of radio and television are closely linked to production, although they are not strictly production departments. They decide in conjunction with top management when programmes should be scheduled for transmission. They decide what goes out when, and in fact determine the shape of the overall picture of a day's viewing or listening. In addition, they have responsibility for the allocation of resources and facilities to departments and programmes.

[1] Since this report was prepared, *Broadcasting in the Seventies* has been published, resulting in a number of changes in the organization of the BBC, particularly as far as regional broadcasting is concerned.

Managing Director, Radio

- Engineering Operations and Maintenance[3] (radio group)
- Programmes and Planning
  - Radio 1
  - Radio 2
  - Radio 3
  - Radio 4
  - Presentation
- Local Radio Development
- Midlands[2]
- North[2]
- N. Ireland[2]
- Scotland[2]
- Wales[2]
- South and West[2]
- Supply and Services
  - Radio Production Services
  - Drama
  - Educational Broadcasting
    - School Broadcasting[1]
    - Further Education
  - Gramophone Programmes
  - Light Entertainment
  - Music Programmes
  - Light Music
  - Outside Broadcasts
  - Popular Music
  - Religious Broadcasting[1]
  - Talks and Current Affairs
- Administration
  - Administration
  - Production Planning
- School Broadcasting Council (Seconded BBC Staff)

Managing Director, Television

- Engineering Operations and
- Maintenance[3] (television group)
- Programme Groups and Departments
  - Planning
  - Presentation
  - Drama Group
  - Light Entertainment Group
  - Outside Broadcasts Group
  - Current Affairs Group
  - Features Group
  - Documentary Programmes
  - Children's Programmes
  - School Broadcasting[1]
  - Further Education
  - Religious Broadcasting[1]
- Programme Servicing Departments
  - Film Operations and Services
  - Design Group
  - Studio Management
  - Scenic Servicing
  - Artists Bookings
  - Script Unit
- Administration
- Television Enterprises

[1] Parts of Educational and Religious Broadcasting Departments, which cover radio and television

[2] Under Managing Director, Radio but responsible to Managing Director, Radio, Managing Director, Television and Director of Engineering for day-to-day working in their respective branches

[3] Responsible to Director of Engineering for professional standards

Director of Engineering

- Research
- Designs
- Transmitter Planning and installation
- Studio Planning and installations
- Equipment
- Building

- Operations and Maintenance[1] (Radio Group)
- Operations and Maintenance[1] (Television Group)
- Operations and Maintenance (Regions)
- Operations and Maintenance[1] (External Group)
- Operations and Maintenance (Transmitter Group)
- Operations and Maintenance (Communications)

- Engineering Establishment
- Engineering Training
- Engineering information
- Engineering Secretariat

[1] Under Managing Director concerned but responsible to Director of Engineering for professional standards

Managing Director, External Broadcasting

- Engineering Operations and Maintenance[1] (External Broadcasting)
- Services Division
  - English Network
  - African
  - Arabic
  - Central European
  - East European
  - Eastern
  - Far Eastern
  - French Language
  - German
  - Latin American
  - South European
  - Overseas Regional Services
- Programme Division
  - Eternal Services News
  - Programme Supply Department
  - External Programme Operations
  - English by Radio and Television
- Audience Research
- Transcription
- Monitoring
- Administration

[1] Responsible to Director of Engineering for professional standards.

Director of Administration

- Finance
- Staff Administration
  - General
  - Medical and Welfare
  - Grading
- Management Services Group
- Staff Training and Appointments
  - Staff Training
  - Appointments
- Legal Adviser
  - Solicitor
  - Programme Contracts
  - Copyright
- Central Services Group
  - Buying
  - Catering
  - Central Services (Central Premises)
  - Central Services (Television)
  - Facilities

Director of Public Affairs

- Information Services
  - Secretariat
  - Publicity
  - Audience Research
  - Libraries, News Information and Registries
- Publications
  - Advertisement
  - Circulation
  - Distribution
  - Production
  - Radio Times Hulton Picture Library
  - *Radio Times*
  - *The Listener*
  - Educational Publications
  - General Publications
  - *Ariel* (*Staff Magazine*)
- Overseas and Foreign Relations

The operations divisions of the BBC are concerned with the actual mechanics of getting the picture on to the television screen or the sound into the radio. Most people concerned in operations have some kind of engineering training, and to reach a position of any responsibility in the operations divisions, a very high degree of engineering expertise is necessary.

The administration department of the BBC is very complex, and has responsibility for staff, training, finance, legal aspects, and all the other departments which go to make up the administration of a large public corporation.

Chapter II
WOMEN AND EMPLOYMENT IN THE BBC

1. *Historical background to women in the BBC*

From the very beginning, the BBC was unusual in its treatment of women employees. First of all, it established the principle of equal pay from the start, so that one of the biggest obstacles to equality between men and women in the work situation was never a matter of contention. Secondly, the BBC had no ban on married women working, and in fact, in the early days some of the most outstanding women were married. In both these respects, it had a much more progressive policy than the Civil Service.

One of the first five Governors of the BBC was a woman, and there were a number of exceptional women in positions of quite considerable responsibility. In the early days of broadcasting in 1931, the BBC was praised for its policy towards women in positions of responsibility.

> 'As regards women on the staff, the BBC has set an example which is not always to be found among public bodies. Women are not compelled to resign at marriage, and equal pay for equal work is on the whole respected, while married women are not debarred from applying for posts.'[1]

At that time, there were married women as heads of the Schools and Adult Education sections, and there were women executives in the Foreign Department, Publications, Children's Hour, Administrative Branch, and in the regions. In 1931 the Head of the BBC Talks Department was a woman—Hilda Matheson—and her resignation at the end of that year caused a sensation. The *News Chronicle* and *Daily Telegraph* reported in December 1931 that she had had numerous battles on the Corporation Programme Board with her fellow board members who were all men. It was reported that she had pressed her views 'from a feminine standpoint in the face of overwhelming masculine opinion'.

However, by 1936, the *Manchester Guardian* was commenting in a leader that the BBC remained an exceedingly masculine institution,

[1] *Woman's Leader*, January 2, 1931.

and in June of the following year, it headlined an article with 'Does the BBC want women chiefs?' It went on to ask if there was a career at Broadcasting House for women. 'In the early days there were almost as many women chiefs of departments as men, but gradually this has been changed, until it looks as though every one of the higher-paid jobs at Broadcasting House will soon be in the hands of men.' Throughout the 1930s there were continual press comments on the lack of women broadcasters or commentators.

However, the 1939–45 war offered women the opportunity to break into positions of responsibility and into fields where they had hitherto been banned. At the time, it looked as though women grasped this opportunity with both hands and, in fact, a number of women holding highly responsible positions today managed to get their toes in the door because of their work during the war. The numbers of BBC staff more than doubled from 4,000 before the war to 9,000 in 1941, and the proportion of women staff rose from 7 per cent pre-war to 20 per cent in 1942; women secretaries moved rapidly into jobs as announcers, producers and script-writers. Women were also employed in control rooms, working long hours on complicated technical apparatus, taking over the work of engineers. However, after the war, many of the women who had held posts of some responsibility drifted back to their families again, although some women who had seen their opportunities did stay to move up the promotion ladder.

It has been pointed out by BBC officials that not all the women who had been promoted quickly were of exceptionally high calibre, and it has been suggested that some were promoted beyond their capacities to positions of responsibility which under normal conditions they would never have reached. As a result, some resentment and prejudice against women in senior positions grew up in the years after the war. It is possible that this damaged the chances of promotion of certain women coming up behind them in the post-war era.

However, certain very brilliant women were thrown into positions of responsibility during the war, and it is significant that most of the women in positions of any real seniority today seized the opportunity offered to them during the war to prove their ability to hold senior posts. It is also significant that when this small group of women retires within a fairly short time, there are no obvious women successors to them and, in fact, the number of really senior women will probably fall sharply within the next few years.

After the war, the recruitment of women did not reflect the quality of their work during the war. This was partly due to the fact that men from the armed services were returning to the BBC, and partly due to the fact that there was still quite a fair proportion of women who had stayed on after the war. Women were gradually accepted in fields where they had been unacceptable before the war, but certain engineering fields still remain virtually closed to them, in spite of the engineering work they undertook during the war.

Some of the outstanding women who had been in the pre-war BBC moved on and up, and in 1950 Mary Somerville became the first woman Controller in the BBC when she was appointed Controller of Talks Department. However, since her retirement in 1955 there has been no other woman above the rank of Assistant Controller. Mrs Mary Adams was appointed Assistant Controller of Television in 1953. In 1969 the only woman at this level was Mrs Joanna Spicer who was Assistant Controller (Planning) Television.

In 1954, the BBC started its General Trainee Scheme which will be discussed later in this report, but restricted it to men until 1960. In September 1959, Mrs Mary Hamilton, a former Governor of the BBC wrote to *The Times* about the lack of women in top jobs in the BBC:

> 'Since the days of Hilda Matheson, Mary Somerville, Mary Adams and Isa Benzie women have not appeared in director posts; in fact the BBC lags far behind the Civil Service. There is no Evelyn Sharpe, no Mary Smieton.'

In March 1962 further correspondence started in *The Times*, when Mrs Cazalet Keir, a former woman Governor, wrote to ask why only 4 out of 150 top BBC posts were held by women. She wanted a rule that women should sit on senior post selection boards, more publicity for the BBC's General Trainee Scheme and expanded recruitment for women. The BBC pointed out that the 150 posts did not include all senior posts—for example Assistant Heads of Television and Sound Talks Departments, Diplomatic Correspondent of External Services and so on were all held by women. Mrs Mary Adams replied at some length from her own experience, ending up with the plea to the BBC not to discourage graduate women recruits. 'Only warn them that the outside world, including the BBC and ITV, is a world of, for, and by men.' And the evidence gathered for this report from interviews with both men and women in the BBC suggests that Mrs Adams's comment is still true.

2. *Present position of women in the BBC*

In July 1968, the BBC employed 23,376 people, of whom 14,653 were men and 8,723 were women. Approximately 5,500 were employed in secretarial and clerical jobs, just over 6,000 in manual grade including catering, and 11,612 people in other areas of the BBC—in management, production and operations, of whom 4,681 were in management and production. It is with those people in the management and production area that this study is mainly concerned.

The BBC does not break the figures down by sex, but by grade. The BBC has a job evaluation system in which each job has a grade and a related salary range. There is considerable overlap in salary between the different grades, and promotion from one grade to another does not necessarily mean starting at the bottom of the salary range for the new grade. The grading system was revised in May 1968, and the grades at the time of this research were as follows: A and A plus—special grades for people on special salaries and those in top management in the BBC; MP7—salary rising to £4,675; MP6—salary rising to £3,970; MP5—salary rising to £3,260; MP4—salary rising to £2,965; MP2/MP3—salary rising to £2,705.

In 1969 there was probably only 1 woman in the A and A plus grades out of a total of 102. There were 6 women out of 122 on MP7; there were 17 women out of 378 on MP6; and there were 34 women out of 493 on MP5. Women held a total of 58 jobs out of the 1,095 jobs graded MP5 and above. The proportion of these grades held by women was as follows:

A and A plus	1 per cent
MP7	5 per cent
MP6	5 per cent
MP5	7 per cent

Overall the proportion of the jobs graded MP5 and above which were held by women was approximately 5 per cent in 1969, and this proportion has not changed up to the date of publication.

The vast majority of women in grades of MP2 upwards in the BBC are involved in production or in the planning departments. It is interesting to look at the proportion of producer jobs held by women. A television producer is graded MP5, whereas a radio producer is either MP4 or MP3, and occasionally MP2. This is due to the greater complexity of television production. The picture is somewhat confused by the fact that the following table excludes production assistants and assistant producers in television, who are also on grades MP2, 3 or 4, but the table does give the proportion of women holding positions as producers:

Television	15 per cent
Radio	nearly 33 per cent
Regions (radio and television)	7 per cent

What emerges from these figures, in combination with those in the previous paragraphs, is that the women tend to be found in jobs without departmental or divisional responsibility, although the individual responsibility that they bring to their jobs—for example in the staff and resources they control—may be considerable. There are very few of them in jobs where they have to make policy decisions.

It is difficult to measure the amount of responsibility held by individual people, and this makes the division between people in 'senior posts' and those in less senior posts somewhat arbitrary. Although the job evaluation system with its grades is perhaps the nearest we can get to measuring degree of seniority, nevertheless, there are certainly great differences in the degree of responsibility held by people on the same grade.

For example, a drama director or producer in television may have as many as 200 people responsible to him or her at any one time, including the cast, the technicians, the designer, stage manager, make-up and costumes people and so on. A producer in charge of a long series has responsibility that can only be described as enormous. He or she will work in close conjunction with people with departmental responsibility, but it is the producer who is in charge of the day-to-day working of the programme, and the producer is judged on the quality of the finished product.

However, the producer does not take policy decisions, although he or she may well influence them. It is people in the senior positions —from Assistant Heads of Departments upwards who are involved in policy decisions, and who are also involved in battling for resources for the programmes put out by their department or divisions. These resources are not only financial. Departmental Heads have to compete for filming, editing and recording facilities, as well as for their staff requirements and programme schedules. Producers certainly have to fight for budgets and facilities, but it is the Departmental Head who decides how he will allocate his resources.

Over and above this, there are other groups in competition with one another. For example, radio competes with television, and engineering competes with production. The very top policy decisions are taken by the board of directors.

It is significant that women in the BBC are not to be found at all in the most senior levels, and that there are very few at senior levels with departmental or divisional responsibility.

3. *Methodology*

For the purpose of this study, we had to select a group of women in top jobs. The BBC defined its senior posts as those in grades MP5 and above—a total of 1,095, of which women held 58. However, there is some difference here between radio and television. As we have seen, a television producer is graded MP5 whereas most radio producers are MP4 or MP3, and sometimes MP2. Although it was recognized that television producers' posts are graded according to their greater responsibility, nevertheless it was felt by the BBC and PEP that it would be misleading to exclude radio producers from this study. Therefore, some women were interviewed from grades MP3 and MP4.

A total of 36 people were interviewed. Thirty-three were members of the BBC staff, of whom 22 were women and 11 were men. In addition, 3 former senior members of BBC staff were interviewed—2 women and 1 man.

Of the 22 women interviewed, 4 were in their twenties and had come into the BBC under the General Trainee Scheme (see page 173) while the other 18 were in the 35-plus age group. They were mainly producers, senior producers or editors in television or radio between the ages of 35 and 45, although 4 of the women interviewed held positions of greater seniority. All but one of the women interviewed held posts in the production or planning areas of the BBC.

The men were mainly senior workers in the administrative areas, some of whom had had production experience. Three of the men were still in the production field.

Thirteen of the 22 women were single (including the 4 women who had come in under the General Trainee Scheme); 4 were married with children; 1 was married without children; 2 were widowed with children and 2 were divorced with children.

4. *Careers in the BBC*

Perhaps the striking characteristic of careers in the BBC is the difficulty of discerning any regular type of pattern on the Civil Service model. The very term 'career pattern' is frowned upon, and it was frequently stated that there was no such thing in the BBC. There are a number of reasons for this deviation from the Civil Service.

There is no set entry gate through which all senior staff must come, as there is in the Civil Service or professions. There is no recognized pattern of promotion. There is no recognized necessary set of qualifications for the most senior staff, or even for the more junior staff. There is no laid down procedure for promotion from grade to grade on the Civil Service pattern, and there is no traditional pattern of time to be spent in certain departments or offices. The BBC is a very flexible organization, and this is reflected in its career structure. The system allows for enormous individual differences in career histories.

One of the reasons for this is the way that the BBC has grown up and adapted itself to its changing role and functions. It has developed very much in an ad hoc way, creating new departments and divisions as it has grown, and along with these, new posts of responsibility and power. Empires have risen and fallen, as public taste has changed and as demands have altered. This has meant the very speedy rise of certain people who have literally found themselves in the right place at the right time, when their particular talents were in demand.

Another reason for the lack of discernible career patterns is the BBC's competitive appointments system, by which most jobs are advertised within the organization. This is not really compatible with a system of career planning by management, and it also puts the onus for career advancement very much on the individual. The effects of this type of system are important, and will be discussed in the section on Career Development and Promotion.

The BBC is a very unusual type of organization, and is perhaps unique in the breadth of its responsibilities. It cannot be 'tidy' in the same way as the Civil Service or a large, not very diversified commercial organization can be. It is, among other things a film industry, a music industry and one of the largest publishing industries in the country. It gathers together under one umbrella a large number of specializations, many of which are fairly small and self-contained, so that it is very difficult to have straightforward career lines leading to top management.

Some examination of the careers of the women interviewed shows how difficult it is to generalize about careers in the BBC. Of the 22 women interviewed who were still in the BBC, 6 had come in as secretaries or clerks, 4 as producers in radio, 3 had come in as studio managers (now Programme Operations Assistants), 2 had come into the News Department, 1 had come in as a report writer in the Monitoring Service, 1 as a stage manager and 1 as a programme administration executive. The remaining 4 had come in as general trainees.

Their subsequent career histories show even greater individual variations, and it would be true to say that very few of the women interviewed followed similar careers. (This is of course also true for men in the BBC.) Although most of them were working as producers or senior producers in radio or television when they were interviewed, they had reached their present jobs in a variety of ways. Some had remained in the same field or type of programme, while others had moved from radio to television or from one type of programme to another. Some had been recruited as producers, some had become producers through the attachments scheme which will be discussed later in the report, while others had applied for promotion to specific jobs. One or two had been encouraged to move up while others had fought every inch of the way for promotion.

Some of the women interviewed crossed the paths of others interviewed, which is not surprising in view of the fact that women tend to be found in certain areas of the BBC. However, even those whose paths crossed moved apart again, and it is perhaps surprising that so few career histories bear any relation to others, especially since women tend to be found in these specialized areas.

The promotion system of the BBC, described in a later section, places a great deal of emphasis on individual initiative, and it would perhaps be true to say that people grasp opportunities or seek change at times which are peculiar to themselves as individuals. The Civil Service system of promotion, where individuals are selected for certain posts, and where individual preference or initiative plays little or no part, is the very opposite of the BBC system.

The BBC is also different from the Civil Service in that entry is not more or less bound to a certain age group who will come in at a certain level. The BBC recruits people into management and production jobs at virtually all ages and all levels. It recruits people straight from university or further education, it recruits people with a few years' experience in other fields, it recruits specialists, and until fairly recently it had a tradition of recruiting men from the armed services and colonial service.

The BBC is changing in its attitude towards its staffing policy. The traditional attitude was similar to that of the Civil Service—that people coming in were embarking on a life-time career. However, the peculiar demands of a public entertainment industry have led to a new look at employment, and it has been recognized that it is not always in the interests of either the BBC or its employees to confine people to established posts until retirement. This has led to an increasing tendency by the BBC to take staff—particularly production staff—on short-term contracts.

The BBC is also very different from the Civil Service in that it offers no expected pattern of promotion to its recruits. The prospects for each new recruit are different, and depend to a much larger extent on personal ability and ambition than in the Civil Service. A new recruit coming into the BBC at the age of about 22 or 23 as a Programme Operations Assistant (a recognized entry gate for graduates and those of similar calibre) could literally go more or less anywhere in the BBC. Most of them, it appears, hope to make their names in production fields. Some will stay as P.O.A.s, while others may rise to the top of the management ladder. They may move very fast or very slowly.

All this analysis is designed to show how very difficult it is to make categorical statements about careers in the BBC for either men or women. The general impression must be one of individual ability, initiative and ambition against a continually changing background, in which help is given in moving up the ladder, but no posting or placing exists.

Chapter III

ENTRY GATES, TRAINING, CAREER DEVELOPMENT AND GRADUATE RECRUITMENT POLICY

1. *Entry gates*

a. Training schemes

General Trainee Scheme. In 1954, the BBC started its General Trainee Scheme, which was designed to recruit outstanding graduates from all disciplines to be its top managers and star producers of the future. The scheme was restricted to men until 1960, when it was opened to women as well. Between 1954 and 1969, 99 graduates were selected, of whom 7 were women. The following qualifications are required:

> 'Applicants should be not less than twenty-one years of age on 1st September and not yet twenty-six years on the previous 1st March (with certain exceptions). . . . Candidates should be of high academic standard and must show that they possess not only marked practical initiative and imagination, but at least the capacity to develop leadership either in managerial terms or in the field of programme ideas, editorial judgment, and production techniques. The primary considerations will be the qualities of mind and character of the candidates, and their capacity to make full use of the training given. . . .'

Since women perform so poorly when the future top management and star producers of the BBC are being selected, a more detailed assessment of the situation is indicated in the final part of this section.

Table 1 gives an analysis of the General Trainee Competition for the years 1966–69 inclusive.

Trainee Programme Operations Assistants (*Radio*). The General Trainee Scheme is clearly not the main source of potential top talent in the BBC, since the number recruited under the scheme is so small. A generally recognized 'second-tier' scheme for recruiting graduates and similar calibre entrants in their early twenties is the Trainee Programme Operations Assistant (Radio) Scheme.

> 'Programme Operations Assistants (P.O.A.s) are responsible for the technical and artistic presentation of all studio programmes in

TABLE 1 *Analysis of General Trainee Competition*

	1966			1967			1968			1969		
	Men	Women	Total	Men	Women	Total	Men	Women	Total	Men	Women	Total
Total application	322	182	504	344	171	515	460	255	715	444	118	625
Preliminary interviews	109	31	140	125	40	165	106	26	132	105	11	116
Short-listed for final board	20	4	24	23	4	27	26	5	31	21	3	24
Selected	5	1	6	6	0	6	7	0	7	6	0	6

radio. . . . The work is partly artistic, in that a P.O.A. working to a producer must be able to interpret the effects the latter wishes to achieve, and partly technical in that this effect can only be obtained by the knowledgeable and intelligent operation of the equipment.'

This extract from the official description of a P.O.A.'s work shows that it is a good background for a producer, and, in fact, a sizeable proportion of both radio and television producers have been P.O.A.s or studio managers, as they used to be called. It is regarded by graduates who do not fulfil the exacting requirements of the General Trainee competition as an alternative way into the BBC, and it is perhaps most interesting that it is a much easier way into the BBC for women graduates. In 1968, 83 P.O.A.s were appointed, of whom 41 were men and 42 were women—an intake of women of approximately 50 per cent. Fifty-eight of the successful applicants were graduates who had just left university, while the rest mainly had further education of some kind. In 1969, 46 were selected, of whom 27 were women. At present, there are about 325 P.O.A.s in radio (in both domestic and external broadcasting) of whom nearly one third are women. P.O.A.s can apply for a production attachment in either radio or television, and their requests are regarded sympathetically.

Other trainees. Each year the BBC selects a number of people between the ages of 18 and 25 to be trained in three aspects of film-making—Assistant Film Cameramen, Assistant Film Recordists and Assistant Film Editors. The camera and recording fields are limited to men only, but both men and women may apply to be Assistant Film Editors. However, very few women do apply, and opportunities for them are limited in the Film Department.

There are occasional opportunities for women to be trained as Make-up Assistants. This is clearly very specialized work and prospects are usually limited. However, the Head of Make-up Department's post is one carrying a great deal of responsibility and a high salary.

Each year the BBC's Engineering Division recruits a number of graduates in Electrical Engineering or Physics and a number of school leavers with 'A' level Mathematics and Physics. None of these traineeships are open to women.

Women are considered for traineeships in the Design Department, and in fact some of the outstanding designers in the BBC are women. Minimum requirements are a good general education to GCE 'A'

Level and art or architectural training or some professional experience in an allied field of design.

b. Direct entry to a specific job

When the BBC feels that it cannot fill a vacancy from inside or it wishes to attract applications from outside, it advertises the job concerned in the press, notably in the general section of the Situations Vacant columns of the *Daily Telegraph* on Wednesdays.

Through this method of recruitment the BBC hopes to attract people with specialist qualifications or expertise in some particular field, as well as graduates with experience of work outside the BBC. It does not stipulate that applicants should be trained or experienced in television or radio to be considered for a production post. It is perhaps more interested in injecting fresh ideas and a different outlook than in attracting broadcasting expertise for its own sake. In this respect, opportunities for graduates in their middle or late twenties without specialized training are probably greater than they would be in, say, industry, and are certainly greater than in the scientific field.

c. Unsolicited applications

The BBC Appointments Department receives about 1,500 unsolicited applications each month. Many of these are unqualified for the type of posts they would like, but a proportion of them are put forward for Boards for posts for which they are qualified if a vacancy occurs.

d. General reserve scheme

This is a system by which the BBC employs people for whom it has no immediate vacancy, but does not wish to lose. It is generally reserved for someone who is outstanding in his particular field—a reporter, for example.

e. Administrative reserve scheme

Under this scheme, a number of young men and women are taken into the BBC who have had some experience in personnel management or an allied field. They are usually professionally trained in personnel work, management techniques or organization and methods.

f. Monitoring services

There are a number of vacancies each year in the monitoring service of the BBC for report writers or sub-editors. A foreign language is not essential for these posts, but is useful. However, a good background in international affairs and interest in politics, economics and science are considered necessary.

g. Secretarial/clerical

It is possible to enter the production/management ladder from being a secretary. This was a fairly common pattern for women some years ago, but as the opportunities—particularly for graduates—have increased in other fields, so the proportion of women coming into production via secretarial work has dropped.

2. *Training*

For the schemes outlined above there is a wide variety of training courses and, naturally, a great deal of training in the job. Courses are designed not only for new entrants but also for people who have been in the BBC for some time. There are about twenty different types of courses run for staff in the production and management fields.

3. *Career development and promotion*

It has been pointed out in this report that one of the reasons for the lack of discernible career patterns in the BBC is its competitive appointments system, in which the vast majority of jobs are advertised internally and are open to competition. This system is very different from the planned career system used in the Civil Service and in many large firms, where the employer can move employees around within the organization. There are advantages and disadvantages in both systems, but the BBC is convinced that its competitive appointments system, backed up by continuing assessment of staff, is the most suitable for its needs.

At present in the BBC it is usual for applications to be made through the applicant's Establishment or Personnel Officer. It has been the general practice for people to apply on their own initiative for the posts they want. Occasionally, candidates are encouraged to apply for a vacancy either by their Establishment Officers or by a Head of Department. Some of the women interviewed thought that this ought to happen a lot more often than it did. They felt that not enough thought was given to possible career paths open to people, and that neither men nor women were given enough advice on possible strategies or moves which could be made to further their careers.

There are undoubtedly advantages in the system of promotion by application and competition, as opposed to the 'planned career' system. It means that people are seen and considered who are not obvious choices for the post, but who may have talents which are being hidden where they are at present employed. It also means that it is very difficult to have a list of 'golden boys' or high-fliers who are going to be moved into chosen positions.

However, the system also has its disadvantages. The very fact that it is difficult to plan career paths for high-fliers may become very frustrating for those who have to wait for a vacancy to be advertised, and who may feel that not enough thought is being paid to their career prospects. The system makes it difficult for the management to control its own succession, and the haphazard timing of vacancies prevents an individual from planning his future. There is also the disadvantage that a number of suitable applicants may be missed by the system. Most of the women interviewed said that they thought this particularly likely with women. They thought that women were generally more modest and diffident about their capabilities and were less confident of their chances of being successful at a Board. Many of the women said that they would only apply for jobs for which they had an almost certain chance, whereas they thought that men were much more likely to be aware of the desirability of having been seen by a Board whether they thought they would be appointed or not. The women also said that once a woman had been turned down for a post, she would be more wary of applying for another job, whereas they felt that men would be much more impelled by economic pressure to apply again. Undoubtedly, there are many men who behave in exactly the same way as the women, but this is not the way that the women interviewed saw their behaviour. Senior Establishment Officers pointed out that it was often extremely difficult to persuade well-qualified men to apply for a job, for precisely the same reasons outlined by the women.

Many of the problems of career development in the BBC were discussed at a conference of senior personnel officers held about two years ago. One of the most important objects of the conference was to try to limit the element of chance in the system of selection by Appointments Boards by introducing much more thorough and continuing assessment of staff and their potential.

There is one big drawback cited by a number of people involved in selection—that it is very difficult not to give the job to the person with the most obvious qualifications for the job. This makes it hard to 'talent-spot' and give a job to someone who shows great potential. This system is also thought to activate against women. If the post which is advertised has never been filled by a woman, it obviously requires new thinking on the part of the selectors to envisage a woman in the job. When she is in direct competition with a man and there appears to be little difference in their qualifications, it was felt that the job would probably go to the man—the safer option and the more obvious choice.

The composition of the Boards, particularly those handling the more senior jobs, has often been criticized. A woman writing to *The Times* in March 1962 suggested that there should be all-female Boards for senior BBC jobs, since the reverse so often happened. A senior man involved in selection said that women seemed to do less well in the Board situation, i.e. that they did not perform as well as men in the quick cross-fire of conversation needed in this kind of interview. However, another man who has frequently sat on selection Boards pointed out that some women may do much better than men. The BBC feels that Boards should be constituted from those best qualified professionally to assess candidates and not to represent minority interests of sex, politics, religion and so on. They state that it is the specific duty of the Board chairman to see that *all* candidates are properly considered.

Occasionally there are closed Boards, open only to a limited number of people—sometimes only two—when these are considered the only people suitable for the post, perhaps because of the specialized nature of the work. Sometimes people are promoted without a Board, since they are thought to be the only person who could be considered for the job. This happens more frequently in management posts. There has also been a tendency for new posts to be created with a specific person in mind to fill new needs. This has happened particularly with the expansion of television.

Another method of promotion is through the system of training attachments referred to in the last section. In this case, people may be sent on attachment, usually at their present salary, for six months. This may be extended. They are then expected to return to their old department. However, if a vacancy then comes up in the department to which they have been attached, they stand a very good chance of getting the job, since they have proved that they can do it by actually doing it. The BBC argues that it is a training period, during which the person cannot possibly be doing it as well as someone established in the job. In addition it is designed to help people find their right niche or area within the BBC. The BBC regards it as a supplement to the Corporation's competitive system of promotion, giving to management more flexibility in the deployment of its staff, and to staff a means, through training, to become effective competitors for posts which they might not otherwise be able to obtain.

The Central Attachments Scheme is now open to most members of the BBC staff who have been three years on a grade and who are over the age of 25. During the year 1966, 122 applications and recommendations were received. At the end of the year, 90 of these had been recommended for attachment, while the others had withdrawn or been rejected. Since the Scheme began in 1960, 317 of those recommended have completed attachments and of these 108 have obtained new posts related to their attachment. In addition, the television service also advertises a number of production attachments.

4. *Graduate recruitment policy*

As we have seen, the BBC has designed its General Trainee Scheme to recruit its top managers and star producers of the future. In the section describing this scheme, we gave figures showing the relative performance of men and women at each of the stages of selection. Since the success rate of the women at each of these stages was so poor in relation to the men, we feel that some analysis of this situation would be relevant. The BBC itself is concerned about the fact that it finds it difficult to recruit women of the calibre considered necessary for a General Trainee.

Some reasons for the disappointing performance of women were discussed with BBC officials responsible for the recruitment of General Trainees. It was felt that a number of outstanding women graduates simply did not apply because (a) women were more modest than men and did not feel they stood a chance; (b) a lot of very good women graduates got married either at university or shortly after graduating, and were not attracted by a job which appeared to imply long-term service and prospects. From the interviewing carried out in connection with this study, a number of other points affecting original applications also emerged. Perhaps one of the main drawbacks to the BBC's attracting more applications from women graduates is the fact that they have recruited so few. This is known to the university appointments officers, many of whom actively discourage young women from applying for the General Trainee Scheme. In fact, according to some of the young women interviewed they are told that it is almost impossible for a woman to get into the BBC at all, and that they ought not to consider it. One woman who did get a traineeship was told that she would stand no chance, which only sharpened her determination. 'I watched television non-stop for the four months before the Board. I was determined to prove the Appointments people wrong.' She got in, but most people—men and women alike—do not have her determination. Another girl was told that she would stand no chance on the Scheme, but was advised to apply for the then Studio Manager Competition (now the P.O.A. Competition). She did not like the idea of 'twiddling knobs' and did not apply. However, the day before the applications closed for the General Trainee Competition a friend of hers—the President of the Union—said that he had applied and why didn't she? She was given a traineeship and he was not. However, the BBC nearly missed one of its very few women recruits.

Nevertheless, a certain number of women—about half as many as men—are ambitious enough or encouraged by someone to apply, and yet, as shown in the table the proportion of women left at each stage of the selection process declines rapidly. Taking the 1968 figures, the proportion of women to men at application stage was more than 1·2, at preliminary interview stage it was approximately 1·4, at Final Board Stage it was approximately 1·5, and at selection stage it was 0·7. And this is the usual pattern as can be seen from the figures.

What are the reasons for the disappointing performance of women? First of all, many more are weeded out after the application stage than men, partly because their academic qualifications are not as good and partly because their other interests or extra-mural activities do not appear to be as interesting to the BBC. At the preliminary interview and Final Board Stage they are assessed in a face-to-face situation—first with perhaps only one other person and then with a full Board of up to four or five people. Women are felt not to perform as well as men in this kind of situation, and the question is: Why not?

Certain comments were made by BBC officials. It was suggested by one senior BBC executive that the Alpha Plus graduates who applied were almost exclusively men, that the Alpha graduates were almost exclusively women and the next layer was about 50:50, and that it was the Alpha Plus graduates that the BBC was looking for. The BBC recognized the possibility that an all-male Board might bias the selection process, and in 1967 a senior woman was invited to sit on the selection Boards. She has said that she was cruelly disappointed in the calibre of the girls interviewed.

Certain possible reasons for the poor performance of women at interviews and Boards were put by BBC staff concerned with selection. It was thought that there is in anti-intellectual bias in this country which continues to operate against intelligent women. This might have the effect of inhibiting outstanding young women from appearing too clever or from arguing forcibly with men. It would give them less practice in the cross-fire of argument or conversation and would perhaps detract from their performance at Boards. It was said that women often appeared much less relaxed than their male competitors and would never crack a little joke for example, whereas the men would appear much more at ease altogether. Lack of confidence or actual diffidence was an outstanding characteristic of many of the women interviewed. However, at the same time, a number of women were turned down because they were too aggressive or actively suffragette. It was felt that General Trainees were being selected not only for their capacities and potential, but also for their ability to get on with other people and lead teams. Quite naturally, it was thought that lack of confidence or over-aggressiveness shown in an interview situation were not desirable characteristics for potential high-fliers, particularly those as much under scrutiny as General Trainees.

The performance of the women General Trainees that the BBC has taken on is difficult to assess in a study of this kind, because of the small number of women involved. However, out of 7 women employed since 1960, 4 are still with the BBC, which is not an unduly high turnover of young women graduates, compared with other organizations. One of the others left to have a baby, and the other two for personal reasons.

However, it can be said that none of the women, as yet, is regarded as matching up to the outstanding performance of some of the men General Trainees. Those involved in watching the careers of General Trainees feel that young women find it more difficult to operate within the harsh, competitive world of television which is very much a man's world still, partly because of the large amount of technical equipment and large supporting staff of manual and technical workers who are all men, and partly because of the nature of the work.

Secondly, young women are thought to find it more difficult than young men to separate their work life from their private life; they appear to allow the one to impinge on the other to the possible detriment of both. The men undoubtedly have drawbacks too—over-ambition and arrogance are frequently cited—but these were thought to be more easily controllable and not to affect their work to such an extent. These points, of course, are relevant to the employment of women in responsible positions in general.

This is the picture seen from the employer's side of the fence. There is no doubt that they will continue to recruit young women if they can find them, but it is clear that the BBC is worried that it is not finding enough of the kind of young women it wants.

The women General Trainees in the BBC feel on the whole that the BBC may not really be doing what it promised. In other words, they do not feel that they are being groomed either for top management or for star producer jobs. This may also be true for young male

General Trainees too. In the competitive system of the BBC, it is difficult to groom anyone for stardom, but nevertheless the women see young men passing them by and being promoted above their heads. While under training, they receive excellent advice on prospects and promotion, but they feel that once out in the big BBC world, they are left to sink or swim with the rest—perhaps true of all General Trainees.

The training that the young women received appears to have been very patchy. Sometimes it was clearly excellent, but sometimes it was nearly disastrous. For example, one General Trainee was sent to a Programme Department and was told to do a studio production. 'No one had told me *how* to do it. The secretary said, "You don't mind if I go off and have a drink now, do you?" I said "No", although I minded very much. And then it was sheer goodwill on somebody's part who showed me how to do it. I think it's a bit hit and miss. But without exception I was always shown extreme goodwill in radio.'

In television the picture was sometimes different. One girl was attached to a producer. 'There was a general feeling that General Trainees were there to do the equivalent of washing the tea-cups. They were disliked very much in television, although I think this has tended to change. You were regarded with a bit of suspicion, especially since you had to write a report on your attachment. I had a lot of interesting film research to do, but the producer wouldn't allow me into the gallery or the cutting-room—both pretty essential in training in television production. He had had one before and said he couldn't stand another. I was told that I would have to stay and suffer.'

There are a great many courses on which General Trainees are sent, and they were all considered useful by the trainees interviewed. However, they thought that actually doing the job was different from attending a course, however well designed, and there was a plea from both men and women General Trainees for some greater time and help from those to whom they were attached. It was recognized that a producer doing a full-time job producing a programme did not have enough time to really train a person, and that there were times when having to rely on the enormous amount of goodwill found in the BBC was just not enough.

There can be little doubt that the performance of the women General Trainees can be related to the performance of women in general, and that the factors affecting the employment and promotion of all women are perhaps seen in an exaggerated form with General Trainees. This report has looked at the problem in some detail. Since the General Trainee Scheme is designed to attract the top BBC people of tomorrow, and women do not appear to come through it very well, the implication is that there is not much prospect of change from the present situation of very few women in really senior posts.

However, some senior men have pointed out that the General Trainee Scheme has tended to become a scheme for training men in Current Affairs in television. There are several important production areas in the BBC which will not take General Trainees, so that it is becoming difficult to give them as broad a training as might be desirable. Therefore the failure of women in the General Trainee competition might not be as serious as it appears at the first impression. Their success in the Programme Operation Assistant's competition might perhaps be a better indication of opportunities for young women in the BBC.

Chapter IV
WOMEN IN THE PROMOTION RACE

On paper, as we have seen, women do less well in the promotion race than men. There are clearly a number of reasons for this which are related to the question of supply. First, there are considerably fewer women General Trainees recruited than men; secondly, there are fewer highly qualified women than men and fewer women with some form of higher education which is more and more a prerequisite for the more senior posts (this is particularly true of the 35–45 age group from which much of the material for this study was drawn); thirdly, a fairly high proportion of women in their twenties and thirties leave the BBC when they get married or have children.

However, there are other factors affecting women's prospects in the promotion race which are not directly affected by the question of supply, and we shall look at these in some detail in the following sections.

1. *Certain engineering and technical fields closed to women*

There are obvious reasons for certain engineering and technical fields being closed to women. Women are much less likely than men to have qualifications in engineering and related subjects. Certain engineering work is heavy and dirty, and some work in the technical fields, like pushing heavy television cameras around, is clearly difficult for women, so that it is not surprising that these fields have been predominantly male.

However, there are certain areas in the technical fields where women are accepted—for example as Programmes Operations Assistants in radio where much of their work is of a technical nature, or as Vision Mixers in television.

One of the women interviewed had taken engineering examinations while working in radio as a technical assistant. She saw that the only way up in that department was to get better qualifications so she took an engineering examination and passed. 'I got the bit between my teeth and took the next exam. I passed and caused quite a rumpus. I was sent for by the Head of the Engineering who said "What shall we do with you now? You're a fully-fledged engineer and you're an embarrassment." I couldn't get a job. I suppose I did it really as a protest—to sort out the rules—to show that the system was nonsense—that women could take the exams and then couldn't get the jobs.'

Women have also broken into other areas in the technical field from which they used to be barred. For example, in radio, women studio managers, as they were then called, used not to be allowed to go on Outside Broadcasts. However, one of the women interviewed fought this battle when she was studio manager. 'The older engineers said "A woman can't lift that", so I went out of my way to lift some heavy piece of equipment and just show them.'

In television, women used not to be considered for the posts of Assistant Floor Manager or Floor Manager—the link between the Director and the studio, and responsible for what goes on the studio floor. One of the women interviewed was concerned in changing this, 'Four of us fought for it and they gave us the job on an "acting" basis. Then they got short-staffed and two of us got jobs as Floor Managers. It started in Drama, but then it spread to other departments.'

It seems that in these engineering and technical fields which are mainly closed to women, some jobs are always more likely to be performed by men—the heavier, dirtier jobs and the ones for which most of the qualified candidates are men. However, there do appear to be a number of jobs for which women might be considered in the future, particularly those involving high precision work and those which are really on the fringes of production, but prospects for promotion to the top jobs still look very poor.

2. *Certain areas where women do not do well*

Since production is one of the most important areas in the BBC, and most of the people in top jobs at present have production experience, it would be useful to examine whether women do significantly less well in certain production areas than in others, and whether this affects their opportunities for promotion.

In both radio and television, women have not on the whole done well in the Current Affairs and news areas although there are one or two women in positions of some responsibility in these fields and the situation appears to be changing, particularly in Current Affairs.

A number of reasons were put forward for this by both men and women. Hard news gathering is considered to be a man's job—not only in radio and television, but also in newspapers. The number of women news reporters on national newspapers is very few and this pattern is repeated in the BBC. There are no women reporters on the national news or television, although they are used on such sound news programmes as 'The World At One', mainly on 'human interest' stories. There is also a woman reporter on '24 Hours.' It is argued by men that 'the audience' would not like a woman newscaster or reporter on television, particularly for political or economic items, or for distressing news. Since the field for which women could be used would therefore be so limited, it would be more trouble than it is worth to employ women.

A former Editor of Television News cites the case of fighting for a woman reporter. He eventually introduced her into the news programmes.

> 'Over the dead bodies of my entire staff. I said it was ridiculous that a reactionary country like Spain should have women announcers and we didn't. However, in spite of the fact that she was intelligent, good-looking, the right age, and very good, it was a failure, because the men wouldn't give her the service they gave other men. She came and said to me, "It's not working", and of course it wasn't, because the men were just not cooperating.'

Where women have managed to break through is on the editorial side, and there are women Duty Editors in both sound and television, with wide responsibility in the selection and order of items in news bulletins. However, a newsroom is not everybody's ideal working situation, and men and women thought that undoubtedly some women would be put off by the disadvantages of shift work and an office which might be in use twenty-four hours a day where you could not call even your desk your own because someone else was going to occupy it for the next eight hours. The position of women in the BBC newsrooms is undoubtedly affected by the position of women in the newspaper industry in general, and as long as the image of the rough, tough, beer-drinking, hard-hitting reporter exists, it was felt that women were going to find it more difficult to be accepted in this world than in some others, even on the editorial side.

In Current Affairs there is some extension of this anti-female sentiment. Again they are excluded from reporting on political or economic stories, and are not used as commentators on any serious subject. It is said that they are not used in these capacities in newspapers and therefore do not get the training, but not all radio or television commentators are newspaper journalists. Women, it appears, are held by editors and producers to lack the qualifications, experience and interest in current affairs to be used in anything other than a fairly junior capacity for the most part. One of the women interviewed had tried desperately to break into the reporting field. 'I asked to be considered, and they absolutely refused to see me. They said they wouldn't dream of taking a woman reporter. They couldn't possibly trust a woman on politics.'

There are some women producers in Current Affairs in radio, although the proportion is tiny compared with men, and in External Services the Head of European Talks and English Service is a woman. In television there is one woman producer in Current Affairs and some women Production Assistants. The strain of working in Current Affairs, perhaps on daily programmes, is considerable for both men and women. The hours are long and the competition for inclusion of items is very great. The atmosphere is said to be tough and uncompromising, and most men would wilt under the pressure, which some observers within the BBC claim to be unnecessarily exaggerated. There are also other problems cited in the Current Affairs field—for example, the fact that much of the field covers international news and that a woman cannot be sent abroad easily; that a lot of the work involves filming and that women directors and producers are not easily accepted by film crews; that women simply don't fit into a tightly knit little group of men who are working under great pressure.

Women do not do well in Outside Broadcasts in either radio or television. Again there are obvious reasons for this, although they do not explain the almost total exclusion. Sport is still very much a man's world. It is the rare woman who finds sport as all-absorbing as many men do, and women rarely write about it. However, Outside Broadcasting covers a great variety of other events, from state occasions to ballroom dancing, horse shows to circuses, and there seems to be no lack of interest by women in these events. It is often said by men that women cannot stand the discomfort of the Outside Broadcast life—up early, working under cold and draughty conditions, long hours and so on—but the Producer's Assistant on these expeditions is always a woman, so that this argument in itself does not appear to be valid. Another argument used against the employment of a woman in the capacity of producer in Outside Broadcasts is that she is then the representative of the BBC with outsiders, but again, women pointed out that most producers in other areas are in continual contact with people from outside the BBC, not only when filming but also in the studio.

Light Entertainment is another field in which women do not do well in either radio or television. Women are said to be less attracted by comedy than men. However, there have been one or two outstanding women who have broken into the Light Entertainment field and have been very successful.

Pop Music is a field in radio where women have not done well, although one of the women interviewed came from this area. It seems perhaps surprising that women do not do better in this area, since the 'midwife' qualities needed in a good producer of difficult or temperamental subjects are often said by both men and women to be found more often among women. Perhaps there is a spill-over of the attitude found in the Light Entertainment field . . . that women and show-business for some curious reason do not go together; although the woman interviewed from this area seemed to have had few problems in her job. It is surprising that so few women are found in the Features and Documentary departments in television, particularly because there have been some really outstanding women in the BBC in this area, and also because this is the area in radio where women appear to do well. Few people interviewed were able to give any reasons for this. It is probably in the Features, Current Affairs and Documentary areas that the competition for jobs is greatest, and where this happens, perhaps it is the women who are squeezed out first, or are not allowed in.

3. *Certain areas where women traditionally have done well*

There are certain areas within the BBC where women have traditionally done well. In television, well over a third of the women producers are to be found in children's programmes, schools or further education, and in radio, a similar proportion of women producers are to be found in women's programmes, schools or further education. (There are no longer television programmes designed especially for women.) This pattern is probably to be expected, but one of the questions to be discussed at some length later in this report is whether women find it difficult to move out of these areas, or whether they simply move into them because it is difficult for them to find jobs in other departments.

Women are clearly going to be employed in large numbers in the make-up and costume departments of television, and it is likely that the Head of the Make-up Department will usually be a woman. However, the present Head of the Costume Department is a man.

Women have also reached positions of considerable responsibility in Planning, an area which covers the very complex problems of scheduling programmes, studios, facilities and all the background requirements to programme production.

4. *Certain levels above which it is difficult for a woman to rise*

It is quite clear from the figures quoted at the beginning of this report that it becomes progressively harder for women to reach the next rung the further up the ladder they go. The greatest jump for both men and women to make is above producer level, to Senior Producer, Editor, Assistant Head of Department, Head of Department, and so on to Controller and Director—in other words to holding senior production, departmental or divisional responsibility. We have seen that only 4 per cent of the jobs, 24 out of the 602 posts, of M P6 and above were held by women, and there is no indication that this is going to change. Since this situation is of key importance to this study, it will be examined in some depth in the following section.

Chapter V

REASONS FOR WOMEN FINDING IT DIFFICULT TO MOVE INTO MORE SENIOR POSTS

1. *Specialization*

As was seen in the last section, women are successful in a limited number of fields. This has meant that women have tended to drift towards these areas and have been actively recruited there. However, even there, there are still only a limited number of senior posts. If, however, the able women were spread out a little more over the organization as a whole, perhaps there would be less concentration of women potential high-fliers in one or two departments, giving them more chance of promotion.

Specialization may mean that a person becomes typecast, and spending too long in one department may preclude a man or woman from being considered for jobs in other departments. Since it is in any case difficult for women to get jobs in other departments, some women found it only natural that they tended to stay where they were welcome and did not fight to be accepted in alien communities. This again was felt to limit their prospects for promotion.

Specialization is clearly an increasing problem for both men and women in the BBC, as the subject-matter or treatment of programmes becomes more technical or more influenced by changing fashions. It is very difficult for, say, a drama director to produce a Current Affairs programme, since the expertise required for the two types of programme is so utterly different. The days of the jack-of-all trades radio producer are past, and television, with its greater demands and need for expertise, is putting a much greater restriction on the movement of producers.

It is possible that the women themselves are partly to blame for the fact that they tend to stay put in one area. The men interviewed were much more aware of the problem of being typecast, and there was evidence that they thought ahead more than women did. This man became concerned about being typecast:

> 'After three years of writing scripts I began to feel a bit frustrated. I was 31 and felt I must move. I began to put in for jobs as a producer and television floor manager. I was turned down, and asked myself why I'd had no luck. I decided that it was because I was a

scriptwriter with a label. I was fairly well paid, but I was being paid for my expertise. I was turning into a specialist and I saw the dangers. So I made a calculation and I took a gamble.'

He applied for a job helping to run a radio station in a remote part of the world. The gamble paid off, because he came back two and a half years later with considerable production and management experience. He had virtually been running a staff of 130 and the total output of the station, and from then on he was considered for posts for which he would not have had the slightest chance two and a half years before.

A woman could not do what this man did, but there is the possibility that women could move around a little more than they do. One woman who did move says this:

> 'In 1957 the Establishment people had decided that they should have people who were capable of working in both radio and television, so I was told to go to television. I got a bit huffy about it. "Will you please apply", they said. I was very cross. I had a liking for the Woman's Hour backwater. When I went for a Board for Talks—general programmes—I talked about my experience which was mainly in women's programmes, and they just put me in women's programmes in television. I was typecast—it was the first time that I realized that.'

It is possible that a failure to realize they are becoming typecast is more common with women than men. However, the younger women seemed much more aware of the dangers and were making more conscious decisions on what to do about it—even if it meant actively settling for the field they were in.

2. *Women's own inclination*

Women may simply settle for a field in which they want to work even if the prospects for promotion are slim. Most of the women interviewed stated quite categorically that they did not want a job which took them too far away from actual involvement in a production: 'I should be very happy to stay as a producer. I'm interested mainly in programmes—not in administration.' Another woman said:

> 'I don't want to go anywhere. My main reason for working is that I like the work. I could have applied for the Head of Department job, but I wouldn't like to be away from programmes and meeting such interesting people. I'm not ambitious for power—only that I can do things my way.'

Another woman was offered a very good administrative post outside the BBC:

> 'I couldn't *not* consider it—the money was so good, and it would be dishonest to say that doesn't matter. But I thought of myself and living where I should have to—and I thought of the state of the programme—I'm quite devoted to the programme. . . . I don't think I'm an administrative kind of person. I'm a creative person. I know my limitations. The top people think I'm just thinking small, but I should hate to be Head of my Department. It must be so boring. Heads of Department have to be so political and I'm not. They have to play one person off against the other—that's essential. I shouldn't like that. And now they're paying their top producer well—there's no real financial incentive to be a Head of Department.'

Money was mentioned by a number of women. A radio producer has a limit of about £2,700 in London, a senior radio producer has a limit of nearly £3,000 a year, while television producers have a limit of £3,250 a year. It is quite possible for a successful producer to go on a short-term contract or have a personal grade which would bring her salary up to as much as £4,000 a year.[1] There is clearly not a great deal of financial incentive for a woman who enjoys her job to move up or to agitate for promotion, and a number of women asked why they should bother to make a lot of fuss when it was so difficult to move in any case. It was felt that men were much more likely to be influenced by the financial pressure of keeping a family to seek promotion. A number of women thought other incentives for promotion were less important for women than for men. One senior woman said:

> 'I think ambitious men want power. I don't think this is true of women. I think very few women want power for its own sake. They want it because they want to get their ideas through. A lot of men want power and glory—a big office with thick carpets. Friends would debunk a woman who did want a thick carpet.'

Another reason why a number of women said that they did not want to go any higher was that they saw the characteristics of authority in an unfavourable light. One woman said: 'I think that the traditional characteristics of authority are unfeminine—and this may stop some women from aiming high.'

And finally, there was perhaps the most important inclination of all—the one that removes a very large number of women from the competitive scene altogether and which very much affects the thinking and priorities of those who stay: 'I should much rather be happily

[1] These figures are all higher at the time of publication.

married than in any top job.' It is quite clear that the twin demands of a successful career and a family are still seen by many women as incompatible, particularly by those who were not married.

3. *Women as managers*

A commonly held view, both inside and outside the BBC, is that women frequently lack the qualities of good managers. Within the BBC this opinion was heard from a number of men in positions of authority:

> 'There is generally a greater managerial element (both management of staff and other resources) in the senior posts than in the middle-level posts, and men are considered to make good managers in more cases then women, although some efficient women managers are exceptions to this generalization.'

This whole area of judging whether women lack managerial qualities is clearly one which is very much open to subjective interpretation on what constitutes a good manager. Men often said that women had certain characteristics which militated against their possessing all the necessary prerequisites for good management. Women did not agree, and their views are developed in the section on how they see women in positions of authority.

4. *Difficulties of breaking into a man's world*

Since most of the managerial positions in the BBC are held by men, it is quite clear that a woman is going to experience some difficulty if she manages to break into this world. A man who held a very senior position in the BBC said this:

> 'Some women will get on just because they're so good. But it's the ones just below the Alpha Plus level that are discriminated against. They're felt to be a distracting influence. Take a regular management meeting—every Monday morning, say. It's a closely knit little circle of men meeting—it knows its own mores, language—its own ecology—and then suddenly a species with entirely different reactions is introduced into it. It gets very disturbed and it doesn't like it. It doesn't know how to cope. This is all the more complicated with feelings of necessary chivalry and suppressed sexual attraction and distraction. They don't like it.'

This reaction against women by a group of men was also noted by another man in a senior position:

> 'I think we were a male society. We all worked very closely with one another. We had an unspoken sense of male camaraderie—a kind of lingua franca—a television shorthand if you like. There was a high-powered woman there, but she didn't have it. She didn't speak our language. She would talk very loudly at meetings as long as she could. There was another woman at these meetings. She would sit and write her memos and letters and then she would come out with absolutely devastating comments on the meeting. We didn't like it.'

It is not only on the level of regular meetings that women find it difficult to break in. Senior men clearly felt this fear that women might be difficult to deal with and that they would have to rethink their ways of working when they had to deal with a woman on a senior level. One senior man said:

> 'Probably among the very senior staff there is a feeling that women are more emotional—more dangerous in high office. There have been some very high-powered ladies who have done severe damage for their cause. But with really good women you never think whether they're women or men. There's no danger of emotions or tantrums.'

This woman perhaps sums up the difficulty of senior women operating in a mainly male field. She moved into a new job in a new field:

> 'They were a bit surprised and sweet about my quiet little programmes. The Head of the Department used to kiss my hand. Then I took over a programme and worked seven days a week for six months. I began to realize that I couldn't go on without more staff and more money. I'd been everybody's little friend until I began to ask for more. Women just can't do it. A woman's voice is querulous—it's like a wife—"Here I am all day—struggling away . . .". I could see a tremendous withdrawal. I suppose women nagging sounds like their wives or echoes of their childhood. It makes them become hostile. *Men* can do it—they talk man-to-man about the problem. I didn't get the money. I went from being the most popular girl on the sixth floor to being the most unpopular.'

Women can experience resentment from colleagues when they reach senior positions, but this was not found very frequently in the BBC. One explanation for this was thought to be that women were rarely in competition for the more senior jobs where the resentment might be greater.

The jealousy or lack of cooperation that many of the women interviewed had experienced mainly came from men in the service departments of the BBC—the Engineering and Filming sections which have a tradition of being almost essentially male worlds. This was felt particularly by the women when they were young or inexperienced:

> 'When I started in television, I had a particularly sticky chief technician. I had my own programmes without really knowing much about television—and being a girl made it worse. I think they resent all young directors, but they find it specially painful to be under a woman. I found that I had to play feminine to win much more with the technical people. I had to say "Oh, so-and-so, I know I've been terribly naughty, but could I possibly have an extra day's filming." I know some women just can't bring themselves to do this, and they make absolutely no concessions. But then they don't get what they want.'

The idea that men might not like working for a woman was thought to affect the thinking of people who are allocating jobs on a programme, and most of the women interviewed suspected that it prejudiced their prospects of promotion. Even at a minor level, if there were two people who could go out and film a story, a number of women thought that a man would be sent rather than a woman, and that this was particularly true of filming abroad:

> 'The Editor said to me: no film crew wants to be told what to do by a woman.'

A man said:

> 'I don't think I have any prejudice against women, but I think I should hate working for a woman. I know it's irrational and unreasonable. I've never had to do it.'

And finally, a senior man said briefly:

> 'I should say that some, or perhaps most, men feel uncomfortable when they have to deal with a senior woman.'

It is not only difficult for women to break into all-male meetings which are part of the job, but it was thought to be even more difficult for women to be accepted on an informal basis.

> 'There's an awful lot of this "old-boy" business. The chaps keep up with each other like this—crossing the road to meet people. Women just don't share in this. You see the men chatting away to each other.'

And another woman felt the same:

> 'I know terribly few people. I've never drunk in the right bars. My husband says it's vital, but I don't believe in it. I think I've got here purely on talent.'

Of course, men take part in certain sporting activities from which women are excluded. And there are other social opportunities for men to make friends outside their work.

> 'Now if a woman became great pals with an administrative officer, people would look a bit askance. You just can't become pals as men do. I can't go up to the Assistant Editor and say "Let's have dinner" because if I went out with Mr B., Mrs B would wonder what was happening.'

Yet an increasing number of women do manage to operate in a man's world and seem to do so very successfully. One woman had these comments to make about those who managed it:

> 'One has to be a real politician to get on. You often see it here—the women are very often widowed—been through it all—they've got the balance of a man's world through being married, but now they've got the time and the energy to devote themselves to their career.'

Most of the women interviewed stressed that women were not as interested in the internal politics and intrigues of the organization as the men and that this affected their chance of promotion; nor, perhaps more important, were they so intent on manœuvring themselves into a position from which they could expand their empire. The BBC in the late 1950s and early 1960s experienced a big expansion in television and there was a proliferation of small empires and groups. The women pointed out that they found it significant that even at this time no woman managed to turn her programme into a group or department. However, a man whose career was meteoric at this time says if a woman had had his job in a programme which expanded, there is no reason why she too should not have had sudden swift promotion, but that at that time there were no women running the programmes which expanded. Another woman said:

> 'At one time I should have said that women were discriminated against. Now I should say they don't play the game the right way.'

It was felt generally that the socializing, the drinking in the right pubs and clubs, and above all the easy social contact which men have with one another, all militated against the advancement of women. All these contacts were felt to give men much more opportunity of indulging in internal politics than women could ever have.

The extent to which 'internal politics' exist is difficult to pinpoint. There is clearly more likelihood of internal politics operating in the higher levels of the BBC than, for example, in the Civil Service. Senior Civil Servants too may have to fight to get their policies over, but they are operating in a much simpler environment. Considering the nature of its work, the BBC probably does not engender an unusual amount of office politics, but the nature of the work does mean that a BBC manager has to think up a continual stream of products, turn them into programmes, obtain resources for them and market them not only to higher authority but also to the public. This type of work does perhaps need a much more outgoing and influence-seeking type of behaviour than is needed, say, in the senior ranks of the Civil Service. This behaviour will operate both at an official and at an informal level. One senior man commented, however:

> 'Women don't indulge in politics that count, because they're not in the positions where they could. But if they could get there, they'd do it just as much as the men.'

5. *Women under much closer scrutiny*

It was generally agreed by both men and women that women were under much closer scrutiny than men at all stages of their careers. It was repeatedly said that a woman has to be twice as good as a man to be chosen for a senior post, and has to prove continually that she remains twice as good.

A former Head of the Appointments Department has written:

> 'In a sense it is often harder for a women than a man to get a job above a certain grade. Boards tend to ask themselves twice over, so to speak, whether the woman candidate really is better than her male competitors and really can do the job. In view of their conspicuousness and the debit of failure of their sex (being a pronounced minority, they attract more attention than men; this applies to their successes and to their failures) it is no bad thing in the interest of the women that this extra scrutiny is given.'

One woman in television summed up the thoughts of most women interviewed when she said:

> 'It's still easier for men. A woman has got to be just that bit better than the competition. She's got to be better in every way—at the job, at the kind of success she builds into a programme. If it's bad—she'll hear without a doubt, "Ah well, she's a woman." A man will hear, "Bad luck—bad script." It will be less likely that it will be interpreted as his personal fault.'

An important comment on the nature of the scrutiny was made by one informant who stressed that stereotyped characteristics were attributed to women by men on the flimsiest of evidence. She thought that men tended to generalize about women very much from their own experience of certain senior women who might or might not have been typical.

> 'Perhaps women tend to show their frustration in their private lives more. I think, too, that men expect women to bring their private lives into the office more. My boss is always saying, "Oh you're so feminine—I can't work with you." And really he is very emotional and dramatic himself. It's fatal to burst into tears. I did this once—and got a very bad reaction. He avoided me ever after. And a woman can't drink. We never stop hearing about women who do or did. A woman's private life is under more scrutiny. A lot of things are blamed on just being a woman—like women drivers. People like to put it down to being a woman.'

And it was thought by some that this close scrutiny means that women have to prove themselves doubly before they are appointed to a job:

> 'I'm sure there's no disadvantage in being a woman at production level. A good woman producer is just as likely to get on as a good man producer. But the moment you get to the administrative type of jobs—it's very difficult to show that you can do the job before you actually do it. They don't scrutinize men quite so carefully. They're more prepared to take a risk.'

6. *Appearance of women a disadvantage*

The very femininity of a woman was thought to lessen her chances of being promoted into a position of some authority. It was felt that women look younger and appear to act with less authority—that they just did not 'look the part'. Women thought the selectors felt that people might be prepared to take orders from a very young man, since there was the army tradition of young officers giving orders, but that a woman—particularly a young woman—had a difficult time commanding sufficient respect to maintain the authority necessary for a management type of post. Their attitude to authority was also deemed to make it more difficult for women:

> 'There's a woman in my own unit. She's able and would want a lot more responsibility—she wants responsibility as such. But she won't get all that far. She's in her late forties—unmarried. I was astonished when I found out how old she was—she's got a very

young manner. She's very able, but she won't put on a solemn responsible air. She's very light-hearted. I suppose she just doesn't look the part.'

One senior woman producer thought that this attitude extended outside the BBC:

'I sometimes mind being taken for the secretary. Last time I was out with the film unit directing, it was assumed by outsiders that I was the continuity girl. People would never assume that a young man was junior, but people certainly assume it with a woman.'

And handling the situation was generally felt to be difficult by the women interviewed:

'I think one has to walk a tight-rope, neither being a proxy man nor ultra-feminine. It's only if authority comes naturally to you that you manage to walk it successfully. I've watched good women fail because they either try to be like men or try to achieve everything with short skirts and smiles.'

7. Experience in women's and children's programmes not taken seriously

A point which was raised frequently by women was that the experience that they or their colleagues had had in children's or women's programmes was simply not regarded as being any qualification for anything else. It must be said that the under-valuing of experience in these departments seems to apply to the departments as a whole, and not merely to the women in them. They felt that men found it much easier to move around from programme to programme or department to department simply because it was recognized that their experience was important. Women felt that the women's and children's areas were regarded as second best and it seemed to be thought that standards were lower there. It was also thought that a head of children's or women's programmes would never get any further simply because her management experience in her area would be thought too limited whereas they felt that the head of any other department or group would be considered on his or her individual merits.

One woman who moved out of women's programmes after quite a few years' experience said this:

'It was the first time I'd been outside the women's empire. They didn't take my previous work seriously, in spite of the viewing figures, I was given rather small things to do. I did much less work in my first year here than I've ever done.'

8. *Devotion to work*

Some women felt that they did not rise above a certain level because men believed they would not devote themselves wholeheartedly to their work, and that, particularly if they had family commitments, they would not be prepared to sacrifice the time necessary to function well in a top position. One senior woman said:

> 'I suppose one of the reasons women don't get any further is that they are not usually ready to sink themselves day and night into a job. I think I'm thought to show a lack of keenness. I'm angry if someone rings me up on my days off. I think the organization ought to be able to get someone to take decisions on my days off. I think men like to feel important. I just don't think it's worth being such an eager beaver. I say this—but I'm as bad as anyone really. I've been known to work for a fortnight without a day off. When I've done that, I say "No, never again." I think it's a reflection on your own inefficiency.'

Women felt that a married woman in particular would find it difficult to prove full devotion to her job, and this is covered in detail in a later section. On the other hand, it was thought that some women were not given positions of responsibility because it was feared that they might devote themselves too whole-heartedly to their work. This characteristic seemed to be regarded as laudable in men but undesirable in women.

9. *Commitments*

Married women and women with children will be discussed in a later section, but both men and women pointed out that there were some women in the BBC with great potential who were tied, either practically or emotionally, by the responsibility of elderly parents, and who felt unable to take on additional responsibilities at work.

10. *Power without title*

A former senior man said:

> 'I think men make it very difficult for women. Women in production very often have the power and responsibility without being given

> the post or the title. I can think of a number of women who came up with great contributions to programmes, and were often brilliant driving forces, but they didn't go up to be Executive Producers—in the jumping-off position for management.'

A senior woman thought that women often held key positions and agreed with the opinion expressed by the previous speaker:

> 'I was in fact doing the work of a person with a more senior rank, but they didn't give it to me. I asked the person above me, and he said I'd have had the title if I'd been a man. . . . I was always viewed as the person next in line to the man above me, and then his head would go and someone else would be appointed. There was always the question of whether my head should roll too since I was so closely associated with him, but it was felt that they needed continuity and my supporting role.'

11. *Unwillingness of BBC to take risks*

One man attempted to analyse the attitude of the BBC towards women in senior posts:

> 'Why not women? Opportunity is equal, but there is a funny corollary to this. If you overweigh appointments in favour of women, it's the same as if you did this for coloured people—you're doing damage. You're saying that although they're not as good, we're making an exception. But because you don't want to do that, if you feel that two people are equal—for a senior job—you mustn't take the woman first because she's a woman. The BBC don't give women the chance. I would take an equal risk with either, but the BBC don't take that risk. It's very difficult, with the system we have, not to select the person immediately best-qualified. It's difficult to take the one with the higher potential. Women are up against the clash of the obvious and long-term planning.'

Another former top BBC man said:

> 'The General Trainee Scheme militates against women. We're looking for future Director Generals—and that's by definition a man. Or we're looking for men in the group from which future Directors of the BBC will come. You need a great revolution in society to think women capable of doing certain types of jobs. And inside the BBC, they're not thought capable of top management.'

Chapter VI
WOMEN IN AUTHORITY

Both men and women were asked how they saw the main characteristics of women in positions of authority. It was felt that these perceptions might affect women's attitudes towards promotion and the attitudes of men towards accepting women in positions of authority.

Certain characteristics were attributed to women in authority both by men and women, but the interpretation frequently differed according to the sex of the respondent.

One of the most common characteristics noted was the attention to detail shown by women—not only those in authority. This was thought to go hand in hand with a conscientious approach to work and an ability to be accurate and meticulous. This was seen by the women to have great advantages, and was also appreciated by the men. But the men felt that sometimes the attention to detail could be reflected in an inability to see the wood for the trees and a tendency to miss the most important policy-making point. A woman Assistant Head of Department endorsed this feeling:

> 'Women take time and trouble over things that don't matter. Men are much more intelligent about the things they select and work at. They'll look ahead and set an objective—see what's valuable and useful to them—avoid clutter. I think that this selection of objectives is vital—refusing to be cluttered by a lot of subsidiary things which *are* important, but not in the same way.'

The men said that the woman's eye for accuracy and detail was often most useful in a secondary although complementary role, whereas men were more capable of looking at the broad field and making managerial decisions. Some men stressed the key position held by many senior secretaries in the BBC, who were indispensable because of their detailed knowledge and because of the complementary nature of their functions. A woman producer in drama also referred to this difference between men and women in authority:

> 'I think lack of experience of the size of the thing makes it difficult for women. A lot of women are frightened by the size and complexity of the work, but not many men are. I think men are more

inclined to think in realistic terms—£x thousand and so many people to control. Men cut corners and skip where they can. I think women can get bogged down in detail.'

Women thought that women producers were often more painstaking about the accuracy of their programmes. A number of them felt that men sometimes went too far in the emphasis they were prepared to put on a subject if they felt that it made 'better television', and that women were more honest in their approach to a subject and more concerned that nothing should be distorted. They felt that women had higher values in this respect than men.

Women also spoke of the warmth and humanity towards colleagues and subordinates which senior women often showed. Most of them thought that women were often much more sympathetic towards people's problems than men were. They thought that women were much better at picking up atmosphere than men, so that if trouble was brewing in a department or programme they were aware of it at an earlier stage than their male counterparts. However, it was recognized by the women themselves that these characteristics could easily get out of hand and that concern with the feelings of others could detract from a woman's performance in her job. If a woman was over-involved in the problems of another person, it was thought she might be unable to take essential decisions about that person. A former senior BBC woman said that the time when she realized that she had managerial ability was when she first took the decision to sack someone, in spite of the fact that this person had certain personal problems of which she was aware.

Both men and women recognized the dangers that some women in positions of authority tended to develop over-emotional reactions towards people, in which they took things too personally and were inclined to 'have favourites' or to discriminate against people. Although the women were aware of these dangers, they felt that the type of woman who reacted in this way was a dying breed. They felt that the 'modern woman' was less prone to emotionalism of this kind, and that if she suffered from it, it was unlikely that she would reach a position of authority in any case. Men were much more worried about what they saw as the over-involvement and tendency to take things personally among women in authority, and there was a strong impression given of a number of highly emotional women in the past who had been remembered more for their emotional unpredictability than for their good work.

However, women felt that this very sensitivity towards the feelings of others was a positive asset in a producer. Most of the women interviewed stressed that they felt that a good woman producer was more capable of putting people at ease and getting good performance out of amateurs than all but the very best men. It was felt that women were more flexible when confronted with another's point of view, and that although this might not necessarily be a good thing when dealing with colleagues and staff, it was a great advantage when producing a programme. It certainly was felt to help in dealing with non-professionals who might be a little out of their depth in the unknown atmosphere of a television or radio studio. One high-level woman producer said:

> 'I think women are very well-suited as Talks producers which is really a midwife job—not truly creative like writing or painting. I think a producer's job is very well done by women—arranging and organization and getting on well with people.'

A number of women said that it was sometimes easier to work with or for other women. One young woman said: 'Men think it's expected of them to be slightly sexual', and other women mentioned how difficult some men found it to treat them as normal working colleagues and not as something rather special. The majority of women thought that senior women were often more businesslike than men, and that they were usually better organized. They also thought that women 'got on with the job'. They thought that men were too fond of meetings and committees which took up far too much time, and had an obsessive love of taking 'epic minutes'. One senior man thought that women would be just as fond of meetings and committees if they were allowed to go to them more.

A general comment from the women was that they thought they were much less formal than men and less eager to build rules and regulations around themselves. One senior producer said:

> 'I think women have less time for the kind of protocol than men build up around themselves. I think women are more realistic—they look twice at protocol and see whether it's worth bothering about. I'm always breaking rules that the Administration dreams up. Women come across this protocol less in their formative years. Boys' schools have much more rigid strata. Men are very good at building structures around them—look at the trade unions.'

Women mentioned men's concern with the outward appearance of power, such as thick carpets and secretaries in outer offices, and said that women were less aware of status symbols. A number of women mentioned the BBC's custom of calling senior members of staff by the initials of their jobs, for example, DG for Director General. They felt this became ludicrous when applied to people with very long titles, particularly when they addressed each other in public by their initials. Some women were struck by the frequency with which men sent memos when they themselves would have used the telephone, and in general, the senior women interviewed thought that senior men were often much less well organized than they were themselves.

Both men and women thought that women were more loyal, reliable and dedicated than men, but that this had its positive and negative sides. One senior woman thought that this characteristic had turned into single-mindedness on her part which she thought the BBC was only too ready to exploit. She thought there was a great danger in the fact that certain women in responsible positions were eager to devote themselves whole-heartedly to their jobs to the complete exclusion of everything else. She felt that she herself had been guilty of this, and that it could affect the way in which women treated subordinates who were not so dedicated to their work. On the other hand, some of the women thought that some women in authority were not taken seriously because they were not prepared to devote themselves as whole-heartedly to their work as men were.

One characteristic mentioned by both men and women was the tendency that they saw in certain senior women to talk too much. One women called it 'this nag, nag, nag quality' and two men cited this as the one reason they could not bear the thought of working with or for a woman.

One thing which some women found very difficult to come to terms with was that they felt that characteristics of authority which were acceptable in man were very often not found acceptable in women. They thought that ambition was regarded as a desirable characteristic of a man but that it was regarded as something rather undesirable in a woman. One girl said:

> 'I think it's partly that we are brain-washed—feminine women are not top women—and don't want to be. I don't know many women who would say, "Yes, I'm very ambitious." People say that I am ambitious, simply because I have the job I've got. It's partly sour grapes—men have to attach this awful label of "career woman".'

A number of women said that men could be far more authoritarian and brusque with other people than senior women could. They felt that people were used to taking orders from a man and that if a woman wanted something done she had to approach the problem in quite a different way.

A high proportion of the women interviewed mentioned that they thought that women had more stamina than men and were more capable of absorbing crises than many men in their experience. The men, on the other hand, frequently cited woman's over-emotionalism and tendency to burst into tears. Only one woman interviewed mentioned tears, whereas most of the men mentioned that women were prone to tears, however senior they were.

Most of the women interviewed thought that they were earning very good salaries, although they realized that men in their position would not necessarily feel the same. They thought that women in senior posts were less motivated by money than men and that this lack of economic pressure was reflected in their attitude towards their work. They felt that women were less competitive than men and less aggressive and cut-throat about their work, and that an important reason for this was that most women did not have to support a family.

There was a marked tendency on the part of the men interviewed to look at the prospect of more senior women from their own experience with a very limited number of senior women. They were inclined to generalize about women's characteristics from those of a very special little group of women, each of whom appeared to have had some distinct disadvantage. The typical picture of a woman in a senior post then emerged as an amalgam of all these characteristics, and this was a fairly fearsome creation.

Women were more inclined to point out certain 'typical' characteristics and then say that there were many women who did not have these characteristics. Women would also point out that many men were very similar to many women, and talked of the number of men they knew who were sticklers for detail and highly emotional. They thought that these characteristics were often overlooked if the men concerned had other positive attributes, whereas they would be held against a woman in line for promotion.

Chapter VII
MARRIAGE, CHILDREN AND WORK

Of the 22 women interviewed who were still working for the BBC 13 were single (including the 4 General Trainees), 5 were married, 2 were widows, and 2 were divorced. Of these 9 married, widowed or divorced women, 8 had children. Of the women with children, 4 had taken the minimum amount of time off to have their babies and had come back to work, 1 had lived abroad a lot but had been able to combine bringing up a baby with a variety of part-time and full-time work, two had worked freelance or part-time for the BBC, and the other had come back to the BBC when her children were out of the baby stage. All the women with children thought that if a woman wanted to stay in the running for the good jobs she had to take as little time off to have her children as possible. Their own reasons for returning to work were rarely clear-cut, however. They either felt they had to work for economic reasons or they believed that their function in the family was one of bringing stability—either financial or emotional. None of the women interviewed said that she had returned to work because of sheer love of the job or ambition, although these might have been secondary factors. None of the women with children who had worked through showed any real regrets about it, although they felt that they had missed certain things through not having brought up their children all the time. However, they thought that there might be certain advantages to the children:

> 'I think that when the children were very little, they would rather have had me at home, but when they got to about 9 or 10, they were proud of me. I think I possibly make a better mother to older children. My own mother was a very motherly mother. But when I was about 11 and started asking lots of questions to which they didn't know the answers, my parents felt threatened. Now when my son knows more than I do I'm glad. I have an assured position. My assurance of my own status has made them rather arrogant perhaps—they don't accept things on trust.'

Another woman had very definite views on why she had worked:

> 'I feel temperamentally the need for a very stable kind of existence with the assurance of a settled income. My husband is a brilliant

man but a freelance by nature. This left me with three ways open to me—(a) sitting at home biting my nails, (b) nagging him to try and make him my kind of person, or (c) provide what I wanted in my life myself, and I opted for the last one. I'm not unhappy—I've enjoyed myself enormously because he backed me up.'

This support from husbands was frequently mentioned as a desirable characteristic, although not all the women had received it. The husband was sometimes not as successful as his wife:

> 'I think there are very few women who have gone ahead where the husband has also gone ahead. It's very difficult to think of families where the two are both successful. A lot of women won't admit that in some sort of way they are supplementing what the husband doesn't provide—in some cases because of bad health or bad luck.'

The women were asked how they thought marriage and children affected women's opportunities for promotion. The women with children thought that marriage as such did not have much effect on how women were treated, but as soon as they were pregnant it was assumed that they would leave. If they came back they thought that the BBC was perhaps fairer than other organizations they knew of. If they showed that they could do their jobs, the BBC did not display an unreasonable interest in how they ran their homes. However, they did feel that if a woman with children applied for promotion, then the fact that she had children would become an important factor, and that, given the choice, the Board would be more likely to give promotion to a man than to her. They felt that this was not always fair, and that it reflected a general tendency among men—particularly among older men—to react against working mothers in principle. They felt that men often built up an elaborate set of reasons for not giving a job to a working mother, such as the likelihood that the mother would stay at home if the child was ill or that she could not run a responsible job and a home properly, and so on. Most of the women said that given the kind of money they were earning, it was highly unlikely that they would not have made adequate arrangements for running their homes and their children's lives, and that crisis points occurred only rarely. They felt that men were just as likely as women to take time off at crisis points, and a number of women said that men were much more likely to take time off to go to school speech days or sports days than they were, because as women they were under closer scrutiny.

A widow described how she met men's resentment of her working. As soon as she gently let it be known that she was a widow, she felt this resentment evaporate and the men's attitude change. She was then regarded as a necessary breadwinner like themselves and a brave little woman. One senior woman described how she planned her career so that while her children were small she deliberately kept herself in a backwater, doing a job which was well within her capacity. She back-pedalled and spent as much of her time as possible writing her scripts from home. She felt that she could have got a lot further in the BBC if she had not taken this conscious decision to 'level-peg' instead of moving forward at the same pace as her male contemporaries. She saw this as the real problem for young women—that at the time when they were having their babies the young men were sorting themselves out into the successful and the not-so-successful. By the time the women were in a position to move back in, all the good jobs had been taken and the highly competitive situation in the BBC did not leave much room for people to come back.

The problem of coming back into the BBC, having left it for even a short period of time, was put to the women. All of them thought that leaving for more than the minimum maternity leave would put paid to a woman's prospects of getting on. They thought that this was becoming more true than it used to be. The days when producers of 40-plus were appointed were thought to be over, and the new emphasis on youth in responsible jobs was bound to militate very much against women who wanted to take a few years off to have families. Both men and women interviewed thought that this was not only true of women, however. They cited instances of people moving out of the BBC and being forgotten and unable to come back. They felt that fashion, particularly in television, changed so fast that even two years out would make a producer old-fashioned and possibly unable to get a job. Senior men responsible for appointments said that only the better men were sent abroad to help underdeveloped countries set up radio and television stations, because it was so difficult to fit the mediocre man back into the BBC. The increasing competition for jobs and the cult of youth and the tendency to burn people up fast in television were all thought to make it very difficult for women with children.

The possibility of part-time or freelance work was also discussed with both men and women. Two of the women interviewed had done part-time work for the BBC while their children were small. Both these women worked in External Broadcasting, where the opportunities for freelance or part-time work were generally considered to be greater than in any other part of the BBC. This was because of the many different types of programmes and output of the External

Services and the enormous number of programmes containing small items which could economically be covered by a freelance or a part-timer. The kind of work was interviewing, writing short items, producing on short-term contracts of three months at a time, or working as a holiday relief.

Both women had enjoyed doing freelance or part-time work because of the freedom it allowed them as far as school holidays were concerned, and for working from home and when they liked. They had both returned to full-time work as producers when their children were older. They both felt that freelance and part-time work were rather underpaid for the work involved. They thought that the fact that they had continued to keep in touch with the BBC had made it easier for them to move back into full-time work. They both felt, however, that their chances of getting any higher than producer level would have been strongly inhibited by the fact that they had not had a continuous career. They felt that this would have been true of anyone—high-flier or not.

Senior men were asked whether they thought that broken career patterns would affect a woman's chances of reaching senior posts. The general consensus was that it depended on the woman and her field and how long she was away, but that her chances would be greatly diminished the longer she stayed out of the BBC and was not working in any related field. There was no question of bringing a woman back in a senior position simply because five years before she had shown great potential. She would have to apply in the usual way and take her chance in the normal competitive channels. However, if she had had a good record and still showed potential, it was likely that she would be looked upon sympathetically, although she could not expect preferential treatment. She could not apply for an internally advertised vacancy unless she had left within the previous six months.

The relative lack of opportunities for freelance or part-time work was criticized, particularly by the younger women interviewed. They felt that their generation of women were much more eager to continue to do something while they had young children, so that they did not become 'captive wives', but nevertheless they were conscious of the responsibilities of mothers towards young children. They felt that an artificial barrier had been put up so that women were forced into a position of either working full-time or not at all. They felt that an organization like the BBC could provide far more opportunities for freelance or part-time work, and mentioned the fact that much of this work was given out on what they called the 'network' basis rather than in an official or organized way. Most of the women interviewed stressed the necessity of keeping up good contacts with colleagues if they wanted this kind of work. This meant that a woman really ought to think of moving into a department at the beginning of her career where the opportunities of part-time or freelance work were greatest.

The single women on the whole did not feel very great sympathy towards married women with children who wanted part-time work. They felt that the administrative difficulties involved were too great, and that part-time work as a producer was not really possible, since someone had to be available most of the time. Even on a big team it was thought that someone else would have to do the work when the part-timer was not in. Single women also thought that a working mother should not expect any concessions and ought to be treated in exactly the same way as other women. It was curious that they had the impression that married women *did* get extra concessions, whereas the mothers interviewed stressed how they went out of their way to show that their work came first when they were in the BBC. The mothers pointed out that they had a great sense of responsibility towards their work, and that this was not incompatible with having a great sense of responsibility towards their families. They felt that the question 'which comes first—family or work?' was rarely relevant. There was no doubt in most of their minds that their families came first, but they thought that the number of situations in which this dramatic choice would occur was very limited, and that this kind of question should also be asked of men with children.

Senior men interviewed were often ambivalent in their attitudes towards working mothers. Although they went to great lengths to explain that the BBC was not interested in the private lives of its staff, nevertheless most of them expressed some concern at the thought of mothers of young children working, although they stressed that they did not think that this would affect their attitude to such a mother at a Selection Board. Some of them said that they would feel bound to ask what arrangements she had made for her children although they accepted that this was not perhaps directly relevant to the question of whether she was the best qualified person for the job.

In comparison with industry, the BBC appeared to be less influenced by the marital status of women, and the general attitude towards mothers working seemed more open-minded. The general atmosphere was generally less censorious. There was a feeling that men did not allow their private lives to intrude on their working lives as much as women did, but nevertheless some senior men mentioned that women were never known to go to their Establishment Officers with drink or debt problems. In fact, women were thought less likely to take their personal problems to their Establishment Officers than men. Certainly the women interviewed showed a marked reluctance to confide in their Establishment Officers or ask them for advice particularly about anything concerned with the twin demands of work and family. They felt that this would emphasize the problem with which they were living and perhaps give the impression that they were unable to cope with it.

One senior woman thought that the BBC could do a lot to help women who wanted to keep in touch with the BBC although not doing a full-time job:

> 'I think there's got to be a great deal more flexibility about hours. Married women will come in for a four-, five-, six-hour day. An intelligent woman has infinite value. I think employers will find they have to work in teams. We're analysing skills and work now. If we get as far as analysing jobs, why don't we analyse the timetable? We'll have to re-design the jobs—it goes right the way through. We could look at this department and parcel out jobs—and they don't all have to be 9 to 5.30 jobs.'

She had this advice for young women who wanted to do well in the BBC, but at the same time felt a strong sense of responsibility towards their families:

> 'I think they ought to hang on as long as they can—get themselves into a backwater where the job is well within their capabilities and then come back in as strongly as they can. If not—then they should leave, but use their network to get some kind of part-time job—keep their minds alive—it's the best possible way to get back in. If you have a degree and have worked for the BBC, it's a very good jumping-off point for all kinds of other things. But they can't expect the world to re-design jobs for them unless they have gifts and usefulness that people want.'

Chapter VIII
CONCLUSIONS

The main question to be asked at the end of a report of this kind is whether women have done as well in the BBC as might be expected, considering the fact that many able women leave when they get married or have babies. The question must be underlined by the fact that most of the very senior women in the BBC are going to retire fairly soon, and that there are no obvious female successors to their posts. There is also very strong evidence to show that women are reaching positions of less responsibility than they were even fifteen years ago, when Mary Somerville had Controller rank. There is certainly no reason to imagine that anything like the situation in the early 1930s, when almost half the departmental heads in the BBC were women, could be repeated in the near future.

A senior BBC official has suggested that there are no obvious successors to the senior BBC women because there are so few women in the middle management ranks. It is certainly true to say that there are few women at this level, but the question is, why is this so? The figures quoted at the beginning of this report show how the proportion of women declines the higher the grade, and the greater the responsibility. The general consensus of opinion was that up to a certain level—that of producer or its equivalent grade—women had more or less equal opportunity to men, although in certain jobs and in certain areas women were probably in a weaker position than men even at this level. Above this level, where jobs normally included at least some element of managerial responsibility, it was generally agreed that women were at a disadvantage, and that the higher the jobs were in the management structure, the greater the disadvantage.

What are the reasons for this? There are certainly historical reasons for the number of women in very senior positions who are retiring at much the same time. This report has shown how a number of outstanding women seized their opportunities during the war to start on the ladder to management. The question arises whether in fact there have been other women working in the BBC since then, who would have proved to be of similar calibre if they had been given the opportunities, or if they had been pitchforked into situations where they could have seized these opportunities. There is clearly some anomaly when a generation of women who are in general much better educated and more confident than the previous generation cannot throw up outstanding women of the type who are shortly retiring. There are the possibilities that the BBC's promotion system does not work to the advantage of women, and that the BBC's recruitment policy does not find women of the calibre of this group of senior women.

The BBC's recruitment policy has been examined in this report. Are the top women of tomorrow being recruited today, and if not, what can be done about it? This report has shown that there are two main paths into the BBC for ambitious young women straight from university or further education—as a General Trainee or as a Trainee Programmes Operations Assistant. The General Trainee Scheme and the successes and failures of women have been reported on at some length. If the BBC stresses the importance of its General Trainee Scheme in selecting its future top management, it is not unreasonable that a report of this kind, concerned as it is with women in top management, should spend some time looking at the performance of women in this scheme. It is possible that the BBC does not know how to select women for a scheme of this kind, that women are not suitable for a scheme of this kind, or that there is something wrong with the scheme itself.

The other method of entry—as a Trainee Programme Operations Assistant—certainly appears to give a good training in radio operations, and there is little doubt that there is ample opportunity and encouragement given to able young women—and men—who want to move into radio or television production, but perhaps not every high-flying woman is attracted by the idea of putting on tapes and pressing buttons, and it is possible that the BBC does not attract as many of the really bright women as it might if it offered a different type of entry gate. It is interesting to note that as many women as men are recruited for this scheme at present, and it could be a very illuminating exercise to follow up the careers of a single year's intake.

It seems surprising that these are the only two main training schemes in production which are open to graduates. There really does appear to be an enormous gap between the General Trainee Scheme, with its emphasis on outstanding qualities and top management potential and the technically orientated Programme Operations Assistant Trainee scheme which is limited to radio. Since women are notably unsuccessful in the General Trainee competition, and possibly fail to see the advantages in becoming a Trainee P.O.A., there would appear to be a good case for offering an entry gate somewhere between the two. This could be a training scheme in radio and/or television production, but it would not, of course, be limited only to women. It is quite probable that the BBC cannot afford to lose some of the men whom it now rejects for General Traineeships, who do not attempt the second course available—the P.O.A. Competition—but turn their attention to the management training schemes of other organizations, where the rewards are higher and more immediate than through the P.O.A. scheme.

If the BBC is serious about its stated desire to recruit young women of high calibre who could be potential top management, it ought perhaps to examine its methods of recruitment and training of young women. It is also possible, as stated by some women, that University Appointments Boards could do more to channel women into applying for the BBC General Trainee Scheme.

One of the main problems which obscures the issue is that the BBC has what appears to be a wealth of talent applying to it, and there can be no doubt that young men and women with excellent academic and extra-mural records are turned down by the BBC without even having an interview, simply because there are applicants with even better qualifications. It could be that among those turned down at all stages of selection, especially among the women, who have been shown to be more diffident and less ambitious, there are potentially very bright managers. It might be worth the BBC's while to encourage some of these people to reapply when they have 'cut their working teeth' elsewhere. The BBC has so many unsolicited applications that it might well shudder at this possibility, but in the case of women in particular it could pay dividends.

Both the occupational and family case studies carried out in conjunction with this survey stress that girls' career plans often have a less clear direction and strength of motivation than those of either men or of older women. There have been several references to the 'instability of young women' in this report. Perhaps if the BBC wants the same sort of career commitment as it gets from men it should concentrate on older women entrants, who often have more balanced personal lives and who could bring greater maturity to their work. These women should have the chance to come in as trainees, not only as qualified professionals, since it is again a characteristic of women to switch professions, or at least not to settle finally for a particular profession, at a later age than men. Married women can often afford to retrain at 27 or 28 plus, where men could not, because they have their husband's financial resources behind them. They are often also more willing than men to restart relatively low down, especially if they can see that, if their merits justify it, they will be accelerated up when their training is completed. It could be that the BBC could pick up some of the very bright women mentioned in the report who apparently get married as soon as they leave university and do not apply for the BBC along with the other graduates. It appears to be very likely from much of the evidence collected in this survey as a whole that the recruitment of married women in their late twenties or early thirties who have had their families might bring in some women with top management potential who are prepared to offer the career commitment that younger women graduates are not This point could also be underlined with the observation in the report that older married women and widows who have got the measure of a man's world are the best able to cope with it.

The possibility of recruiting older married women rests on the acceptance by the BBC that women have different career cycles from those of men. It also requires some examination of the apparently generally accepted view that producers are getting a bit past it by the age of forty, which means that those women—or men—who have a different working pattern from the normal and reach the experience and qualifications needed for promotion relatively late do not merit consideration. In this respect, the BBC appears to be changing, since it used to make a point of taking on retired officers from the armed forces into its administrative departments, and indeed, one or two of the more successful women in the past were not recruited until they were over 40. It could be argued that both in the national and the BBC's interests, manpower resources need to be conserved, and that any employer who disqualifies certain candidates simply on the ground that the rhythm of their life is different is not giving proper attention to the conservation of human resources.

This report has looked at some length at the problem of married women and their children. Although the BBC is an enlightened employer as far as working mothers are concerned, nevertheless the onus and the decisions rest very much with the individual woman and her prospects depend very much on her standing within the organization. If she is respected and wanted, the rules are bent slightly at times—but this is true for any trusted employee of the BBC who gets into difficulties. At the moment, the system of dealing with a woman who wants to continue working after having a baby or who wishes to return to work after a break appears to be haphazard. If the BBC wants more top women managers, it ought to find ways of encouraging some of its potential talent to stay with it, if only in a part-time or freelance capacity for a number of years, and then giving women with this talent the opportunity of coming back into the promotion race. Again, if the BBC wants to conserve talent it could look more closely at the possibility of rationalizing employment of freelance and less than full-time women. *Working Wonders* made the point very strongly that many top quality women are available only on the condition that they are not willing to do a full-time job. However, at the moment, work of this kind is usually only available through the 'old-boy' network or contacts of this kind.

These jobs need only be at a fairly junior level. It would undoubtedly create difficulties if heads of department worked less than full-time, but it was pointed out in a number of interviews that not all jobs in production required constant attendance during office hours. Indeed, many members of production teams, both male and female, regularly spend some time out of the office working on scripts or ideas, and there are a number of programmes where some kind of shift work exists in any case. Very often flexibility of hours is all that a woman needs to make her feel that it is possible to continue working with a family. Research work, too, can often be handed out on an ad hoc basis, and it is probable that some women would be satisfied to earn quite a lot less and have less responsibility for a while, if they had the opportunity of coming back on a full-time basis later. It is possible that it would be in the BBC's interests to create these kinds of opportunities for women so that it did not lose valuable members of staff.

These points are all concerned with recruitment and conservation of resources, but there are a number of comments to be made on promotion prospects for women already in the BBC.

There can be no doubt that things *have* changed and that in a number of respects women have moved forward, in that they do lift heavy weights, hold down jobs as producers, and deal satisfactorily with the managerial element in these jobs. But all this has happened by accident through individuals' ambition and drive, difficulty in filling certain posts, or the fact that women seized opportunities during the Second World War. However, the BBC do not seem to have a thought-out policy to this end. It should be asked whether it is likely if the BBC had had such a policy some of the obstacles to women's advancement which still exist would have proved as mythical as those which have been removed.

It appears that lack of experience in 'women's areas' of radio and television is not a bar to men's promotion, but that lack of experience in 'men's areas' is a bar to women. This inconsistency appears somewhat bizarre.

BBC officials apparently accept that there is resistance to women in a number of quarters, not on the basis of their actual capacity to do the job, but of the tradition that certain areas are male clubs and that in others the number of applicants far outruns the number of jobs, and that those in possession accordingly set up artificial barriers to keep women out. The BBC seem to accept this as a fact of life.

There appears to be a tendency, in considering women's potential performance, to stress the alleged defects of typical or modal women—over-attention to detail, emotionality and so on—but to pay too little attention to the corresponding defects in men as noted by women informants. There was a strong tendency to stereotype individuals, especially women, in terms of certain characteristics, and some evidence to show a more open eye for points which favour men and disfavour women. A special aspect of this is one which has been observed in other occupational studies in this survey. There is fairly substantial evidence that higher paid and better qualified women are being considered not on the characteristics of their own class, but on those of the much more numerous women who are lower paid and less well qualified. The higher paid women, for example, have and use better facilities for coping with the problems of working while having young children. They lose far more by staying out of work, and in fact, there is evidence collected in other parts of this survey to show that they are much less likely to stay out of work than those with poorer qualifications. A young woman earning over £2,000 a year in a production post in the BBC faces the prospect of having her family income at least halved when she has a baby. She has considerable financial incentive to go back to work, or at least to try and earn some money to keep the family's standard of living from dropping dramatically. This very important point was not always appreciated, particularly by some of the older interviewees.

There is also evidence to show that women perform well in jobs into which they may have been pitchforked, and this is borne out by the experience of women in the BBC during the Second World War. It was pointed out by several informants that management was less prepared to take a risk of putting a woman into a job with an element of managerial responsibility in it, but was prepared to take this risk with men. There seems to be no reason why they should not take the risk with women too.

If there were more women in managerial positions or even in areas where women are not readily accepted, it would certainly be easier for the women following them to behave naturally and to be accepted by men. There would be less fuss about femininity or intrusion into a man's world, and less emphasis on the question of whether women and authority go together. In fact many of women's problems would disappear if there were more of them around.

In general, the BBC ought not to assume that it has equal opportunity for women, but should examine what it means by equal opportunity. It cannot ignore the long-term consequences of losing or not recruiting high calibre women. There is perhaps a case for special treatment for special women. The point was made by BBC officials that there was often a clash between a long-term consideration of this kind and the need to justify a particular appointment in terms of immediately apparent considerations. There can be little doubt that the BBC has great responsibility as one of the most prominent showcases for the policy of public enterprises on equal opportunity and the conservation of manpower resources. In addition, in examining its attitude towards women, it might be able to recruit or keep some top-quality talent which it has hitherto neglected.

Part Four

WOMEN IN THE ADMINISTRATIVE CLASS OF THE CIVIL SERVICE

PREFACE

This is a study of women in the administrative class.[1] The 220 women members of the class are not the only women in the Civil Service, nor are administrative Civil Servants who totalled about 2,600 on January 1, 1969 numerically the largest group in the Civil Service. Most of the other functional groups in the non-industrial Civil Service outnumber the administrative class. And many of the classes comprising these groups have a higher proportion of women members. For instance women form 8 per cent of the permanent members of the administrative class, 20 per cent of the permanent members of the executive class, 44 per cent of the permanent members of the clerical class and 9 per cent of the permanent members of the legal class.[2]

In effect women administrators are a minority within a minority. Both minorities, that of the administrative class and that of its women members, have an importance that belies their numbers. The administrative class has long been regarded as the elite of the Civil Service and as one of the prestigious occupations in our society. Women administrators have jobs of considerable responsibility and they work under formal conditions of complete equality with men. This study, which draws upon questionnaire and interview responses of men and women administrators as well as published material on the administrative class, seeks to enquire into the performance of women in the administrative class: what positions they have attained, how well they appear to carry the role of administrator, how comfortable they feel in the administrative world and how well the occupation combines with the responsibilities of marriage and family life.[3] It is important that this study of women administrators should not lead to them being regarded as an isolated minority. They are women but they are also administrators, working along with men at a highly demanding occupation, being contained for most of their working

[1] The study does not embrace the administrative grade in the Diplomatic Service.

[2] More extensive figures on staff groups in the non-industrial Civil Service and the number of women members, 1968, are given in Appendix 1.

[3] See Appendix 2.

lives by the same occupational world. Hence as far as possible this study seeks to view women administrators within the context of work and careers inside the administrative class and to note the similarities between men and women at work as well as the differences.

Chapter I
THE HISTORICAL PICTURE

CHAIRMAN: 'Are women admitted to all of these examinations you have been talking of?'
SIR STANLEY LEATHES: 'I am afraid not!'
CHAIRMAN: 'Do you see any reason why they should not be?'
SIR STANLEY: 'Well, it is a very revolutionary proposal is it not?'
CHAIRMAN: 'We are living in revolutionary times are we not?'
SIR STANLEY: 'Perhaps!'

Royal Commission on the Civil Service, 1912.

1. *Introduction*

Over a period of ninety years the Civil Service has moved by a number of steps from being a totally male institution to a position where it is accorded accolades for its employment practices in relation to women.

Women were first employed in the Civil Service in the 1870s; during the next fifty years they were employed in limited sectors of the Civil Service where they received lower rates of pay than men doing comparable work. Initially women were permitted to marry and to continue work, but from the 1890s onwards it became usual for departments to insist on retirement at marriage. After the First World War women were allowed to enter the administrative, executive and clerical classes of the Civil Service but they still had to resign at marriage, received lower pay than the men and were prohibited from holding certain posts. In the 1930s reforms resulted in the majority of Civil Service posts being opened to women and men equally.[1] Then several major steps were taken after the Second World

[1] Categories of Non-Industrial Grades in the Civil Service in which recruitment is still wholly or partly restricted to men are (excluding Post Office): Agricultural and Fishery Specialists (a limited number of grades); Cartographic Surveyors and Reproduction Staff Grade A in the Ordnance Survey Department; Chaplains; Customs: Outdoor Service Grades and Water Guard; Immigration Service;

[*footnote continued overleaf*]

War: in 1946 the insistence on retirement at marriage was dropped and equal pay for women was granted in 1955 and finally achieved in 1962.

Present circumstances perhaps lead to a benign view of history in the Civil Service as well as in other elements of British society ('there is an element of myth in common notions about the British capacity to settle their political and economic differences through peaceable, fair and democratic processes')[1]: the Civil Service has not moved to its present position on the employment of women without arguments of great bitterness.

During the late nineteenth and early twentieth century the Civil Service was a major target for feminist organizations which felt that the State was more likely to be pushed into an acceptance of the principle of equality of the sexes than were private employers. The Civil Service did not accede readily to the demand that it should treat men and women according to universal criteria. Rather, it resisted the notion that it should be expected to act differently from other employers; the Treasury argued before various Royal Commissions[2] that the loss involved in upsetting any status quo in favour of the principle of equality of the sexes was of a more certain nature than any benefits that the wholesale recognition of the principle could bring the Civil Service. For a variety of reasons, however, the Civil Service has, over time, yielded ground to the universalists. It seems that the Service was moved by a changed interpretation of its

Industrial Foremen; Instructing Staff in the Home Office and Service Departments; Managerial and other Staff in exclusively or mainly male establishments; Marine Staff and Ships' Crews; some Museum Staff; Overseas Survey Staff; Radio Operators; Repository and Research Room Attendants in the Public Records Office; Royal Observer Corps; Security Grades; Storekeeping Grades; some Technical, Engineering and Inspecting Grades.

[1] Barrington Moore, Jnr., *The Social Origins of Dictatorship and Democracy*, Allen Lane, The Penguin Press, 1967.

[2] The following Royal Commissions deliberated about the employment of women in the Civil Service: Royal Commission on the Civil Service, 1874–75 (Playfair Commission) Report 1875; Royal Commission on the Civil Service, 1886–90 (Ridley Commission) Report 1890; Royal Commission on the Civil Service, 1912–15 (MacDonnell Commission) Reports 1 to 6, 1912–16; Royal Commission on the Civil Service, 1929–31 (Tomlin Commission) Report 1931, Cmnd. 3099; Royal Commission on Equal pay, 1944–46 (Chairman: Sir Cyril Asquith) Report, 1946, Cmnd. 6939.

In addition Civil Service Whitley Councils considered aspects of their employment, see: *Reorganisation of the Civil Service*, Report of the National Whitley Committee, 1920; Report of the National Whitley Council Committee on Women's Questions, 1934; *Marriage Bar in the Civil Service*, Report of the Civil Service National Whitley Council Committee, Cmd. 6886 (London, HMSO, 1946).

economic self-interest in addition, and perhaps in preference, to considerations of principle.

The most specific and insistent reforming pressure on the Civil Service came from the two women's associations within it. The larger, the National Association of Women Civil Servants, recruited from clerks and typists, had evolved through various changes of title and structure from the first women's association, that of the Women Clerks in the Post Office, formed in 1901. The second, The Council of Women Civil Servants, recruited from women in the professional, administrative and higher executive grades, took this title in 1925, having originated in 1920 as the Standing Joint Committee on Women in the Higher Grades of the Civil Service. This had been formed so that women in the higher grades 'could formulate and give expression to their views on matters relating to women in the Civil Service and could watch their interests generally'. At times these two associations received support from Members of Parliament, from the predominantly male Civil Service unions and rather indirectly from notable feminists inside the Service such as Sir Warren Fisher.[1]

There do not appear to have been very strong active links between the associations and national feminist organizations such as the Fawcett Society and the Association of Business and Professional Women. Some individual members had links but the occasions on which the Civil Service women's organizations ventured into general rather than occupational agitation were very rare. The most notable occasion was that of the Equal Pay Campaign after the Second World War. On their side the feminist associations confined their activities *vis à vis* the Civil Service to protesting, in their evidence to the several Royal Commissions on the Civil Service, against the inequalities borne by women within it.

2. *The main milestones*

The Civil Service first became an employer of women fortuitously. In 1870 the State took over the telegraph companies which employed women. Some officials were quick to see the providence of an accident and in the 1870s promoted the employment of women as clerks in the Post Office: they argued that the employment of women as clerks clearly served the Service's interests as an employer.

> 'In the first place, they have in an eminent degree the quickness of eye and ear, and the delicacy of touch, which are essential quali-

[1] Sir Warren Fisher's espousal of the feminist cause is demonstrated in his evidence to the Tomlin Commission on the Civil Service.

fications of a good operator. In the second place, they take more kindly than men or boys do to sedentary employment, and are more patient during long confinement to one place. In the third place the wages, which will draw male operators from but an inferior class of the community, will draw female operators from a superior class. Female operators thus drawn from a superior class will, as a rule, write better than the male clerks, and spell more correctly; and, where the staff is mixed, the female clerks will raise the tone of the whole staff. They are also less disposed than men to combine for the purpose of extorting higher wages, and this is by no means an unimportant matter. On one other ground it is especially desirable that we should extend the employment of women. Permanently established Civil Servants invariably expect their remuneration to increase with their years of service, and they look for this increased remuneration even in the cases, necessarily very numerous, in which from the very nature of their employment they can be of no more use or value in the twentieth than in the fifth year of their service. . . . Women, however, will solve these difficulties for the department by retiring for the purpose of getting married as soon as they get the chance. It is true that we do not, as the companies did, punish marriage by dismissal. It is also true that we encourage married women to return to the Service; but as a rule those who marry will retire, and those only will return whose married life is less fortunate and prosperous than they had hoped. On the whole, it may be stated without fear of contradiction that if we place an equal number of females and males on the same ascending scale of pay, the aggregate pay to the females will always be less than the aggregate pay to the males; that, within a certain range of duty, the work will be better done by the females than by the males, because the females will be drawn from a somewhat superior class; and further, that there will always be fewer females than males on the pension list.'[1]

Related arguments about the specific appropriateness of women led to their employment as inspectors of female poor law institutions (first appointment 1873), female educational institutions (first appointment 1883), and of industries employing predominantly female labour (first appointment 1893). Hence when the MacDonnell Commission looked at the employment picture in 1914 they found

[1] This passage, attributed to Mr Scudamore, 'a Post Office official of eminence', is quoted in Hilda Martindale, *Women Servants of the State, 1820–1938*, London: Allen & Unwin, 1938.

besides female clerks, typists, domestics, prison and hospital workers, more than 200 women inspectors, 'much more important than women clerks by reason of the responsibilities of their duties'.[1]

The employment of women in the Civil Service gave rise to a 'segregated' structure—one of separate and unequal opportunities for men and women. Before the First World War the service had two establishments, male and female. In the main structure of the service the division was along the following lines;

Male Establishment	*Female Establishment*
First Division	
Intermediate Class	
Staff Clerks	
Second Division	
Superintending Assistant Clerks	Assistant Superintendents
Assistant Clerks	Principal Clerks
	Women Clerks (First and Second Classes)
	Shorthand Typists
	Typists
	Writing Assistants

This overall picture was the product of the ad hoc decisions of departments that certain posts should be designated for men only or that regulations governing admissions of candidates through competitive examinations should exclude women. Initially segregation involved the physical cloistering of men and women: this practice ceased to be operative by the twentieth century (the ladies at the War Office 'who thought they would like to be mixed up in their work more with the men'[2] winning the day). This was long before the social principles of segregation, i.e. that men and women should not compete with one another and that they should be placed on separate seniority lists, were abandoned.

The MacDonnell Commission on the Civil Service (1912–15) considered the employment of women within the Civil Service at great length. The arguments of the impressive array of social reformers who gave evidence to it were that women should be employed in the same jobs as men, assessed according to the same standards and subject to the same privileges and constraints in their work. They

[1] Royal Commission on the Civil Service (1912–15). *Majority Report.*

[2] Royal Commission on the Civil Service (1912–15). *Evidence of Secretary to the Army Council and Permanent Under Secretary of State.*

sought to persuade the Commission that the State would benefit greatly from the presence of women at all levels of the machinery of government and that it should seek to set an example to private employers. The majority of the Commission, however, were not persuaded. Their report, in 1912, recorded their opinion that 'the object should not be to provide employment for women as such, but to secure for the State the advantages of the services of women whenever these services will best promote its interests'. They accepted the arguments of their Civil Service witnesses that 'the evidence shows that in the power of sustained work, in the continuity of service and in adaptability to varying service conditions the advantage lies with men . . . except in certain limited spheres of employment, areas concerned with the home, the work and institutional life of women and children'.[1]

The MacDonnell Commission did not seek to force a reluctant Civil Service to change its attitude towards the employment of women. In the event the First World War created such a manpower shortage that the Service was forced to employ large numbers of women. In August 1914 the Service employed 192,800 men and 36,000 women: by January 1918 the total of men had dropped to 136,300 and that of women had risen to 144,600. Another effect of the war was to move women in staff and inspectorship positions over into administrative and executive posts. Such transfers helped to undermine the kinds of arguments against the fitness of women for these positions that had been aired before the MacDonnell Commission. This is not to say, however, that after the war the admission of women to executive and administrative posts on the same terms as men was plain sailing.

The Report of the Re-Organisation Committee of the National Whitley Council, issued in the post-war atmosphere of reform and reconstruction, advocated the virtually unlimited interchangeability of men and women within the Civil Service general classes. On the question of how women were to be admitted, the Report followed the recommendations of the official side and proposed that subject to quinquennial review (this was later made triennial by Parliamentary amendment) women should be chosen on the basis of interviews by selection boards rather than, as in the case of men, by an open competition by written examination.[2] The Civil Service, it seems, wanted to exercise special care in choosing the women who were to enter an almost totally male preserve. After the first three years of

[1] Royal Commission on the Civil Service (1912–15). *Majority Report*.

[2] From the 1920s onwards an interview was added to the written examinations held for candidates to the administrative class.

special competitions, however, women were allowed to enter the open competitions along with men.

From 1925 to 1939, after which the war led to the temporary abandonment of competitions, men and women competed equally in the open competitions for the administrative class. Contemporary observers however were disappointed by the rate of flow of women into the administrative class. Professor Kelsall in his study of Higher Civil Servants[1] points out that:

> 'Over the whole period 1925 to 1939 inclusive, out of some 490 competition appointments, only 35, or 7 per cent, were given to women. . . . By 1939 there were only 43 women in the administrative class, or not much more than 3 per cent of the total. Thirty of them were open competition entrants since 1925. . . . . Three were successful candidates at the special competition of 1922–3. The remaining 10 had either been given administrative appointments after previously holding specialist or executive class posts in the Civil Service or had been brought in direct from the outside without examination.'

The disappointingly small number of women entering and working in the administrative class before the Second World War was generally attributed to the small numbers of women initially applying, rather than to their performance in the selection process. The low proportion of women at Oxford and Cambridge, then the major source of recruits to the class, was partly responsible for the small number of applicants. Contemporary observers also felt that qualified women were dissuaded from applying by their commitment to teaching careers, their lack of knowledge about the administrative class and their uncertainty about the promotion chances of women in the class.

In 1929 another Royal Commission on the Civil Service, the Tomlin Commission, again considered its employment practices in relation to women. The major reform that it advocated was the 'aggregation' of Civil Service posts. As a result the surviving elements of the 'segregated' structure, the separate male and female establishments which had grown up prior to the First World War were almost totally dismantled during the 1930s. The entry of women into the administrative class in the 1920s had not been accompanied by the creation of a segregated structure, though it had led to the institution

[1] R. K. Kelsall, *Higher Civil Servants in Britain*, London: Routledge & Kegan Paul, 1955, pp. 171–5. This study is a source of historical information on attitudes to recruitment to the Higher Civil Service.

of male and female Establishment Officers in the departments where both sexes were employed. Establishment posts specifically designated for women were gradually abolished in the 1930s, the last one disappearing from the Treasury during the Second World War.

Despite the pleas of many witnesses, the Tomlin Commission did not advocate the removal of the two conditions of employment common to all women in the Civil Service, resignation at marriage and unequal pay.

The operation of the marriage bar was governed by Treasury regulations made in 1921. These specified that women holding established Civil Service posts should be unmarried or widows and that single women should resign their appointments on marriage. If they had service of not less than six years prior to marriage, they would be eligible for a marriage gratuity.[1] These regulations superseded an 1894 Treasury minute on the subject: both rulings formalized and extended an ad hoc departmental practice. At the time of the Treasury ruling (1921) the Service was preparing to accept the regular entry of women into the administrative and other general classes. There were many reformers who interpreted the coincidence of the two events in the same way as Sir Samuel Hoare, who commented in a Parliamentary debate that in the Civil Service there was still 'solid opposition to the entry of women in any large numbers', hence attempts to hedge the newly conceded entry of women 'with every kind of restriction [to] make it impossible for women to enter save in exceptional cases'.[2]

A battle over the marriage bar was waged until 1946 when women who married were given the option of continuing in service or resigning and, if they had the requisite years of service, taking their gratuities.[3] Until this time the Service as employer maintained that it stood to gain very little from a change in ruling. Most women, it was claimed, would in any case resign on marriage; where they resigned and subsequently found themselves without means of support there were mechanisms for compassionate reinstatement and where the Service could not face the loss of the women there were opportunties for keeping them on a temporary basis. Other benefits

[1] The marriage gratuity was calculated at the rate of one month's pay for each complete year of established service, not exceeding in the whole a maximum of 12 months' pay, see *Marriage Bar in the Civil Service, op. cit.*, p. 4.

[2] Sir Samuel Hoare in Debate on Sex Disqualification (Removal) Bill, October 27, 1919, quoted in Martindale *op. cit.*, p. 150.

[3] It is also possible for a woman to resign for purposes of marriage, to receive her marriage gratuity and then to continue to work as an unestablished Civil Servant.

of the marriage bar were seen to be the improved chances it gave to men's careers (in the 1920s and 1930s the male Civil Service Clerical Union supported the continuation of the bar for this reason), and the fact that the Civil Service would not be saddled with women giving inadequate attention to their work because of their domestic responsibilities. This line of argument was strongly expressed by Dame Maude Lawrence, Director of Women's Establishments (Treasury) in her evidence to the Tomlin Commission; in her opinion married women were a loss to the employers—'one does not get the same efficiency with a person who has two sets of interests as from a person who can give undivided attention'.[1] The main opposition to the marriage bar came from the Council of Women Civil Servants. In evidence to the Tomlin Commission they countered Dame Maude's arguments with the observation that men and women alike 'have their working hours and their domestic hours which are about equally divided in the working day'.[2] Spokesmen of the Council advocated that the choice of continuing in employment should be left to the individual women, some of whom had a greater aptitude for serving the State than they did for bringing up their children.

In its opposition to the marriage bar the Council for Women Civil Servants was supported by the professional and administrative staff associations, the Institution of Professional Civil Servants and the First Division Association respectively, who saw the retention of the marriage bar as 'inimical to the real interests of the Civil Service'.[3] The male and female clerical associations however pressed for the retention of the bar. The predominantly male association, the Civil Service Clerical Association, was worried by the possible impact that the removal of the bar would have on the career prospects of their members. The women on the other hand were concerned that the removal of the bar would eliminate the opportunity for marriage gratuities. The initial Treasury pronouncement (Minute, March 17, 1894) on the subject of marriage and marriage gratuity presented the latter as compensation for enforced resignation. It was felt by many women, especially those in the lower grades, that the lifting of the marriage bar would lead to the withdrawal of the gratuity system. And given the routine nature of their work and the limited nature of the promotion opportunities they did not relish the loss of the opportunity for very early retirement with a golden handshake. Women in the administrative class, with their greater career rewards, criticized the marriage bar much more vociferously. In 1929 they

[1] Evidence of Dame Maude Lawrence to the Tomlin Commission.
[2] Evidence of Council of Women Civil Servants to Tomlin Commission.
[3] First Division Association, *Annual Report*, 1946, Appendix IV.

won a limited concession from the Tomlin Commission which recommended a procedure whereby married women could be retained if the 'interests of the public service' demanded this. Between 1934 and 1938 8 married women were considered indispensable. The real breach in the prohibition against married women occurred in the Second World War. Then married women formed a sizeable proportion of women recruited on a temporary basis at all levels and it was found that the alleged obstacles to their efficient operation in the Civil Service were far from insuperable. Subsequent to this experience the Treasury quietly dropped the bar but continued to grant marriage gratuities.

After the dropping of the marriage bar in 1946, the major issue remaining to be settled was that of pay. In this case though some arguments appeared in the correspondence columns of the journals of the Civil Service associations, the main conflict was not as with the marriage bar, between different grades of the service, but between the Civil Service staff as a whole and the Chancellor of the Exchequer. The House of Commons had resolved in favour of equal pay for Civil Servants in 1920. Successive Chancellors, however, both Labour and Conservative, insisted that given the state of the economy and the government's other commitments, the necessary money could not be found. A steady campaigning pressure, was kept up by reformers in and out of Parliament and in particular was brought to a head by the general election of 1929 and the appointment of the Tomlin Commission on the Civil Service. The Commission was split on the pay issue. By the 1930s there were signs that the general rule of inequality was cracking. To that date the main exceptions to the rule of unequal pay were medical and dental staff for whom the BMA had been able to negotiate equal rates using the black list vigorously when necessary, and the Factory Inspectors Grade II. When after the Second World War the first women reached Deputy Secretary Grade, this and the Permanent Secretary Grade were also automatically assumed to have equal pay. In 1937 it was agreed by the National Whitley Council that women should not be paid at less than 80 per cent of the corresponding men's rates and that the cash gap should not exceed £175 per year. In a number of grades this led to a substantial improvement for women. From the time when the Tomlin Commission was taking evidence onwards women's organizations promoted the idea that if expense was so much of a problem, equal pay might be introduced by equal stages over a number of years; at times a period of as long as fifteen to twenty years was mentioned. Arguments, apart from the question of the state of the economy, were of the kind that might be expected. On one side it was argued that men were more likely to have dependents and need more, on the other that the actual degree of inequality of pay contributed little towards the real cost of maintaining a family and that tax and family allowances could do the job much better.

At the end of the Second World War the issue of equal pay became more prominent. In 1944 a Royal Commission on Equal Pay was set up and its Report seemed to favour the introduction of equal pay in the public services. In 1944 the Civil Service women's associations joined with many other women's groups to form the Equal Pay Campaign Committee and from about 1947 onwards they channelled much of their agitation over pay through this body. On the issue of pay post-war governments were subject to divided pressures. The women's associations worked mainly through the Equal Pay Campaign Committee and demanded equal pay immediately. Large public service unions, amongst them the Clerical Association and the Society of Civil Servants, were members of a rival Equal Pay Co-ordinating Committee which drew its constituent organizations from the National Staff side of the Whitley Council, and which pressed for equal pay by stages.

Post-war Labour Chancellors took the same line as Conservative Chancellors before the war on the need to give priority to other things. Labour was, however, visibly wilting under the equal pay pressure by 1951 and in the first post-war Conservative Government 1951–55 the pressure built up strongly. In 1954, for instance, both Equal Pay Committees presented petitions to Parliament. 'It was arranged that the two petitions be delivered separately at Westminster on the same day, 8th March, and formally presented on 9th March, "Equal Pay Day". The Campaign Committee lost the competition for signatures by 80,000 to 600,000, but won the competition for newspaper space. Its representatives delivered its petition in three horse-drawn carriages. The representatives of the Co-ordinating Committee took a taxi.'[1]

The Conservative Chancellor, R. A. Butler, edged gradually towards a decision and in 1954 the government permitted negotiations to take place in the National Whitley Council for the gradual implementation of equal pay in the Civil Service. Whilst these negotiations went on, a split appeared between the constituent associations of the Equal Pay Campaign Committee over the issue of the timing of equalization. On the whole the local authority and Civil Service bodies were more inclined to accept implementation by stages than were the women schoolteachers. In the event the solution

[1] Allen Potter, 'Equal Pay Campaign Committee: a case study of a pressure group', *Political Studies*, vol. V, p. 55, 1957.

reached in the case of the Civil Service in January 1955 to introduce equal pay in seven annual instalments set the pattern for the other public services.

The achievement of victory in the mid-1950s seems to have stemmed from the pre-election competition of the two major parties in a situation of economic optimism and easing of post-war austerity. It was also more of a victory for the policies of the Equal Pay Co-ordinating Committee than it was for those of the Campaign Committee. According to Professor Allen Potter, 'it does not follow that only the Co-ordinating Committee was an effective pressure group. In theory, the adoption of a compromise formula by the Government may result from an attempt to deal with pressures from powerful advocates of opposing extreme policies; the correspondence of the formula with the policy of a moderate group may have no significance.'[1]

With victory on the pay issue the two women's Civil Service associations decided to disband. They had existed as pressure groups to achieve specific ends, for instance the aims of the National Association of Women Civil Servants were:

> 'To remove the artificial restrictions placed on the employment of women in the Civil Service;
>
> To secure that their remuneration for services rendered should not be differentiated by reason of sex;
>
> To secure the free and unfettered admission of women to all appointments in the Service;
>
> To protect and promote the common interests of women in the Civil Service;
>
> To secure the removal of all civil and political disabilities of women.'

By the late 1950s the first three highly specific aims had been achieved in the main and both associations were faced with the decisions about their future. In disbanding in 1958 (NAWCS) and 1959 (CWCS) they rejected the notion of maintaining themselves as watchdogs of women's interests inside the Civil Service as some members urged that they should. In part this was because it was recognized that the main issues having been won, the associations' drawing power on new members would fade, but there was also a feeling that in the brave new Civil Service world of complete equality of the sexes

[1] Allen Potter, 'Equal Pay Campaign Commitee: a case study of a pressure group', *Political Studies*, vol. V, p. 63, 1957.

women's associations would have the appearance of skeletons at the feast. The disappearance of the women's associations was welcomed by the main staff associations because it helped to close staff ranks. With one exception the women's associations had not ventured on the staff associations' ground—they had no say in pay negotiations and they were not represented in the Whitley machinery. The exception concerned typists, an occupational group composed predominantly of women. In this instance the NAWCS secured the right of being the representative in pay negotiations and consequently earned the hostility of the Civil Service Clerical Association which lost no opportunity to broadcast its opinions of the 'inept and bungling way' it considered the NAWCS handled pay negotiations.

3. *The past and the present*

What emerges from this brief account of the incorporation of women into the administrative class is that the Civil Service has travelled the road to complete equality of the sexes in a resistant, hesitant manner. In its movement towards this it has been pressurized by feminist organizations, Civil Service women's associations and staff associations, and Members of Parliament and Ministers acting in different combinations and alliances. The summary given in the preceding pages is only a general and brief account of the build-up of opinion and pressure prior to the various decisions to extend the rights of women in Civil Service employment. Nevertheless it is possible to discern the more important elements in the situation. One, undeniably, has been the conservatism of the 'Service attitude': it may well be that on the particular issue of female employment the Service has displayed its general tendency to find good reasons for not doing things. Whatever the explanation the Service, when dealing with the various women's rights issues, has shown itself unwilling to contemplate change and determined to interpret change as for the worst. These attitudes emerge clearly from a reading of the evidence that the Treasury and various Permanent Secretaries presented to the different Royal Commissions which examined the question of the employment of women. Representatives of the Foreign Service (now the Diplomatic Service), which was the last part of the Service to admit women, went to laughable extremes at various times to emphasize 'the grievous dangers, moral and official, likely to follow the adoption of so extraordinary a course', i.e. the admittance of women.[1]

More typically, however, the Service sought to clothe its conserva-

[1] Foreign Office, *Report* of Departmental Sub-Committee set up to review the admission of women, 1936.

tism in arguments of expediency to itself as an employer. Initially it argued that it could not afford to employ women in responsible positions because they were not fitted for them; then it argued that it could not employ married women because they did not give value for money. Given that the service refused to test these propositions it was in as good a position to uphold them as other people were to refute them.

Conservative though the Service was, changes wrought by forces beyond its control weakened its ability to follow a restrictive employment policy in relation to women. The forces of reform played their part in altering the environment of opinion in which the Service was operating: they contributed to the enlightenment of public opinion thereby making the Service's attitudes appear increasingly anachronistic. More important, the pressure of war-time shortages of labour forced the Service to test and to find wanting the arguments that it had advanced about the drawbacks of women employees. The fact that single women in the First World War and married women in the Second served successfully as administrators forced the service to withdraw its arguments against them. It did not necessarily, at least after the First World War, make the institution accept change gracefully: the Service managed to delay the admission of women to the administrative class by the same route as men from 1920 to 1925. After the Second World War the Service attitude to the conditions of women's employment seemed considerably softened compared with its attitude in the 1920s and 1930s. In the 1940s the Service quietly dropped the marriage bar and in the 1950s the government of the day went ahead of the private sector in granting equal pay to women. The explanation for this change lies in alterations in the environment in which the Service was operating: the 1930s were a time of surplus labour whereas in the post Second World War period, the Service was, according to one Treasury Civil Servant, 'quicker than other employers to grasp the consequences of full employment.'[1]

Since the granting of equal pay to women the Civil Service now treats sex differentiation in its employment practices and the working life of the Service as a non-issue. The relative merits and rights of men and women in employment are acknowledged to have raised a great deal of dust in the past. But the question is recognized to have been decisively settled in favour of the universalists. This being so the Service now acts in a way it so fiercely resisted, i.e. according to 'higher principles' than those which guide private employers. As part of cheerfully shouldering the communal cost of employing women on

[1] Interview with Michael P. Fogarty, 1967.

equal terms with men, the Service seems studiously to avoid too much attention to the costs: it appears to keep no running account of the relative wastage of women and men and to avoid scrutinizing statistics on job performance and mobility and sick leave on a sex basis. In fact attempts to obtain such figures seem to be interpreted as challenges to what is now an article of faith in the Civil Service, that women's work experience is in no way different from men's.

The Service now employs a considerable number of women. In April 1968, 24 per cent, 157,425 out of 667,112 permanent non-industrial Civil Servants were women. In 1950 women constituted 30 per cent of this labour force; in 1939, 27 per cent; in 1927, 24 per cent; and in 1919, 24 per cent. In addition the Civil Service has a large non-industrial work force of temporary status which has always swollen during wartime. In 1950, as a result of the Second World War, temporary staff totalled just over half the number of permanent staff and just under half of the temporary staff were women. In 1968 the ratio of permanent to temporary staff in the non-industrial Civil Service was 3:1 and women comprised just over half of the temporary labour force.

When one looks at the administrative, executive and clerical classes separately it becomes clear that the pattern of female employment in the Service reflects that within society at large, women have moved in greatest numbers into the low status jobs whilst males have moved into higher status employment. Thus in 1968, considering the permanent staff, 8 per cent of the administrative class, 20 per cent of the executive class and 50 per cent of the clerical staff were women. Table 1 gives a more comprehensive picture for the last forty years.

One interesting feature of the incorporation of women into the administrative class in the last twenty years emerges from this table. The increase in the number of women over the period—in the order of 33 per cent—has taken place in a class that has remained virtually static. Hence women have actually replaced men—though this has hardly happened to the extent that one can talk about the feminization of the Service. This replacement of male by female administrators has happened during a period in which evidence suggests that the status of the administrative class *vis-à-vis* other higher occupational groups has fallen.

The post-war change of stance was probably also influenced by the high abilities of several of the early women competition entrants. The first 4 women competition entrants, Enid Russell-Smith, Alix Kilroy and Mary Smieton in 1925, and Evelyn Sharp in 1926 eventually became respectively Deputy Secretary in the Ministry of Health, Under Secretary in the Board of Trade, Permanent Secretary in the Ministry of Education and Permanent Secretary in the Ministry of Housing and Local Government. These were very talented and determined individuals who were striking witnesses to the superior administrative talent that could be found amongst women.

The present population of women administrators can be divided into entrants from four different time-periods. First there are those women aged 50 and over who were recruited to the class in the 1920s and 1930s. Numbers of this generation have already passed out of structure, amongst them Baroness Sharp, the first women Permanent Secretary. Whilst this cohort were pioneers—a small highly visible group of young women competing with men from entry onwards,

TABLE 1 *Number of women compared with men in clerical, executive and administrative classes in 1929, 1939, 1949, 1959 and 1969—permanent staff only*

	1929 April	1939 April		1949 Jan.	1959 Jan.	1969 Jan.
Administrative class						
Men	1,076	1,993	(1,926[1])	2,504	2,186	2,376
Women	18	75	(41[1])	154	194	221
Executive class						
Men	4,164	4,413[1]		22,103	28,522	39,101
Women	163	337[1]		5,405	7,423	10,172
Clerical class						
Men	17,240	29,287[1]		43,841[2]	47,776	33,230
Women	6,026	10,677[1]		22,939[2]	26,156	31,725

[1] April 1, 1938.
[2] April 1, 1950.

Source: Civil Service Dept. Figures compiled for this study.

and occasionally being highly successful—they were not strictly the first trailblazers. This position was held by women who moved into the administrative class from other classes during the First World War and afterwards. By the 1930s a handful of women from this entry had reached the rank of Under Secretary and equivalent level posts: most had retired or died by the early 1950s. The second cohort in the present population is that composed of women who entered the class in the war years as temporary Civil Servants and who then became established in the late 1940s. They were part of a flood of women entering the Service, and they were the first generation of women who had the opportunity of staying in the class after marriage. In their way these women too were pioneers, often determined, according to one male contemporary, 'to make this business of being a married women administrator work and sometimes having their lives made hell by spinsters of about fifty, who thought that married women Civil Servants were an abomination and let the side down'.[1] By the 1950s the flow of women into the administrative class was somewhat reduced (between 1948 and 1951 women averaged 12 per cent of the entrants and between 1952 and 1963, 8 per cent). Women who entered between the early 1950s and 1960s provide the third cohort. In these years of entry they entered the class in very small numbers. In this sense there were similarities between the women of this period and those of the 1920s and 1930s, but in the later period women were entering a class in which the major victories had already been won by other women. Finally from 1964 onwards there has been an upsurge of women entering the class; from 1964 to 1967 they averaged 18 per cent of the entrants and in 1968 were 25 per cent. Hence, at present, a substantial number of the generation embarking on a career in the administrative class are women. They have entered the class with the knowledge that they will not be a pioneering minority and the expectation that their sex will in no way hinder their career achievement.

It is impossible to predict with certainty what their experience will be. In considering what lies in store for a modern young woman administrator, however, one can gain some guidance from the experience of older women in the class. The experiences which distinguish cohorts are likely to be important, but it is also likely that the experience of older women administrators has implications and lessons for those now embarking on careers. Chapters III and IV consider aspects of the careers of women administrators now in the class. The next chapter describes some features of work in the administrative class so that the ensuing discussion of career experience can be seen against this background.

[1] Interview with author, October, 1968.

Chapter II
THE WORLD OF WORK

> 'Civil Servants are naturally no more of one type than lawyers or clergymen. But the practice of any profession develops certain qualities of mind and character in those who practise it and tends to repress others. The object . . . is to enquire what sort of mind and character is found predominant in the higher ranks of the home Civil Service. The answer to this question is clearly a matter of observation and opinion and not of statistical fact.'
>
> H. E. Dale, *The Higher Civil Service*, 1938.

The administrative class has often appeared as the tip of the iceberg of the British Civil Service, and it has attracted a great deal of scrutiny and comment. For a number of reasons the class constitutes a 'concentrated' occupation. First, the practice of the occupation is confined to one organizational setting—national government, and predominantly to one place—London. Second, its numbers are small, hence the contacts of an administrator with his fellows are likely to embrace a much higher proportion of practitioners than is likely in many other occupations. Third, the majority of its practitioners (61 per cent) have experienced no other occupational world apart from that of the Civil Service:[1] according to the Survey of the Civil Service 'the administrative class has a smaller proportion of staff who have worked for other organizations than the average firm's staff of managers or board of directors'.[2] And finally the majority of administrators have passed through a limited number of educational institutions, for instance 56 per cent of the class were educated in the private sector (i.e. direct grant, public and other fee paying schools)[3] and just under half of the class have degrees from Oxford and Cambridge.

Administrators have entered the class by a variety of routes. The majority (61 per cent of the Fulton sample of administrators)[4] have taken that of direct entry into the administrative class whereas the

[1] *Committee on the Civil Service* (Fulton Committee), vol. III(1), *Surveys and Investigations: Social Survey of the Civil Service,* London: HMSO, 1969, Ch. 3 *passim.*

[2] *Ibid.* [3] *Ibid.* [4] *Ibid.*

rest have entered it indirectly from other classes in the Civil Service. Direct entrants pass in after success in one of a number of competitions. These are:

1. Method I (discontinued after 1969) and Method II open competitions recruiting to the Assistant Principal grade of the class.
2. An open competition to the Principal grade for candidates aged 28–35 (introduced in 1964) and a special competition for candidates aged 31–51 (since 1965) and for former members of the Forces and Overseas Civil Service.
3. Occasional open competitions for recruiting Assistant Secretaries.

Entrants from other classes either pass into the Principal grade of the class by the mechanisms of departmental and central transfer and promotion or they pass into the Assistant Principal grade after success in a limited competition confined to candidates from the Civil Service.

In the last few years the administrative class has taken in about 250 people annually. The breakdown into the various routes of entry for 1966 is illustrative of their relative importance:[1]

Direct entrants:

1. Open competitions to Assistant Principal grade
   Method I = 18
   Method II = 94
2. Open competitions for entrants aged
   30–35 = 11
   31–51 = 51 including former members of the Forces and Overseas Civil Service
3. Recruitments to Assistant Secretary posts = 2

Indirect entrants:

1. Promoted or transferred to other classes = 71
2. Recruited from limited competitions = 8

In any one year the route by which the largest number of recruits have entered is that of direct entry to the grade of Assistant Principal after success in the Method I and Method II competitions.

After 1969 Method I competitions were abandoned. Between 1948 (when Method II competitions were introduced) and 1969 candidates could try either or both Method I and Method II competitions. The main difference between the competitions was that whereas Method I featured written examinations in academic subjects similar to degree

[1] Figures supplied by Treasury.

examinations, Method II candidates sit a qualifying examination followed—for those who pass the qualifying stage—by tests and interviews over two consecutive days.

These are arranged by the Civil Service Selection Board which is advisory to the Final Selection Board, the body that interviews those candidates recommended by the CSSB and awards marks on the basis of the candidate's records, their performance in the competition so far and the interview itself. Candidates who have failed to obtain at least a second class honours degree are automatically disqualified. Those who already hold first class honours degrees are exempted from the Qualifying Examination, as also are those with approved postgraduate qualifications.

The Method I and II competitions have been the best known routes into the class, being the modern descendants of the 'periodical examinations of a literary character' which Northcote and Trevelyan suggested should be held to secure 'the services of the most promising young men of the day . . . young men of general ability which is of more moment than their being possessed by any speciality'.[1] They are not the only routes but they are regarded as the core to which others are supplementary. The other routes generally bring in more mature recruits either from other classes of the Civil Service or from other occupations. Of recent years there has been a shift in the supply of direct-entry Principals: the predominant source of the 1950s, members of the Armed Forces and overseas Civil Servants, has been less productive and eligibility for late-entry competitions is not now limited by previous occupational experience. Applicants are informed that 'the standards required for admission to the administrative class are high' and that recruitment is 'normally to the grade of Assistant Principal for young university graduates of first or second class honours standard. Candidates in the present scheme need not have a degree but they will be expected to show evidence that they possess similar intellectual qualities and have had appropriate experience of responsible work at a senior level.'[2]

Entrants to the Administrative Class normally start in the grade of Assistant Principal or Principal. These are the lowest ranks of a hierarchy of six grades which divide members of the class in layers of responsibility. [The grades are shown on the following page.]

In addition to being placed in a grade, entrants are assigned to a government department. Departments differ in the proportion that

[1] Northcote–Trevelyan, *Report on the Organisation of the Permanent Civil Service*, reprinted in *Fulton Committee Report*, vol. I, Appendix B, p. 114.

[2] Civil Service Commission, *Recruitment of Men and Women Aged Thirty and Over*, Publication 594/68, p. 1.

	Total numbers July 1, 1968	Salary range July 1, 1969	Annual leave
Permanent Secretary	29	£10,400 £9,800 £9,300	6 weeks
Deputy Secretary	76	£7,100	
Under Secretary	283	£6,000	
Assistant Secretary	836	£4,045 × 6 to £5,200	5 weeks; after 10 years total service 6 weeks
Principal	1,110	£2,599 × 9 to £3,596	
Assistant Principal	323	£1,071 × 14 to £1,827	4 weeks and 2 days[1]

[1] After 6 years total service 5 weeks; after 20, 6 weeks

administrators form of their total staff and in the number of administrators of each grade that they employ. The majority, however, employ members of every administrative grade, and the same administrative units, though with slight variants of terminology. The usual pattern is for a department to be divided into a number of divisions headed by Under Secretaries. Deputy Secretaries coordinate the work of divisions. Each Under Secretary has within his division up to four Assistant Secretaries who in turn are directly superior to between one and four Principals. Within their sections Principals have one or two Assistant Principals and depending on the kind of work, anything from a few to a few hundred Executive and/or Clerical Officers.

It is easier to present a simple account of the routes of entry to the administrative class and of its structure than it is to give such an account of the work and career experience of administrators. The difficulty in any brief discussion of work and careers in the administrative class lies in the problem of conveying an adequate sense of both the central tendencies and the range of experience. What follows in the rest of this chapter is a very general consideration of the kind of work administrators do, the training they receive, the kind of promotion procedure that operates in the class and the different careers it is possible to perceive within it. The final section consists of a consideration of the ethos of the class and the nature of the class as occupational milieu for women.

Basically the jobs of the administrators derive from the special functions of the class 'which seldom have any precise counterpart in outside organizations, particularly in the industrial and commercial sphere, until you get right up to board level'.[1] The official definition of these functions is that they comprise 'the formulation of policy, the coordination and control of government machinery and control of the Departments of the public sector'. The Management Consultancy Group of the Fulton Committee saw the activites of administrators as falling under three main heads—Finance, Policy, and Personnel and Line Management. Traditionally it is the policy and finance work which have absorbed the efforts of the majority of administrators at all levels. Jobs which involve the working out of new lines of policy carry a cachet in the administrative world; they are seen as embodying the essence of administration which is 'first, to give the Minister the facts; secondly, to give him the limitations on those facts—the economic considerations, the statistic considerations, recruiting considerations, and so on. Then, having fed in the information and explained the restraints, the job is to analyse possible courses of action, find out which the Minister wishes to take and explain to him the difficulties surrounding that course. Having made sure that he fully weighs the position and realizes the dangers, then one accepts his decision and works straight to that end. Certainly one often disagrees with what he decides. At a guess 10 per cent of the time. But one's duty is not to make policy but to carry it out.'[2] At any one time very few administrators are engaged full-time on such activities, many more are involved in the activities which spring from the running of existing policies, budgeting and supervising expenditure, overseeing the management of organizations such as employment exchanges or post offices, answering Parliamentary Questions and letters from MPs, and advising on individual cases which raise policy issues.

The hallmark of the advice that administrators give their ministers is that it is intelligent general advice resulting from a scrutiny and assessment of all of the specialist considerations 'the economic considerations, the statistic considerations, the recruitment considerations and so on' which might affect an issue. The aids that they use in this process of analysis and decision-making are their logical analytical minds, their trained ability to consider a mass of detail and to extract from it the salient considerations and their capacity for 'sound' judgment. These tools have been labelled on the one hand 'amateur' and on the other those of one of the 'most professionally competent power groups' in Western Europe. The debate rages as to

[1] Sir Laurence Helsby, Evidence, Sixth *Report* from the Estimates Committee, August 1965, p. 162.

[2] Sir Maurice Dean, Permanent Secretary at the Ministry of Technology, quoted in 'What's Wrong with Whitehall', *The Sunday Times*, October 1, 1967.

the value of generalism but there is no doubt that up to now it has dominated the organization of work in the administrative class.

In the administrative class the grade that demarcates the experience of the many from that of the few is that of Under Secretary: this grade and the two above it represent the top management and policy levels of a department. The difference in the work experience between these and lower levels of the hierarchy lies in the amount of organizational responsibility that they carry and the broadness of the issues with which they are concerned. The top administrators of a department are more actively engaged than are the rest of the department in working with the Minister. Ability to work with Ministers and a highly developed sensitivity to the political side of administrative work are prerequisites for the incumbents of these posts. As a working rule it seems that questions of changes of policy are considered by the head of a division, an Under Secretary, who then refers his consideration to the Permanent Secretary and the Minister. One respondent[1] said that 'as a rule of thumb an Under Secretary alters policy, an Assistant Secretary tends to adapt situations to the policy that he finds and a Principal has final responsibility for the less tricky situations', another described the hierarchy in a division as operating as a team: 'your team will probably work as a fairly close knit unit from about the Principal up to the Under Secretary or Deputy Secretary, each doing the kind of job at his own different level'.

Administrative expertise is primarily fostered and acquired through practice. The Assistant Principal grade is regarded as a training grade, and those who enter it spend up to five years working in a number of sections in a department and attending formal courses. All Assistant Principals who have survived a two year probationary period, and nearly all do, attend a twenty weeks' course on economics and statistics. This course is designed to furnish recruits with a basic grounding in economics, now seen as indispensable to an administrator. Most administrators welcome the advent of formalized training which helps to reduce both the element of chance present in on-the-job training and the isolation felt by a new recruit to a government department. Since the early 1950s nearly all Assistant Principals have experienced between one and two years as Private Secretary to the Permanent Secretary or some Junior Minister or as Assistant Private Secretary to the Minister: the official justification for such experience in the training period is that it gives the new recruit a bird's-eye view of the department as a functioning whole and it is not felt to be very demanding work intellectually, though it can be

[1] See Appendix I.

extremely exhausting in time and energy. In other grades of the class there is a slowly growing tendency for administrators to attend formal training courses in specific subjects or techniques.

Above the entrants to the Assistant Principal and Principal grades there stands the hierarchy of grades through which they will eventually move. In the course of an administrator's career major decisions on the nature and timing of posts he is to occupy and the timing and extent of his promotion within the class are taken by other people. Administrators generally do not apply for posts within the class and they certainly do not apply for promotion to another grade. In the case of postings within grades decisions about moving administrators are made by the Establishments Officer, sometimes in consultation with other administrators and, where an important posting is being considered, e.g. Principal Private Secretary to a Minister, after consultation with the Permanent Secretary. Most administrators accept that Establishments divisions will attempt to accommodate their feelings on the subject of postings to the extent that they involve personal issues, e.g. their ability to get along with another Civil Servant, but that preferences about the nature of the work, etc., will rarely be given much attention. Indeed, most administrators rarely express such preferences for they accept that as general administrators they should be able to get to grips with any subject area in the purview of the administrative class. It has been the usual practice in the class for administrators to develop their general administrative skills and to demonstrate their versatility by changing posts about once every two or three years during most of their career. Thus there is a great deal of lateral posting within a grade in the class, both within and between departments.

Inside the Civil Service below the administrative class there is a set of formal procedures governing promotion between grades. When vacancies occur in any grade a Promotion Board is appointed to advise the head of the department on filling them. The Promotion Board generally consists of a member of the Establishments Division and two or more other department members one grade above that to which the promotion is being made. Staff Associations have no representation on Promotion Boards. It is the function of the Promotion Board to fix a field of seniority from which candidates will be considered for promotion. Seniority is dated from the day of a Civil Servant's entry into a grade and is calculated in terms of years. Hence the Board has to determine a cutting point in the line of seniority and then assess the candidates. The assessment is based initially on a standardized, annual report completed by the officer for whom the Civil Servant works. Part of this report is an assessment of fitness for promotion made on a four point scale, Highly Qualified, Qualified, Likely to Qualify in Time, Unlikely to Qualify. The Board should interview those designated as Highly Qualified and make recommendations about the filling of the vacancies from these candidates.

In the administrative class the procedure follows the spirit rather than the precise form of the above outline. For vacancies in the Principal grade a field of seniority is fixed, report forms scrutinized, but candidates are rarely interviewed before recommendations are made. For vacancies in the other grades the system operates even more informally. Annual reports are rarely written on people beyond the first Principal years: for Assistant Secretary vacancies the Establishments Officer and other senior officers in the department make 'soundings' and recommendations to the Permanent Secretary; for Under Secretary vacancies the Permanent Secretary makes the decisions though the consent of the Prime Minister is required for some of them and this is sought through the Civil Service Department. Permanent and Deputy Secretary vacancies are filled by Ministers after a process of consultation involving the head of the Civil Service and the Prime Minister. The procedure of delimiting a field of review or seniority is followed and generally the most able of the most senior candidates is chosen. However, in many cases the field of review is determined not so much by considerations of seniority alone but also by that of officers' merit.

In the administrative class within the Principal grade one encounters high-fliers, administrators considered so exceptional that they are promoted along with more senior administrators. Departments differ according to the extent that they are prepared to let people 'fly'. But looking at the Service as a whole it is possible to perceive three streams of administrators. The bulk of the administrators follow the middle path—they are currently made Assistant Secretary in their late thirties and most of them then serve as Assistant Secretaries for the rest of their careers apart from a few who serve as Under Secretaries for the last ten years of their careers. A few of the class 'fly'. They become Assistant Secretaries in their mid-thirties and if they go on flying, which not all of them do, they become Under Secretaries in their early forties, Deputy Secretaries three or four years after this and Permanent Secretary by their late forties or early fifties. A small minority of the class stay at the level of Principal for the whole of their careers.

Stemming from the streaming process in the class there are two discernible administrative career profiles besides those of the 'failures' —the people who do not go beyond Principal. First there is that of the 'bread and butter' of the class, the man or woman who rises to Assistant Secretary and perhaps Under Secretary at the end of their career. They will have entered the class in their early twenties, have spent about five years as an Assistant Principal and, within this period, eighteen months or so in the private office of the Minister or the Permanent Secretary. After becoming Principal at the age of around twenty-eight they will then spend about ten to twelve years in this grade, holding three or four different jobs, one of which may be in another department. Generally, he or she will be promoted to an Assistant Secretaryship in his or her late thirties and early forties. It is possible to be made an Assistant Secretary up to the age of fifty-five but the chance of promotion to the grade decreases rapidly after forty-five. When serving as an Assistant Secretary the average Civil Servant has a small chance of making the grade as Under Secretary for the last seven years or so of his career. Otherwise, he will retire at sixty or so as an Assistant Secretary.

The fliers spiral to different heights than those attained by the main body of the class and the path of the spiral tends to go through specific postings noticeable for their demanding nature and for the broad scope of their concerns. The high-flying spiral is also more likely to lead an administrator into two or three departments so that he can gain a sense of the interdependence of government departments. The Civil Service Department actively concerns itself with the staffing of top departmental posts, and hence tends to cultivate the careers of departmental fliers, for example by suggesting interdepartmental transfers.

In terms of the attainment of top jobs in the Civil Service, fairly crucial decisions are made about the individuals in their middle and late thirties. The important evidence on which these decisions are based is performance during the first five or six years of the Principal grade. These, probably more than any others, are the proving years for the administrator. Obviously, individuals shine as Assistant Principals but on the whole the responsibilities of the majority are not seen as significant tests of their administrative ability. Chance appears to play a large part in the winnowing process in the early Principal years: the character of the luck, or lack of it, derives from the foibles of the political process to which the administrative class is so closely attuned. Principals can find the responsibilities of their sections suddenly meriting considerable political interest. Obviously not all postings become politically important by chance, the interest in some can be predicted, in which case more than the usual element of care is exercised in choosing the incumbent of such posts. Whether the hum of political activity around the post is foreseen or not, the incumbent is well placed, if he seizes the opportunity, to make a good reputation for himself, for such work commands what all administrative work does not, a powerful audience at the top of the department. Private office postings which most Assistant Principles obtain in their fourth and fifth years of training are also seen to hold out such opportunities. Given the young Principal who makes a reputation for himself, the organization generally seeks to test his mettle and to make full use of his services by posting him to other demanding jobs. Thus the road to success contains the stiffest hurdles, each hurdle is both a gesture of confidence and a further test of ability. Failure to surmount any of these hurdles clearly throws doubt on an individual's capacities to get to the top, because as people move into the middle and higher echelons it is the same general qualities, rather than mastery of any particular field, which are being tested.

It is difficult to be precise about the skills and qualities that are likely to take people into the top posts of the class. Administrators, when questioned about this,[1] gave some very general replies. The flavour of their descriptions is probably best conveyed by a selection of them.

> 'Intellectual power, courage and unselfishness and complete support from your wife if you have one.'
>
> 'Clarity of thought and speech, courage, equanimity and concern for the community.'
>
> 'It is more easily recognized than described! The main qualities are—ability to reach the heart of a problem, and to ask the right questions; to see that the questions are answered; to delegate and devolve; to provide leadership.'
>
> 'Self-confidence, good presence, fluency, sheer ability.'
>
> 'A combination of intellectual resource, drive and good judgment of people and situations.'
>
> 'High speed input and output. Common sense. Sensitivity to political issues. A thick skin. Capacity to sway people in rational argument.'
>
> 'Stamina. A good physique and the ability to "compartmentalize", i.e. to concentrate on an issue and then switch one's attention completely to the next problem. Other qualities, intelligence, perseverance, are obviously necessary but are shared by others throughout the Service.'

[1] The questionnaire sent to a number of administrators in connection with this study contained the question 'Do you have a clear image of the characteristics needed to become a "high-flyer" in the administrative class? If so, what is it?'

> 'Ability to seize and concentrate on the essentials of problems, to get things done, determination and tenacity, intellectual honesty, willingness to initiate and to take responsibility, good negotiator, ability to keep one's emotions detached from one's work, a certain broad humanity.'
>
> 'Ambition, stamina, intelligence of the "converging" rather than the "diverging" order, concentration, patience.'
>
> 'A clear, trenchant yet flexible mind. The ability to deal calmly with crises and to cope firmly and diplomatically with e.g. Ministers. Hardworking, ambitious, scrupulous about ends but not too fussy about means. A good memory. An infinite capacity to be willingly bored. Not too much sense of humour. Considerable self-confidence and self-esteem.'

In the course of their working lives administrative Civil Servants whether or not they get to the top experience common demands and expectations which gradually mould the ways in which they behave and think of themselves. In the first place they are expected to be the servants of the party in power and the electorate that put them there. A sense of service bites deeply into the lives of administrators: they are expected to be loyal to their masters, to give advice to the best of their ability, to accept that it may be rejected and then to work loyally for any policy that may be accepted. The role of the Civil Servant is formally defined in terms which make him an anonymous neuter, one who lives to serve and who begins all of his public letters with 'The Minister instructs . . .'. Administrators, whilst obviously not swallowing the administrative fiction whole, nevertheless define their work role in self-effacing, accommodating terms. According to one respondent 'administrators are the oil which enables the machine to work without themselves being a component'. This theme of being there to serve and to assist others tends to appear in an administrators' attitude to postings and work allocation: he or she is prepared for others to make these decisions, to judge how best he can serve the machinery of government.

The service ethos of administrative life is part of the explanation for the long hours of work which many administrators are prepared to undertake. Top administrators in particular are subject to 'unrelenting and unremitting'[1] strain of work, for they live to serve and feed their Ministers, responding to demands for information and advice at whatever hour of day or evening it is called for.

The pressures of work experienced by administrators seem broadly to divide into two. First, those which fall on certain posts and func-

[1] Sir Laurence Helsby, *op. cit.*

tions that are close to the cut and thrust of politics. There are a few posts in any department which are particularly sensitive to ministerial pace, e.g. the Permanent Secretaryship and the Private Secretaryships. The latter in particular carry with them the expectations of twelve- and fourteen-hour working days. The more junior of the secretaryships are staffed by people in their late twenties: because of the relatively delayed age of marriage amongst administrators, the experience up to now has been that both male and female junior Private Secretaries have been unmarried. Principal Private Secretaryships are held by administrators in their middle and late thirties. Where the incumbents are married, and the majority of them are, the expectation and experience is that family and domestic life go by the board.

There are other posts where, because of the politically sensitive nature of their function, e.g. industrial relations, or something to do with regional distribution of industry and/or employment policy, a pretty constant stream of pressure issues can be expected. There are those pressures which fall somewhat less regularly and insistently on the majority of other posts in the class. Administrators in many posts are liable to sporadic exposures to the heat of the political process. In some posts, e.g. those connected with finance, this is fairly predictable because of the calendar of events. Thus between April and July those working on the Finance Bill can expect long working hours, working weekends and attendance at late night sittings of the House; the same kind of pressure will fall on those working with local government finance between August and December. In other posts the pressure blows up unpredictably as the result of events, e.g. the Court Leys Approved School case.

There are a minority of posts in the class where work can be conducted at a leisurely pace, but on the whole the experience of administrators seems to be that they are faced with a stream of deadlines—papers to be digested, memoranda to be written, parliamentary questions to be answered. Most administrators are in the position of having their work load and flow directed by demands and initiatives generated by events outside the administrative machine, and some are in posts geared to fast moving events. During the 1960s the work loads of all administrators have been affected by the fact that the amount of work undertaken by the class has definitely increased whereas the number of administrators has not.

It remains to be said that individual administrators differ in their subjective response to the work loads that they carry. In considering the ingredients of success many administrators commented that intense love of work and readiness to sacrifice other aspects of one's life were necessary to sustain the pace in posts which lay on the route to the top of the class. Naturally enough, those in such posts differed in the extent to which they saw their work demanding 'sacrifices' of them. Similarly there were different responses on the level of effort demanded by the everyday aspects of administrative work. Most administrators described times when seasonal or unexpected pressure necessitated evening and weekend work so that they might for a few weeks at a stretch be working a sixty- or seventy-hour week. But the periods and sense of pressure seemed to last longer with some administrators than others. Some saw themselves able to cope comfortably by working a forty-hour week at the office plus, perhaps, five hours a week in addition to this. Others conveyed a much greater sense of working against time and of regularly needing to add ten to fifteen hours to their basic working week.

Administrators are expected to be loyal and dedicated servants, but not weak sycophants. The emphasis is that they should serve Ministers with fearlessness, honesty and integrity. In ideal terms the administrator is supposed to combine the characteristics of a trusted loyal servant with those of an independent discerning trusted adviser—the old retainer who dares to tell the young master he is being a fool but who serves him with dogged devotion. The security of an administrator's job is supposed to enable him to speak his mind without fear of jeopardizing his livelihood and he is given the freedom to decide whether what he is asked to do can be squared with his own conscience. Administrators formally have the option of resignation and, beyond this, it seems, as a recent anecdote related about a prominent Civil Servant illustrates, that they have other strategies for demonstrating the independence of mind that they retain in a serving capacity.

> 'Each day between the invasion of Suez and the resignation of Anthony Eden the Treasury's head of overseas finance wore a black tie to work. The tie symbolized the disgust he felt for the Suez fiasco, and not least for the role he had personally been assigned in it. . . . [He] thought hard about resigning but in the end he settled for the black tie.'[1]

Honesty and integrity are important themes in the administrative world: administrators, in common with all Civil Servants, are supposed to act with complete probity and uprightness in their dealings with the public. They are also expected to act with honesty towards their political heads. Ministers have to be able to trust the advice and

[1] Eric Jacobs, 'Cleaning the Corridors of Power', *The Sunday Times*, September 15, 1968.

information that they are given. They want the assurance that they are not committing themselves to a course of action some of the facts affecting which have been conveniently overlooked. One of the greatest sins that a Civil Servant can commit is in any way misleading a Minister with the result that the Minister is made to look a fool before other colleagues, the House of Commons and the public.

Most administrators if describing themselves would add a third category to that of Ministerial servant and trusted adviser—that of 'realist'. The theme of realism runs strongly through all accounts which administrators give of their work. They see the making of recommendations and decisions as their *raison d'être*. They are not there merely to find out, to analyse, to warn, but also to work through to solutions which, whilst not ideal from every point of view, satisfy the most important considerations. As one administrator put it, administrators need 'to dissect problems realistically and to make a constructive contribution to their solution which falls in line with reality (a political situation) and actually works'. A strong sense of realism is regarded as vital equipment for the administrator giving him the flexibility necessary to operate in a world of compromises, adjustments and half measures and the resilience to survive the kind of occupational hazards that are seen as the lot of the administrator. These are best described in the words of administrators themselves:

> 'In this work one has to undo what one did yesterday and like it.'
>
> 'It isn't the problems which are intellectually insoluble which are so difficult as those where it is difficult to know what to do next, the next step doesn't seem obvious. One can eventually get down to say, "Well there are no right solutions here but I think this is the best we can do", but very often there is something wrong or something that needs doing but it is not obvious to one what is the best way to tackle it.'
>
> 'It implies a good deal of compromise and adaptations and that you don't have to do if you are doing academic work. We have to take into account political considerations which you wouldn't have to do. But I don't really mind that. It is part of the great game that you play and it's fun. I am not a purist in that sort of way. I am realistic about what has to be done. I don't have any tremendous illusions or ideals. I know the context and I know the limitations, I hope. If you don't you are desperately frustrated. There are times when you really do begin to believe in something, then you can't perhaps achieve it and then you do feel very frustrated. They don't like Civil Servants, I don't think, to get too deeply believing in things. The kind of Civil Servant who does get dedicated . . .

won't reflect the changes of policy at the top. You want him to know a lot about the subject but you don't want him to be too deeply involved in it emotionally. He must be flexible, he must be able to accept someone else's point of view and apply it. I am talking generally now, not about my own particular job, you go to your Minister or your senior officer and you argue your place and at the end of the day you lose and he says I'm sorry I don't agree and that's got to be done, and you have to go back and you have got to do that and apply it to the very best of your will and ability. If you are terribly emotionally involved you would find this very difficult. So you learn at a very early age to get that out of your system.'[1]

In conclusion, how does the administrative class appear as a world for women to work and succeed in?

The public service bureaucracy within which administrators work has features which operate against the most blatant forms of sex discrimination. The Civil Service is committed to impartiality and equity, to acting towards persons in accordance with standardized rules and procedures. The rule is that men and women are to be judged solely in terms of their demonstrated merit: the Civil Service cannot afford to have its general reputation doubted by being less than scrupulous in any one aspect of its behaviour. In fact the essence of the role of a Civil Servant in our society is that he or she is bound to put into effect general policies and decisions with which he may not necessarily agree. Civil Servants are used to distinguishing between their personal feelings and judgments and their obligations as officials; and their habit of making such distinctions probably has its uses, in contributing to the fair consideration of women. Civil Servants certainly see the system in which they work as highly meritocratic: such a system proscribes certain forms of competition and this probably helps the working relationship of men and women. People cannot be seen to 'fix' things for favourites, and members of either sex cannot use traditional techniques such as 'sitting on the boss's knee' and 'drinking with the boys' to get ahead unfairly. The process by which demonstrated merit is determined in the Civil Service does not preclude the possibility that errors of judgment take place. But the Civil Service is not marked by the grosser forms of partonage which often appear in other work environments and are there held to effect the relative progress of the sexes.

Another feature of the public bureaucratic context as opposed to

[1] These quotations are taken from interviews conducted by Drs Rhona and Robert Rapoport in the course of the PEP project on *Women in Top Jobs*.

other work environments is the security of tenure accorded to office holders. The Civil Service has ways of getting rid of highly unsatisfactory employees. But it does not have the opportunity, as do many business firms, to decide that women can be treated as lightweight employees, to be jettisoned in a time of retrenchment or when they start to raise families.

The administrative class itself has both positive and negative features from the point of view of women wishing to succeed in it. On the positive side there are within the administrative class conventions about relationships between colleagues and the manner in which business is conducted which help to temper the climate of the work world to the traditional but still strongly held notions of feminine behaviour. The emphasis in the Civil Service is on quiet, restrained, polite behaviour, on behaviour which preserves appearances and does not force breaches in relations; 'we are', said one administrator, 'very kid-glovish'. In part such conventions probably stem from the gentlemen's world to which Civil Servants once belonged. In part they stem from the roles which Civil Servants are ascribed and ascribe to themselves—conciliators, compromisers, servants.

The administrator's role might seem a highly suitable one for women. Baroness Sharp once wondered aloud whether women were not more suited than men to playing the 'super secretary' role that fell to administrators. Perhaps it is more realistic, however, to take the view that the administrative role demands a combination of culturally defined 'masculine' and 'feminine' qualities and that such a combination is as likely to be found amongst women as it is amongst men.

There are several features of work and careers within the class which could be construed as working against women's chance of success. Much of the work of administrators brings them into contact with spheres outside the Civil Service. For women this presents special problems for they cannot work solely within a world where formal recognition of the equality of the sexes has been granted. It may be that their effectiveness as administrators is affected by the resistance to women in positions of authority that is said to exist in sectors of industry. It is also possible that dealing with women administrators may make anti-feminists in industry change their ideas. The postings policy in the class is by no means wholly disadvantageous to women: for instance it works against the possibility of their being persistently blocked by one superior with a low opinion of women at work whatever their capabilities. Job mobility within the administrative class also has the big advantage from a married woman's point of view of not being tied to geographical mobility.

The administrative Civil Servant does not, like many industrial managers, have to move around the country in order to move up the promotion ladder.

It is possible that one of the central features of careers in the class poses particular problems for women. The administrative class is a highly unitary structure. In each department there is one top post with a handful of supporting posts, and it would seem that there is one predominant route to these top posts. This lies through a series of demanding 'front room' jobs concerned with the issues closest to the Ministry's political heart. There does not appear to be within the class a number of differentiated hierarchies which provide different routes by which administrators can travel to the top. It is possible that such a career structure may well operate to inhibit women's attainments: women administrators have to travel the route historically dominated by men, they cannot carve specialized routes for themselves.

Chapter III

THE CAREER SUCCESS OF MEN AND WOMEN

'The Government is very much ahead of industry in recognizing the equality of women; the pay is the same—and several women in the Civil Service have been Heads of Department.

Somehow their sex is quite irrelevant and men don't mind taking orders from them. The fact that they are women never intrudes though I certainly don't mean that it is necessary for a woman to become in any way masculine in a position of authority.'

Sir Paul Chambers,
The Times, July 16, 1968.

'The Civil Service is a particularly enlightened employer of women, making no ostensible discrimination against them in pay and prospects . . . even so all the signs are that they compete on less than equal terms with men.'

Fulton Committee,
Survey of the Civil Service, Summary and Conclusions.

How well do women do in the Administrative class? How does their work experience and success compare with that of men? This chapter seeks to provide answers to these questions. It compares the performance of men and women at two stages, that of entering the class and that of working within it. In conclusion it suggests reasons for the apparent differences between the career success of men and women administrators.

1. *The entry of men and women to the class*

The routes by which the present population of male and female administrators have entered the class are those described in Chapter II.[1] The oldest serving members of the class entered in the late 1920s and early 1930s. It is impossible, however, to count the total number of men and women entrants by all of these routes since this period.[2]

[1] See Chapter II, p. 242.

[2] One difficulty is that the staff record tabulations recording transfers and promotions by sex for the years before 1964 have been destroyed.

Even without these figures two points are clear. First, the major route by which men and women enter the class is the open competition held for 21- to 27-year-olds. Second, the number of women coming in by all of these routes has always, with the exception of the war years, been much smaller than the number of men. For instance in 1966, 45 men and 3 women were promoted from the executive class, 19 men and 4 women were transferred from other classes and a total of 161 men and 23 women were successful[1] in examinations conducted by the Civil Service Commission.

From figures published in the Annual Reports of the Civil Service Commission it is possible to analyse the relative performance of men and women in these competitions from 1948 to the present day. Between 1948 and 1967 a total of 1,316 men and 190 women succeeded in the Method I and Method II entry competitions. Hence in this period for every woman entrant from these competitions there have been 6 male entrants. Table 2 gives a more detailed breakdown of the figures between the Method I and the Method II competitions and different periods of time.

TABLE 2 *Number of successful candidates in Method I and Method II Competitions 1948–67*

	Method I		Method II	
	Male	Female	Male	Female
1948–51	160	22	78	10
1952–55	121	16	98	9
1956–59	85	13	98	9
1960–63	85	15	196	15
1964–67	80	13	315	68
1948–67	531	79	785	111

Source: Annual Reports of Civil Service Commission 1948–67.

The small number of women entrants compared with men is basically the result of two processes: application and selection. Smaller numbers of women than of men apply to enter the competitions. Between 1948 and 1967 women formed about one fifth of the candidates in both the Method I and the Method II competitions. In addition women candidates have, for every year between 1948 and 1967, been less successful than men candidates in both competitions.

One cannot give definite answers to the questions as to why fewer women than men apply and fewer women than men succeed. In the

[1] Those successful in the examinations do not always enter the class.

case of applications the size of the female undergraduate population has an effect: women have for most of the post-war years formed about 25 per cent of the undergraduate population. Possibly also the number of women coming into the class has been affected by the fact that the administrative class has drawn the majority of its applicants and its entrants from Oxford and Cambridge: these universities have a smaller proportion of women students than do other British universities. In recent years the Oxbridge predominance in applications and successes has diminished.[1] This has coincided with a more rapid rise in the number of women applicants compared with men.[2]

It is not easy from published information to determine the different propensity of male and female students at the various universities to furnish applicants for the administrative class. It is clear however, that whatever university they attend female students are much less likely than male students to apply for the administrative class.

The evidence for this conclusion is drawn from a comparison of a series of published and unpublished statistics obtained from the University Grants Committee and unpublished information supplied by the Civil Service Commission. The University Grants Committee material distinguishes men and women graduating with first and second class honours degrees in the Arts and Social Sciences in each year from 1961 to 1967 inclusive. Effectively this is the population from which men and women are drawn into the administrative class. The Civil Service Commission information shows the total number of male and female applicants[3] from 1961 onwards regardless of whether the individual applied for one or both methods of entry.

Table 3 compares the proportion of suitably qualified male and female undergraduates who have applied for the administrative class competitions from the years from 1961 to 1966 inclusive. The figures in the table show that in the years under consideration a smaller proportion of suitably qualified women than of men have con-

[1] 'In 1966, for the first time, there were more applications from Redbrick than from Oxbridge. This year the figures went up again and, although the non-Oxbridge applicants are still not so successful, they had half as many acceptances this year, compared with a quarter four years ago. Only in the Diplomatic Service is the Oxbridge candidate still undoubtedly dominant', Patricia Rowan, *The Times*, November 2, 1967.

[2] Between 1964 and 1967 the number of males applying to the Civil Service Commission for the Method I and/or Method II examinations rose by 50 per cent, and the number of females by 150 per cent.

[3] Where a person made two applications, for Method I and Method II, as most do, they were only counted as one applicant.

sidered a career in the administrative class seriously enough to go to the stage of applying to enter the competitions.

The reasons for women's lower rate of application to the class can only be surmised for we know nothing in detail about female student's attitudes to employment in the administrative class as opposed to other occupations. One would assume that the Civil Service's reputation as a fair employer of women and the service orientation of

TABLE 3

Academic year	No. of graduates with first and second class honours degrees in Arts and Social Science subjects	Year of application to CSC	No. of applicants	No. of applicants as percentage of no. of graduates
MALES				
1960–61	4,858	1961	587	12
1961–62	4,699	1962	582	12
1962–63	4,749	1963	546	12
1963–64	5,049	1964	530	11
1964–65	5,539	1965	574	10
1965–66	6,421	1966	645	10
FEMALES				
1960–61	2,254	1961	91	4.0
1961–62	2,347	1962	90	4.0
1962–63	2,643	1963	107	4·0
1963–64	3,152	1964	104	3·0
1964–65	3,701	1965	166	5·0
1966–66	4,230	1966	179	4·0

Sources: Civil Service Commission, information supplied to author; University Grants Committee, *First Employment of University Graduates*, HMSO, and information supplied to author.

much of the work would make it highly attractive to women, compared with industrial employment. On the other hand perhaps many women opt for teaching because contemplating the administrative class involves setting their sights high. It requires their participation in entrance competitions that are regarded as stiff and challenging. And it involves them desiring for themselves a work life based on the metropolis and the corridors of power.

During the 1920s and 1930s the numbers of women applying for the class were regarded as disappointing compared with the numbers of women eligible to apply.[1] The unequal pay and marriage bar provisions operating in the Civil Service were assumed to affect the rate of application amongst women. But the fact that these operated in many other occupations that women entered led observers to conclude that women preferred the role of teacher to that of administrator. In the post-war years these discriminatory provisions have been dropped but this does not seem to have had the effect of making the administrative class as attractive an occupation to women as it is to men. In the last two or three years it is noticeable that women are forming a higher proportion of the applicants to the class. Between 1948 and 1963 women formed 18 per cent of the applicants, between 1964 and 1967 they formed 21 per cent, and in 1968 32 per cent of the applicants. This might be indicative of a shift in the horizons and preferences of female undergraduates but it seems likely that it is also, if not solely, a result of the fact that in the last few years the number of women graduating with first and second class honours degrees in Arts and Social Sciences has risen more rapidly than the number of men obtaining such degrees.[2]

The point was made earlier that the proportions of men and women entering the class are affected by the poorer performance of women in the Method I and Method II examinations. Between 1948 and 1961 women formed 22 per cent of the candidates[3] in the Method I examination but provided only 15 per cent of the successes: in the Method II examinations over the same period they were 19 per cent of the candidates and 14 per cent of the successes. Table 4 provides a more detailed break down of the picture between 1948 and 1967.

It is easier to show that women do worse than men in both competitions than it is to explain why. There are two possible lines of explanation. Compared with men, women may as a group possess less of the attributes which appear to be associated with success in the competitions. They may, alternatively or in addition, perform less well in the selection process. The kind of long-term research necessary to scrutinize the relative performance of the sexes has not been undertaken.[4] Were such research to be done it might throw light

[1] See Chapter I, p. 231.

[2] Between the academic years 1962–63, 1963–64, 1964–65, and 1965–66, the number of such male graduates rose by one fifth and the female graduates by one third.

[3] Not all applicants for the Method I and Method II examinations reach the stage of being interviewed or examined as candidates.

[4] It seems that very little is known about the operation of CSSB procedures. 'From papers presented in vol. IV (of the *Fulton Committee Report*) we know something about the way in which the CSC says selection procedures are operated, but we badly need a socio-psychological study of those procedures and of how

on the reasons for the marked improvement of women's performance in the Method II competitions since 1964 and the fact that as Table 5 shows in these competitions between 1948 and 1968 the comparative failure of women was overall slightly more marked in the written qualifying examination stage of the process than it was in the face to face interview.[1]

The other entry routes to the class can also be broken down into the two stages of application and selection. In all of them the smaller number of women passing through is a result of there being fewer women in the eligible populations both inside and outside the Service. One does not know whether in addition the women eligible

TABLE 4 *Female candidates and successes as proportion of total candidates and successes in Method I and Method II examinations 1948 to 1967.*

	Percentage of candidates		Percentage of successes	
	Method I	Method II	Method I	Method II
1948–51	24	25	12	11
1952–55	20	19	12	8
1956–59	24	16	13	8
1960–63	17	14	15	7
1964–67	22	22	14	18
1948–67	22	19	15	14

Source: Annual Reports of Civil Service Commission 1948–67.

to apply to enter the Limited and Late-Entry Competitions are less likely to apply than men in equivalent positions. In the case of transfers and promotion the distinction between application and selection is rather blurred. It does seem, however, that in the Executive Class at least women in the eligible grades are less likely to be promoted than are their male colleagues. In the case of Limited and Late-Entry Competitions an analysis of Civil Service Commission statis-

the selectors are selected, their attitudes, predispositions etc. We may be forgiven our scepticism in the face of the CSSB Chairman's bland assurance "that there is little doubt that the procedure has been acceptable and has worked well": we have no means of judging', Maurice Wright, *Administrative Research,* paper presented to the Civil Service Department: Public Administration Committee Conference, York, April 1969. The *Report of the Committee of Inquiry into the Method II System of Selection* (Davis Report), HMSO, 1969, Cmnd. 4156, has recently gone some of the way to answering these points.

[1] See Chapter II, p. 244.

TABLE 5 *Men and women candidates in Method II competitions: their success at different stages*

	Stage I: Taking Written or gaining exemption from it		*Stage 2*: Called to Civil Service Selection Board		Candidates at Stage 2 as a percentage of those at Stage I		*Stage 3*: Final Selection Board: Numbers successful		Number successful at Stage 3 as percentage of those at Stage 2	
	Men	*Women*	*Men*	*Women*	*Men*	*Women*	*Men*	*Women*	*Men*	*Women*
1948–68	6,821	1,712	3,290	691	48	40	859	137	26	20

Source: Civil Service Commission, information supplied to author.

tics indicates that in contrast to the Method I and Method II competitions women fare at least as well as men. The evidence for this conclusion is shown in Table 6. There is unfortunately no information which suggests explanations for the differences in the relative performance of the sexes in the various competitions

TABLE 6 *Percentage of male and female candidates declared successful*

1. *Limited competitions* (1956–67)

	Male	Female
Method I	7·7	14·2
Method II	3·0	4·1

2. *Open competitions for principal posts*

	Male	Female
Aged 30–35 (1964–67)	18·2	25·0
Aged 31–52 (1965–67)	7·5	7·0

Source: Annual Reports of Civil Service Commission 1956–67

In brief it appears that the small number of women in the class (221 out of 2,597 administrators on July 1 1969) is partly a function of their lower application rate and partly of their lower success rate. In the last few years an upswing has occurred in the number of women applying to enter, and entering, the class such that in 1968 women formed 25 per cent of the entrants to the class. Once in the class men and women appear to experience different rates of wastage[1] and different rates of promotion. These latter differences are explored in the following section.

2. *The career success of men and women in the class*

The data in this section on promotion experience are drawn from three recent investigations. Two of these, the Social Survey of the

[1] From figures derived from a follow-up study of entrants to the administrative class from Method I and Method II competitions between 1948 and 1956, it appears that of the men and women who took up appointments in these years, the following percentages had left by 1957.

	Method I	Method II
Men	16	12
Women	54	43

Source: *Recruitment to the Administrative Class of the Home Civil Service and the Senior Branch of the Foreign Service*, 1957.

Civil Service and the Civil Service Commission Follow Up of Administrative Class Entrants, were undertaken for the Fulton Committee on the Civil Service.[1] The third investigation was undertaken for the immediate purposes of the present study.[2]

The Survey of Civil Servants was conducted in 1966. Its published findings contain systematic and intensive comparisons between male and female administrators.[3] One such comparison is their distribution between different categories of government department. As Table 7 shows the proportions of men and women administrators in 'economic' and 'other' ministries are similar but in the 'technical' and 'social' ministries the sexes part company with the men concentrating in the former and the women in the latter.

TABLE 7

Type of department	Upper grades 1967		Lower grades 1967		All 1967
	Men (%)	Women (%)	Men (%)	Women (%)	(%)
Economic	27	28	30	32	27
Technical	30	18	26	11	24
Social	21	30	23	35	22
Other	22	24	21	22	27
Total	100	100	100	100	100
(N)	(211)	(50)	(196)	(114)	(571)

Source: Fulton Committee, Social Survey of the Civil Service, Chapter III.

When considering individual ministries the numbers shift from year to year. In 1965 the largest concentrations of women were found in the Ministries of Education (17 women out of 100 administrators), Health (16 out of 91), Housing (10 out of 90), the Post Office (12 out of 94), the Ministry of Agriculture, Fisheries and Food (13 out of 113), the Board of Trade (26 out of 178) and the Treasury (20 out of 148).[4]

In addition the Survey presents information on the relative career success of men and women. Table 8, overleaf, is reproduced from the Report of the Survey as is the following comment.[5]

[1] *The Social Survey of the Civil Service,* Evidence to the Fulton Committee, Surveys and Investigations, vol. 3(1). *Administrative Class Follow-up 1966,* Evidence submitted to Fulton Committee on the Civil Service, Vol. 3(2), pp. 106–53.

[2] See Appendix I.

[3] Certain of these comparisons are reported in Appendix 3.

[4] Figures supplied by Treasury.

[5] Fulton Committee, *op. cit.*, Chapter III.

TABLE 8 *Administrative Class: grade distribution according to year of permanent establishment to the Civil Service and to sex*

Present grade	Established before 1940			Appointed 1940–45			Established after 1945		
	Men (%)	Women (%)	All (%)	Men (%)	Women (%)	All (%)	Men (%)	Women (%)	All (%)
Upper grades, Assistant Secretaries and above	70	37	61	73	51	59	38	11	31
Lower grades	30	63	39	27	49	41	62	89	69
Total	100	100	100	100	100	100	100	100	100
(N)	(150)	(49)	(199)	(26)	(49)	(75)	(231)	(66)	(297)

Source: Fulton Committee, Social Survey of the Civil Service, Chapter III.

'The above table shows that, of *surviving* members first established to the Civil Service before the war, a far higher proportion of men than women (70 per cent as against 37 per cent) are now in the Upper grades. Similar differentials in "career success" between the sexes occur for both wartime and postwar recruits. In this case, however, the differences are not statistically significant.'

The analysis of the careers of administrators entering between 1948 and 1963 and still serving in September 1966 made by the Civil Service Commission for the Fulton Committee does not contain a comparison of men and women.[1] For the benefit of this study, however, the research staff of the Commission reworked the raw data to make such a comparison. The text of their analysis is presented in Appendix 4–A and B. The following brief account comments on certain features of the enquiry and the results.

The enquiry sought information on a number of aspects of the work performance of the 1064 entrants by all routes of entry from 1948 to 1963 who were still serving in the class. The aspects were present rank, and a series of assessments made by a superior officer on the individual concerned. These assessments comprised a ranking of the present performance of the individual according to whether it was above average, average or below average, an indication of the highest rank which the individual was thought 'capable of filling successfully' and a more detailed grading of the individual's performance in terms of seven characteristics.[2]

In Table 9 a comparison is made of three of the ratings accorded to 554 men and 42 women competition (i.e. Method I, Method II and Limited Competition) entrants still in the Service in 1966.

On each of the three measures the distribution of men and women differs in a similar fashion. A higher proportion of the men are placed in the top categories: 28 per cent of the men are now Assistant Secretaries compared with 12 per cent of the women, 42 per cent of the men are rated as above average compared with 38 per cent of the women, 56 per cent of the men as opposed to 33 per cent of the women are rated as capable of successfully filling posts of Under Secretary level and above.

The third and final comparison between men and women administrators involves several comparisons made in June 1968[3] between aspects of the careers of the 23 women administrators who were established as Assistant Principals in 1947, 1948, 1949, 1953 and 1954

[1] This is very much in line with Service policy of assuming that nothing remains to be said about the differences between men's and women's careers.

[2] See p. 280 following.

[3] See Appendix 2.

and 23 male administrators who were established as Assistant Principals in the same year. First information was obtained about whether the individuals were Assistant Secretaries and if so the number of years they had served before achieving this grade, and their age when they became Assistant Secretaries. The differences between men and women are shown in Table 10.

Finally it was ascertained whether the men and women had, either as Principal or Assistant Secretary, served as Principal Private Secretary to a Minister. Six of the 23 male administrators had held this post and none of the women.

TABLE 9 *Competition entrants, 1948–63* (No adjustment made for length of time in the Service)

	Males		Females	
	Number	Percentage of total	Number	Percentage of total
Rank reached				
Assistant Secretary	157	28·3	5	11·9
Principal	330	59·6	30	71·4
Assistant Principal	67	12·1	7	16·7
Total	554	100·0	42	100·0
Present performance				
Above average	234	42·2	16	38·1
Average	262	47·3	22	52.4
Below average	58	10·5	4	9·5
Total	554	100·0	42	100·0
Future potential				
Under-Secretary or above	312	56·3	14	33·3
Assistant Secretary	218	39·4	25	59·5
Principal	24	4·3	3	7·1
Total	554	100·0	42	100·0

Source: Civil Service Commission, information supplied to author.

The preceding information on the career success of men and women administrators refers to pre-1939, 1940–45 and post-1945 entrants to the class. The information on the entrants in the two earlier periods of time is drawn from the Survey of Civil Servants which was based on a sample of Civil Servants, administrators included. The authors of the Survey are certain that the differences in career success recorded in the case of the pre-1939 and war-time men and women entrants to the class are features of the total population of such entrants and not just of the sample. In the case of the post-1945 entrants, however, the authors of the Survey are not completely certain that the differences they record between men and women actually exist in the total post-1945 population of entrants.

The Sample Survey is not the only source of information on the career success of post-1945 entrants. The two other investigations cited both refer to post-1945 entrants. The information presented above is limited to their evidence on entrants from competitions only.

TABLE 10

A. Comparisons of timing in careers of men and women administrators

	Not yet Assistant Secretary	Number of years as Principal before made Assistant Secretary			
In service 14 years					
Women	6	4	0	0	2
Men	8	1	0	0	7
In service 15 years					
Women	4	1	0	1	2
Men	3	1	0	0	2
In service 19 years					
Women	4	1	0	2	1
Men	6	0	1	4	1
In service 20 years					
Women	6	1	4	0	1
Men	4	0	1	3	0
In service 21 years					
Women	3	2	1	0	0
Men	2	0	1	1	0
Total Women	23	9	5	3	6
Men	23	2	3	8	10

B. Age at which made Assistant Secretary

	Total	Under 36 years	36–39 years	40–45 years
Women	14	0	7	7
Men	21	3	11	7

Source: Women in Top Jobs Investigation, 1968.

In the case of the third investigation reported, the findings of differences between men and women competition entrants can only be taken as suggestive and not as conclusive. This is because whilst the information relates to a total population of women entrants, the men were chosen in such a way that leaves one unable to calculate the extent to which they are likely to be representative of the total population of male competition entrants. The second investigation, however, presents information relating to all male and female administrators who entered by competitions in the period between 1948 and 1963. One is not dealing with a sample and the information can be treated as a reliable guide to the experience of a population—male and female administrators who entered via competitions between 1948 and 1963. But one would not be justified in generalizing from these results to a larger population, e.g. all male and women entrants by all routes during all periods of time.

With these comments on the validity of the evidence in mind one can use the information to draw a picture of the career experience of the men and women. It seems that the women reported on have not progressed through the administrative world with the same success and mastery as men. The differences between men and women seem most pronounced in the case of pre-1939 entrants. Two thirds

TABLE 11 *Comparisons of number of men and women administrators*

Staff group and grade July 1, 1969	Men	Women	Total
Administrative			
Permanent Secretary	29	0	29
Deputy Secretary	74	2	76
Under Secretary	274	9	283
Assistant Secretary	773	52	825
Principal	968	93	1,061
Assistant Principal	258	65	323
	2,376	221	2,597

Source: Civil Service Manpower Statistics.

of the women entrants from this period covered by the Survey of Civil Servants were still serving as Principals whereas only one third of the men entrants were. Women entering subsequently have not done as badly as this; nevertheless they appear less likely than men to provide the 'flyers' of the class. The women who become Under Secretaries seem more likely to attain this post at the end of their career rather than as an early step to higher things. This is not to say that women have never broken through to the top of the Service. There have been 2 women Permanent Secretaries in recent years and there are at present, as Table 11 shows, 2 women Deputy Secretaries and 9 women Under Secretaries. Nevertheless the chances for a woman making the breakthrough to the top are much slimmer than those for a man.

3. *The reason why*

Why is it that women, even when present in the administrative class for their working lifetime, fail to get to the top as readily as their male colleagues? The explanations that one can consider are broadly of two kinds. The career experience of men and women administrators may well differ because the two groups differ in abilities and aspirations and/or they may differ because men and women are treated differently by the environment. It is very difficult to gather completely objective information on either of these issues.[1] The account that follows is of the perceptions which men and women administrators have of the treatment and the relative abilities of men and women in the class. The account is based on two sources, the questionnaire and interview responses of men and women administrators contacted in the course of the *Women and Top Jobs* enquiry and responses to the questions that the Civil Service Commission asked of administrators in their Follow-up Survey.[2]

Traditionally the world of the administrative class is a male world; today women are still very much a minority and as a group heavily dependent in the course of their careers on the appraisal and judgments of men. Are the judgments made felt to contain an element of sex bias? Hardly any women respondents could recall any incident which they felt sprang from intense or unreasoned hostility to them as women. Such male attitudes were seen to have passed out of the Service as the old guard, occasionally incensed to the point of apoplexy at the thought of women in the class, retired from the Service. This is not to say, however, that women had not been aware of resistance to themselves operating as administrators. On the whole the focus of this resistance was seen to be in relationships with outsiders, e.g. business, trade unions, local authorities, foreign commercial, governmental or professional bodies. Many Principals found themselves representing their department in the routine but none the less important contacts with outsiders. Very often the man or woman on the Service side was appreciably younger than the 'top brass' who tended to represent the outside world: a woman therefore often combined the problem of showing her convincing currency through the disadvantages of youth and sex. Most women interviewed recalled incidents of mistaken identity, for example when leading a delegation in negotiations they had initially been mistaken for the personal secretary of one of the Civil Servants who was in fact subordinate to them. They noticed a tendency for queries and conversation to be

[1] The Survey of Civil Servants does in its analysis of the administrative class seek to establish which of a number of 'background' educational factors is most closely associated with career success. It is impossible to tell from the analysis, however, whether the lower career success of women is in any way associated with the distribution of these factors.

[2] See Appendices 2 and 4.

addressed to one of their male advisers rather than to themselves. In such situations women were conscious of the determination needed not to let the situations slip out of their control. Their most frequent technique in such situations was 'knowing their subject backwards', their experience having proved in the majority of cases that technical virtuosity helped them to command the respect initially withheld because of their sex. In considering the problems of their relationships with outsiders, most women found their frequent changes of posting a disadvantage: the accommodation that a woman won for herself with one set of clients could rarely be transferred and the problem would often have to be faced again with another industry or another country.

The attitudes of the outside world have their impact on behaviour inside the Service. The closest link appears to operate within the Ministry of Defence where arguments about the impropriety of women operating in a man's world appear both to have made women administrators in the Ministry a rare occurrence and to have encouraged male members of the Ministry to a somewhat patronizing attitude towards women administrators encountered in the course of their work. Some other ministries face the dilemma of whether, initially at least, they should affront the susceptibility of their clients by presenting them with a woman administrator. When asked about posts informally barred to women, Establishment Officers most often responded by naming posts where the client group was especially sensitive to the issue. The solution favoured by most departments seemed to be that of having both men and women in a branch so that some flexibility was possible over the question of who should see whom about what.

There may well be departmental traditions with respect to the treatment of women. It was pointed out earlier that women cluster in 'economic' and 'social' ministries. It is possible that this concentration and the relatively long association of women with these ministries means that women members of such departments stand better chances of promotion than do women administrators in say Customs and Excise or the Ministry of Works. Within the administrative class there is a folklore which distinguishes between ministries in this way but it would be very difficult to obtain the kind of data that would prove or disprove the assumptions of the folklore.

The question of posts where informal understandings operate so as to bar women is also a difficult one to pursue conclusively. Obviously there are posts in the administrative class that no woman has yet held: one needs a detailed knowledge of the organization to identify these posts. There do seem to be posts where there is more conscious deliberation about the qualifications of possible women incumbents than of possible men. Those with sensitive clients and/or those which involve heavy travelling duties come most readily to mind. The post of Principal Private Secretary to the Minister is one where both these considerations combine and where there has been a rather noticeable absence of women. The explanations given for the negligible number of women ever holding this post most frequently touched on the enforced intimacy of the Minister and his/her Principal Private Secretary, speech writing in hotel bedrooms, etc. and the need for politicians to be, like Caesar's wife, above suspicion. To a lesser extent these kinds of considerations were seen to affect the posting of women Assistant Principals to the Minister's office: it was felt that women more frequently ended up as Secretary to the Permanent Secretary. One cannot gauge how far the scruples which operate about placing women in Ministerial Secretaryships, especially the Principal one, take the edge off women's chances of success. People must reach the top who have not had this experience: nevertheless it is distinctly regarded as a grooming experience, the person who has proved himself as Principal Private Secretary being seen as admirably placed in terms of contacts and performance for high-flying.

Women still encounter doubts within the administrative milieu about their fitness for some postings. When it comes to the broader question of fitness for promotion the evidence discussed earlier shows that women's attainments fall short of men's within the administrative class. Perhaps the most salient evidence in this respect is the evaluations of the future capabilities of men and women collected by the Civil Service Commission. The predominantly male evaluators rate men as more likely than women to function successfully at the top of service: they saw 56 per cent of the men as capable of being Under Secretary, compared with 33 per cent of the women. It may be, as a member of the Civil Service Commission staff remarked, that these differences are accounted for by the expectations on the part of the evaluators that women will have on average a shorter working life than men, or alternatively, a career interrupted by periods of special leave whilst having babies. But the question asked was not about the posts that subjects were thought likely to attain during their careers, but about the posts they were thought *capable of filling successfully*. Granted one does not know how the respondents interpreted the question. Nevertheless one is probably justified in interpreting the responses as evidence that women are not considered as capable as men of operating at the level of Under Secretary and above. The point that such evidence raises is whether these evaluations are related to objectively identifiable differences in the work performance of men and women or whether they appear more related to a willingness on the part of men to recognize capacity for administration more readily in their own sex.

Such issues can hardly be settled conclusively. Amongst the responses of male administrators in questionnaires and interviews there was an identifiable, though minority, train of thought which saw the qualities for high office as sex-linked. The comments which revealed such thinking tended to cluster around two disadvantages supposedly linked with the female mind. First its inability to 'think big':

> 'Women are much more predisposed than men to get excited about detail—they have less capacity than men to operate on a broader plain.'
>
> 'There are few women in the class and so one has only limited evidence to go on of their abilities. But within the small sample I have known very few show any willingness to "think big". They are tidy and efficient administrators but I do not know any personally who could initiate really major policy changes.'
>
> 'Many even of the able women seem to lack a sense of proportion, a "feel" for what goes.'
>
> 'Few [women] in my experience have the top management ability to see the essentials à la Weinstock.'

Second, and closely linked, the inability of women to operate with the necessary detachment:

> 'Women do not have the requisite thick skins, they take contrary opinion as personal criticism.'
>
> 'Women get too emotionally involved in their work.'

Virtually no women were prepared to support such judgments of their sex. It is true that one or two in describing what they saw as a successful administrator distinguished between those who felt themselves to be successful 'voluble, self-important administrators treating every task as tremendously important and consequently over-administering everything and becoming blinkered by the system', and those who really were effective, 'able to weed out the very important things, not terribly accommodating, a bit lazy and not terribly popular with superiors though the really clever person can be both apart and not suspect'. The one or two women who perceived these categories felt that women were more likely to fall into the first, but they were almost alone in this opinion. Most women perceived women to be more conscientious than men and were inclined to see the attention to detail which could follow from this as a virtue, as one woman put it 'there is a general Treasury fault perpetuated by men to sort out the general line and leave the details to be worked out. This very often stores up trouble.' Similarly what seemed to males as lack of detachment was interpreted by women as the ability to empathize, a quality which they felt could contribute to the successful outcome of decisions.

The women's responses showed them to be sensitive to the shared attitudes and behaviour of their sex which they attributed to their social minority position—women at work in a predominantly male world. Many emphasized the closer scrutiny which they felt their behaviour was subject to because of their sex: several related incidents where they became aware from others' reference to their sex that they were being measured as women administrators. Most women felt themselves to be the objects of such scrutiny and most of them saw it as having an effect on their behaviour: they felt they ran the risk of having their mistakes treated with less tolerance than would be accorded to men. Such expectations were frequently seen as the source of behaviour which gave rise to the belief that women were sticklers for facts or over-insistent on getting the detail right; a concern for consistency was seen as the natural outcome of the judgments that women felt themselves subject to.

The theme of the women's perceptions of differences between men and women administrators was that the differences were not those of fundamental approach or capacity but sprang from the kinds of adjustments that women made to their minority situation. Thus women were conscious that some of the traditional male techniques for softening up the work situation or difficult encounters within it—'talking it over', over a drink or a meal—could not easily and naturally be initiated by a woman. As compensation women saw themselves consciously using their charm to oil working relationships and to help them ride out tricky situations. One respondent captured the experience of many women administrators in the following words:

> 'I am bound to say that when I'm really up a gum tree at the office, I will go feminine. I have discussed this with other colleagues of mine as to whether it is unfair to use one's feminine instincts and so on, or feminine attitudes or manners to get the results that one wanted and I've always said that I did not think this was unfair because one has so many disadvantages anyway being a woman in the office and one had better make the most of the few advan-

tages one has got and the men are just as aware as you are that you are using that technique and there is nothing underhand.'[1]

The major difference that women perceived between sexes in the work situation was that of motivation. Women were more ready than men to look for the explanation of differential performance in terms of ambition. Quite a few described themselves as in the process of considering whether further promotion was 'worth it'. Others referred to women they knew who had turned down the chance of promotion to Assistant Secretary or above. It needs to be said that references were made to men who had done the same thing. Nevertheless the questionnaire responses of men and women on the degree of responsibility wanted seem to indicate a difference between men and women in this respect: a larger proportion of the men respondents than of the women recorded themselves as wanting considerably more responsibility in the course of their careers. From what the women respondents said it did not appear that having made a decision about their sticking level in the organization they then put in the minimum effort requisite to attain or maintain that level, rather the drive seemed to be to do as good a job as one was capable of but to make it known that one was not looking for further promotion.

Most respondents interpreted the apparently greater tendency of women to act in this way as a result of their taking different attitudes from those of men to the costs of moving beyond Assistant Secretary. As one woman put it,

> 'there are not the same pressures on a woman to get on and get up —she is much less likely to have dependents and since people still fall flat on their faces at the sight of a woman doing even moderately well, she doesn't need success to feed her *amour propre* as men do. Many single women of about 40-plus, on an Assistant Secretary's salary, are doing very nicely thanks and see no need to press on into ulcer territory. There aren't many Evelyn Sharpes.'

A few others stressed that the costs of moving into the top ranks fell more heavily on a woman than on a man because they involved the cultivation of 'masculine' qualities of forcefulness, determination and steeliness. Hence in one woman's words, women prefer to see themselves as 'non-dragons' and 'settle happily at Principal or Assistant Secretary level with no wish (and push) to go further'. In addition to this it must be said that many people professed to see no conflict between the capabilities and behaviour necessary to rise to the top of the class and the maintenance of an acceptable feminine identity: explanations of the 'not wanting to be a dragon' type tended

[1] Interview, *Women in Top Jobs* inquiry, 1968.

to be treated as rationalizations of decisions based on the kind of considerations quoted earlier.

Women were conscious of differences between men and women's attitudes and behaviour in the working situation. In addition many of them sensed that some element of disadvantage still clings to being a woman. Almost invariably no dogmatic statements were made about this: rather the question was seen to be one involving nuances and slim margins. Outstanding women, it was felt, had on the whole to wait a year or so longer than an outstanding man for promotion to Assistant Secretary; good, average women seemed to lose out by two or three years in the promotion stakes to good, average men. These impressions were furnished by many of the women respondents: they came most consistently from women clustered around this critical step. All of the women who raised this point were aware of the interpretations that could be given to their doing so: they nevertheless felt that a tendency to discount women against men was present in the process of evaluation.

This tendency in the field of promotion was linked by respondents to a perceived tendency, already described, for men to be preferred for certain postings. Elements of the belief that women cannot be as effective in certain posts as men seem to linger in the administrative class. As a result there appears to be the practice, more pronounced in some departments, of steering women away from tough or crucial assignments. This in its turn is seen to affect women's promotion chances. In one department in the early 1960s the women Assistant Secretaries and Principals (8 in all) wrote to the First Division Association Branch in their department to point out that they felt that the posting and promotion policies were operating against women. The First Division Association departmental representatives then took the matter up and were assured by the Director of Establishments that women were eligible for all administrative posts in the department save one. The writing of the letter is by no means evidence that women were being unduly discounted. It is, however, evidence that the women felt sufficiently sure of their case to make a collective formal statement about it.

It might well be that the considerations which affect the posting of women are highly significant in explaining both the general phenomenon of the lower career success of women compared with men and the specific phenomenon of the much smaller percentage of women recorded as being capable of being Under Secretaries and above in the Civil Service Commission's Follow-Up study.[1] Perhaps it is that women are, on the basis of their sex, ascribed to jobs which,

[1] See earlier, p. 275.

whilst involving work that is of a high grade, are nevertheless not seen as proving grounds for the managerial, aggressive qualities required for the very top posts. Hence, they tend to fall from view when the high-flying appointments are considered. It certainly seems that somewhere in the evaluation process operating within the class the rather intangible factor of sex ascription plays a part. Judgments still appear to be made in terms of 'the proper spheres' of men and women even when there is little convincing evidence that the capabilities of men on the whole and women on the whole differ markedly. This observation is borne out by the analysis the Civil Service Commission made of the evaluations of the work performance of the women and a sample of the men included in their follow-up study.[1] The categories into which individuals were placed are reproduced below.

1. *Short-term contacts*

   Very impressive in manner and address
   Usually makes a good impression
   Handles people quite well
   His manner tends to be unfortunate
   Poor at making initial contacts

2. *Relations with colleagues* (long-term)

   Wins and retains their highest regard
   Is generally liked and respected
   Gets on well with everyone
   Not very easy in his relationships
   A difficult colleague

3. *Paper work*

   Brilliant on paper
   Written work always clear and well set out
   Generally expresses himself clearly and concisely
   Written work just good enough to get by
   Paper work is a weakness

4. *Figurework*

   Exceptionally good at all kinds of figure work
   Handles and interprets figures well
   Competent at figure work
   Handling of figure work leaves something to be desired
   Not good with numerical data

[1] See Appendix 4B.

5. *Meetings*

    Extremely effective
    Puts his points across convincingly
    Expresses himself adequately
    Barely competent
    Ineffective

6. *Drive*

    Exceptional vitality, well directed to the job
    More effective than most in getting things done
    Usually gets a move on
    Rather inclined to take things easy
    Needs constant chasing

7. *Stability*

    Highly dependable; adapts well to new situations
    Takes most difficulties in his stride
    Reacts quite well to normal stress
    Occasionally flustered or put out
    Easily thrown off balance

When the analysis was made it was found that men's and women's evaluated performance could be judged to differ in only one respect—that of stability. Women were deemed more likely than men to be occasionally flustered and easily thrown off their balance. The analysis did not establish whether differences in showing on this factor of stability were highly significant in explaining judgments of future promise. The notion of stability seems to be a very powerful one in the class. If one considers the series of categories above, that of stability is most vague and general. It seems that when comparing men and women in specific aspects of their work the evaluators saw little difference between the sexes. But when faced with a category that called for an overall evaluation of style and approach to work then the evaluators bore witness to strong differences between the sexes. It would seem that women administrators have not escaped society's type-casting.

Chapter IV
THE IMPACT OF MARRIAGE ON WOMEN'S CAREERS

> 'One does not get the same efficiency with a person who has two sets of interests as from a person who can give undivided attention.'
>
> Dame Maude Lawrence,
> Director of Women's Establishments, Treasury,
> Evidence to Tomlin Commission on the
> Civil Service, 1929–31.

Since 1946 women administrators have had the option of combining an administrative career with marriage and childbearing. This chapter seeks to describe aspects of this combination and to determine the kind of impact that marriage and family life has on women's work experience and career success.

One result of marriage and childbearing is that women leave the Service. In 1947, 1948, 1949, 1953 and 1954 a total of 45 women entered through open competitions and became established. Of these, 15 later married and left the Service at the time of their marriage, or at the birth of their first child or some time in between; 1 of these has subsequently returned to work part-time. Three women married and left when they had had several children, 2 of these subsequently returned to work full-time. In addition 14 women married and have worked continuously up to 1968. Nine out of the 45 women remained single until 1968 and were still working in the Service. In addition 3 single and 1 divorced women left the Service for other occupations.

By 1968, of the original 45 women, just over a third (16) had left the service for marital and family reasons, another 4 having left for what can be called 'occupational' reasons, 16 were married and were working in the class alongside 9 single women from the original cohort.

In the case of this cohort of entrants the married women still working in the class outnumber the single women. This does not seem typical of the majority of women entrants as the figures in Table 12, from the Survey of Civil Servants, show. The comparisons made between men and women administrators in respect of marital status in the Survey indicate that despite a similar age distribution in the two populations the men are far more likely to be married than the women. For instance 81 per cent of the men in the lower administrative grades were married compared with 31 per cent of the women in the same grades.

The Survey of Civil Servants collected information on family size but it has not yet been published. As a result it is impossible to indicate how many married women in the Service have families.

Most of the information in this chapter is drawn from an enquiry which covered single women and married and single men administrators and married women who had left the Service. The numbers were not large enough to permit rigorous comparisons between these categories in terms of career success. Nevertheless the information gathered led to certain impressionistic conclusions about the relative

TABLE 12 *Comparison of women entrants by marital status*

Marital status	Women in administrative class Upper grades (%)	 Lower grades (%)
Single	58	64
Married	32	31
Widowed/Separated Divorced	10	5
Total	100	100

Source: Fulton Committee, Social Survey of the Civil Service, Chapter III.

success of married men and women and single women. It was established in the previous chapter that women's chances of success were less than those of men. It would seem that having children further depresses a woman's chances of moving into the top of the class. But it would not appear that the difference between married and single women is as striking as the difference in career success between male administrators, the majority of whom are married and female administrators, the majority of whom are not married.

The rest of this chapter describes some of the main features of the combination of administrative work and family life as it has been experienced by 14 married women administrators who were contacted in the enquiry undertaken for PEP in 1968.[1] Of the 14, 4 were in their late twenties, 2 being without children, the other 2 having 1 and 2 children each. The remaining 10 were all in their late thirties and forties, 3 of them had no children and the remaining 7 had families of from 1 to 6 children (including step-children and adopted

[1] See Appendix 2.

children). Despite their similarities in age these last 7 women were at very different stages of the family cycle: 2 had recently embarked on motherhood, 3 had the youngest of their families of 3 and 6 children still at pre-primary school age and 2 had their families of 2 and 3 children in adolescence and adulthood.

1. *Staying and leaving*

Most of the married women with children described their decision to combine work and motherhood as being in reality a series of ad hoc decisions made very much along the lines of 'just waiting and seeing how everything works out'. One respondent spoke for others when she wrote: 'I have always said and meant that if some reason for leaving arose connected with my children (physical or psychological problems) they would come first. I have never agonized over this, however, and it's all worked out satisfactorily so far.' One respondent had in fact left the Civil Service when she felt that her arrangements for caring for her young baby were inadequate. Subsequently she returned to the Service. Those prepared to pursue a course of combining motherhood and a full-time career obviously weighed costs and satisfactions of work, family and domestic life differently from the women who left their work. Generally the working women with children emphasized their boredom at the prospect of a domesticated life and stressed by way of contrast their sense of being involved at work in something important—of being close to a world of significant action and events. 'One has', said one women explaining her choice, 'soaked in the Civil Service tradition and one wants to be close to things of importance.' In fact it was this sense of being part of an organized pattern of activities, of being a cog in an acknowledged important machine that seemed a major source of the work satisfaction of these women and of their impetus to continue working. Some of the women mentioned that they imagined gaining the same satisfaction from voluntary public service as, say, a magistrate, school governor or leader of a voluntary organization. But invariably they added that their work had the advantage of being to hand and well paid.

There is no way in which one can compare the capabilities and aptitudes of the women who marry and leave with those of the women who stay. Undoubtedly the decision of some women not to combine work with raising a family drains talent from the class, but the way in which the Service regards this loss tends to change according to the general employment situation. In the mid-1950s, a time of contraction of administrative activities and stagnating promotion in contrast to the 1960s, loss of women administrators through marriage was looked upon as providing welcome slack. In the present situation of labour shortage, especially at the Principal level, the loss is felt more keenly. Either way women who do leave at marriage or at the birth of their first child provide the Service with relatively cheap labour—the 17 women covered by the PEP enquiry who left for family reasons showed an average of five years in the class and only 2 of these collected any superannuation rights in the form of a marriage gratuity.

There can be little doubt but that the basic factor determining a woman's decision whether or not to continue working after children is the attitude of man and wife as to what constitutes acceptable patterns of marital life and child rearing. Such is the pattern of work in the administrative class that a woman with children, who continues to work, must hand over the bulk of the care of her children to someone else. The complex of experiences and values which mould the views of husband and wife on this subject are rather inaccessible even to a study of this nature. What seems to stand out from the information collected is that there is no clear association between the decision made and the joint income level of the spouses and/or the occupation of the husband. Of the 14 women who left to bring up their children and for whom this kind of information is available, 4 married husbands with jobs commanding lower salaries than their own. Eight of the remaining 10 were in fact married to administrative Civil Servants. Thirteen of these leavers lived within easy commuting reach of administrative work, 12 in London and 1 in Edinburgh. If one compares these 14 with the 9 married women with children who had stayed at work until 1968 the contrasts are not striking: 2 of the women in work were married to husbands whose jobs had lower salary scales than their own and 4 of the remaining 7 were married to Civil Servants. Where there did seem some kind of difference between leavers and stayers was in two features of their families of origin. More of the stayers (5 out of 9) than the leavers (4 out of 14) came from a family where the father had a public service occupation, and more of the stayers (6 out of 9) than of the leavers (4 out of 14) had mothers with degrees or professional qualifications. It may be that certain family 'traditions' more than others generate a commitment to careers amongst daughters. But with this kind of study this must remain a surmise.

The strongest impression coming from this study is that the decision of a woman to remain in the administrative class whilst having children, and her decisions at various times to continue, is the result of the highly complex relationship between husband and wife. Even given broadly compatible circumstances between two couples in terms of social backgrounds, age at marriage, occupations of both spouses, assessed competence at work and expressed interest in it, the outcome in terms of the wife's continuation at work may well differ. For the women who continue working it seemed that their relationships prior to and including their marriage combine to make the pursuit of their careers answer an important felt need in their own life and sometimes in their husband's life. Several cases were suggestive of the kinds of situation and the protagonist's perceptions of them that led to a commitment to continue work. In one case a woman described explicitly her desire to gain status and importance for herself via her own efforts because she was not satisfied with her husband's efforts in that direction. In another there was an economic need presented by a relatively late marriage where the husband was in non-pensionable employment. In yet another instance the wife was strongly influenced by her husband's wishes stemming partly from his experience of a previous marriage.

All of the women who continued to work stressed that, given their initial inclination to remain at work, the encouragement and support of their husbands was crucial. Amongst the leavers there were one or two who had left because of strong opposition from their husbands to the idea of their not bringing up their children. In the case of the stayers the husbands' psychological support often seemed to play a crucial role in tiding them over periods of exhaustion when pressure on the work or the domestic scene made the women themselves question the benefits of the combination.

In discussing their own and their husband's attitudes to their continuation at work the married women with children stressed the role played by their own level of earnings in the final decision. In the administrative class they could expect at worst an income rising to just over £3,500 in their early forties (according to the Fulton Commission 46 per cent of administrators earn over £3,500 p.a.). The role played by the woman's salary level in her decision to continue work was that of an enabling factor. In fact a large part of the salary earned by married women administrators with children went, after tax, on domestic and child care help, housing room to accommodate the help and school fees. All three of these items contributed to raising the families' standard of consumption compared with what it would have been on the husband's salary alone. There were no widows or divorcees amongst the women administrators contacted: hence the married women that were being considered were not their own or their families' sole source of financial support. Few women with or without children said that financial benefits were the most important factor leading to their working. Obviously there is the possibility that it was considered undignified to admit to such motives being dominant. But one can consider the responses as further evidence for the conclusion, drawn by Margot Jeffreys in her analysis of the reasons why married women continue to work in the higher grades of the Civil Service,[1] that financial benefits are not the dominant consideration leading married women to continue working in the administrative class, and that this is particularly so in the case of married women with children. The importance of the level of salary which women earn in the administrative class is that it enables man and wife to work full-time and to secure substitute care of the kind they feel necessary to compensate for the wife's absence, *without* touching the husband's salary and the standard of living that they could maintain on that alone. Most couples spend up to £1,000 p.a. in current terms in employing initially, whilst their children are under five years of age, the combination of a nanny and some daily domestic help and subsequently that of a housekeeper/au-pair plus, in some cases, boarding schools. Most of the working mothers made the point that had they had to work full-time in their thirties for a lower income than they commanded in the administrative class then they might well have decided against working full-time. But they were also concerned to stress that until very recently the choice in the administrative class, unlike some other occupations, noticeably teaching, had been full-time work or nothing.

Where the married woman chooses the option of a full-time career the resulting pattern of family life seems to blend features of 'Victorian' and 'post-Victorian' family styles. In these families the 'traditional' professional middle-class pattern is present in the longer periods of separation of parents and children, the highly organized way in which activities are managed, and the use of substitute care. Of the 9 women administrators with children who were interviewed, all had domestic help, usually a non-resident person who cleaned for between eight and twelve hours per week; only in one case was the help provided by a resident au-pair. In addition 5 of the 6 who had some or all of their children under 5 years had a resident nannie who was generally away at weekends. In the sixth case the child was left with a neighbour. None of the families relied on any regular help from relatives. Women administrators with children appear extremely dependent on reliable continuous paid help for the care of their children. Breakdowns in the child-care arrangements seem the most frequent cause of the periods of pressure that respondents

[1] Margot Jeffreys, Research Note, 'Married Women in the Higher Grades of the Civil Service', *British Journal of Sociology*, vol. III, p. 361.

charted in the course of their careers. Several expressed the opinion that as children passed the age of five the problems of caring for them increased. By this age children outgrew the charge of often excellent nannies and had to be cared for out of school hours by housekeepers who were not always willing or able to adopt the role of 'house mother'.

In the administrative class there is a traditional pattern of arriving at the office between 9.30 and 10.00 a.m. and leaving between 6.00 and 6.30 p.m. When the journey to and from work is added to this (only 1 of the 9 women had a central London—S.W.5—address, of the others half lived on the edge of the conurbation and half in the fringe areas), it means that most women leave home about 8.30 to 9.00 a.m. and are not home until 7.00 p.m. By 7.00 p.m. babies and young children are likely to be in bed; in fact most women were accustomed to hardly seeing their young children during the week. By contrast weekends were times for children and were occasions for family togetherness invested with heightened significance because of the weekly separation. At weekends the role of the father was to be with the children whenever possible whereas the wife would devote somewhat more time to oiling the domestic machine. During the week the husbands of 8 of the women were away from home for the same hours as their wives. Such hours plus the presence of domestic help tended to mean that they rarely had routine tasks in the house, certainly not to the same extent as their wives.[1] Where these families appear to differ from the 'traditional' professional middle-class pattern is in the degree of equality and similarity between the role of man and wife and the nature and intensity of interaction with the children when it occurred.

What is striking about the women administrators who combine full-time careers with family life is that in so doing they apply to the total of their lives the skills and techniques appropriate to their work. In the running of their homes they are constantly making decisions about priorities, relying on substantial delegation and seeking to communicate clearly and precisely. One informant described the central place given in her system to a large household book into which every instruction or incoming message was written, in effect a central filing system. Equally, in running the combination of home and work most of the women demonstrate an aptitude for 'compartmentalizing' or 'keeping a lot of balls in the air without getting them muddled': the kind of comment that they frequently made was that they found themselves thinking about them on the way home, but that they rarely thought much about them whilst in the office.

[1] *Loc. cit.*

2. *Impact on their work*

When considering the opposite side of the coin, the impact of family life on the work performance of married women, most respondents felt that domestic and family responsibilities told more heavily on a married woman than on a married man of equal abilities. 'This is not to say', according to one of them, 'that a married woman doesn't earn her pay, but there is a difference between that and the edge required to get to the top.' This theme of 'edge', of the resources of ability, time, energy and will necessary to get to the top of the Civil Service was current in the kind of comments which administrators made on the ingredients of occupational success.[1] In administrative life there are seen to be times and situations when a competitive edge in terms of these resources will help make a person more than ordinarily successful. Having 'edge' is particularly important in the late twenties and early thirties when success as a Principal might well lead to somewhat accelerated promotion. 'Edge' is seen as giving the administrator the extra time and interest to seek to shine at a job that he or she is given. Furthermore it is seen to give him or her the stamina necessary to sustain the kinds of demands made in the particularly onerous jobs which tend to come the way of administrators who seem to be 'going places'.

In the case of women, marriage and family life are seen as making possession of 'edge' all the more unlikely. One woman respondent replying to the question whether women were less likely than men to get to the top of the class said that a smaller proportion of women than of men Principals were likely to get to the top because many of the women were 'odd (i.e. daft) enough to try to combine this job with a family etc. or at least with a husband'.

One way in which family life can take the edge out of a woman's performance is through the effect of pregnancy. The Civil Service allows women two months' maternity leave to be counted against their allowance of six months' sick leave with full pay in any period of twelve months. Beyond the two months a woman may with medical authority take more sick leave, or she may take further leave as annual leave or special leave without pay. Most women seem to prefer to have their leave after the birth of the child rather than before, though some find that a difficult pregnancy necessitates full sick leave or part-time working. Most eventually take more than two months. There is no reliable information on completed family size of married women administrators but assuming the majority have 2 or 3 children, then a woman may be away from work for a year of

[1] See earlier, pp. 251–2.

maternity leave and can well be working at less than full pace for longer than this. Considered against the span of a full working lifetime a year to eighteen months is not a long time. But in an occupation where a lot depends on performance in the late twenties and the thirties then experience of pregnancy and absence during maternity leave may lessen a woman's ability to make an impact. In addition to working themselves back after an absence some of the women found on their return that they had lost the job they had been in: often in the cases where the job was not kept open it was seen to be of a relatively more important, challenging nature than the job taken upon return. On the whole, however, it seemed that in recent years, which have been ones of shortage at the Principal level, women had found themselves able to return to the same posting and respondents did not cite instances in the 1960s, whereas they did in 1950s, of women on leave after childbirth being asked to return or resign.

Once women have children then their family and domestic responsibilities may well help to erode the energy input necessary for them to get well on top of their jobs. One woman Principal, married to another administrative Civil Servant, described the way in which having a child helped to take the 'bloom' off her performance:

> 'There's a lot of hard dull work if you're a Principal not made easier by the fact that secretarial assistance and the telephone service is not good in many Departments and the clerical staff of mixed ability. If you have the ability to arrange your own times to suit your convenience, and you're generally fairly fresh, you can take these difficulties about typing and so on in your stride and you can put in a bit of extra work here and there which will save you a lot of time and trouble in the future. I could do this before I had my baby and my husband can, though he does not need to so much, now. But if you're more rigidly tied to a home timetable and have a lot to do at weekends, it becomes more difficult either to deal with office work absolutely fresh and forcefully or to put in a really useful bit of extra time unless things are pretty well at crisis point. This, of course, contributes to a tendency to follow on, rather than take initiative in one's work, and obviously puts a woman with a lot of home obligations at some disadvantage compared with a man of equal ability. And the effect can well be cumulative if you get used to working in one way, it becomes progressively more difficult to break out of it when or if conditions are different later on. And the fact that most women are conscientious and find it difficult just to cut their losses does not help.'

The conscientious nature of women administrators to which this respondent refers does seem substantiated both by the kind of hours which married women administrators recorded themselves as working and their use of leave allowances. In common with the majority of men and single women questioned on this point, married women worked for some time after six o'clock most evenings of the week and for about three hours in one weekend in a month. One does not appear to find amongst married women as one does amongst married and single men the small proportion who work most nights of the week and most weekends. Married women with children naturally differ from men in their use of maternity and allied sick leave. In addition to annual leave, maternity leave and sick leave, the Service may also grant a maximum of five days' paid leave and further unpaid leave in cases or urgent domestic distress, for example bereavement. There are no Service-wide statistics on the granting of such leave to men and women administrators but judging from responses in interviews women hardly ever used anything beyond annual leave for family matters.

Most of the women with families tended to keep ten days or so of their annual leave as reserve days for family occasions or emergencies. Very often they commended the generous leave arrangements of the service and commented on the willingness of the Service to be flexible if convinced of a woman's determination to remain at work full-time. In this connection they quoted their experience of being able to work odd half days at home, and being able to work part-time over a difficult pregnancy or period of illness.

Whilst the married women administrators might well differ hardly at all from the majority of male administrators in the hours they work, it seems that in the women's lives these hours constitute a greater source of pressure and strain than they do in the men's. Negligible numbers of male and single female respondents felt that their work had an adverse effect on their health; in the case of married women, however, the proportion who felt the adverse effects was over half. The sense of pressure felt by married women is probably a result of the depth of their involvement in the two demanding areas of work and home. Over the long term the married woman may be exercised by dilemmas of commitment to one or the other; over the short term she may be harassed by problems of management—co-ordinating the running of the two spheres of her life. Women with children in the administrative class become conscious of being 'clock-watchers' in a world where according to one woman 'there is a cult of *not* clock-watching which results in caustic comment if one goes too often at precisely the statutorily agreed time'. Most women feel the conflicting pressures of accommodating to the working habits of their colleagues and their own desires to see their children and their unwillingness to impose too many demands on their domestic help. Whatever resolution the women choose—insistence on working standard office hours with very special exceptions, or refusing to so confine their work—seems generally accompanied by some sense of guilt and tension. As described earlier administrative work is subject to frequently unpredictable pressure demands which cannot always be met by taking work home. In fact administrative work seems tied to a marked degree to an office location where files, colleagues and clients converge. Women perceive that faced with the pressure demands they are prepared only sparingly and *in extremis* to work at the office until eight or nine at night and/or come in at eight in the mornings. On the other hand they recognize the times when a family epidemic or difficulties with domestic help have caused their concentration and time input on work to lessen.

For the most part married women administrators seem to maintain their involvement in work and family at the cost of other involvements. For instance compared with male administrators contacted they indicated less leisure activities. They do not appear to have as much 'expendable' time as male administrators: a larger proportion of their lives is committed to the highly salient areas of work and family. Hence the basis for the views often expressed in the work situation that the married woman administrator has no reserves, that she cannot be expected to summon forth the extra effort necessary to hold down some of the highly demanding posts that lie on the route of high-fliers. It does seem, as a result of this view, that other people in the class, Establishment Officers, supervising officers, and colleagues are inhibited in the demands that they make of married women. A comment made by a male Under Secretary on a former subordinate of his shows how sensitive people can be,

> 'Domestic life must have been a bit of a strain for her. . . . One felt a bit that she was working at the limit and that if any crisis came it might just push her over the edge of something, I mean we all have to have a certain amount of reserve at this kind of game. At that kind of level, at that time we used to have a number of adjournment debates and things like that up to 10 o'clock at night, and I didn't really feel that, if she came along, I could ask her to go and sit in the box. I do remember one thing that I particularly wanted her to go to, some conference or something at short notice, to make a statement, I've forgotten what it was; she certainly went very readily. I mean there was no question of her refusing to do

anything. The feelings were on my side that perhaps it was entirely unreasonable, or unnecessary, that she didn't have very much in the way of physical resources.'

From this comment and many others like it, one gathers that such sensitivity is a significant factor in decisions on the placing of married women. If they have a choice administrators would prefer not to place married women administrators with young children in a post that is going to involve overnight travelling, late night or high pressure working. What seems to operate is a form of benign paternalism, whereby colleagues and bosses, operating on the assumption that a woman with children is likely to have commitments and calls on her energy that a man does not have, make the decision about what work loads she can be expected to carry. Such is the procedure of posting in the administrative class, that decisions are generally made without consulting the individuals concerned. One Under Secretary, discussing the posting of a woman with a young baby, said that having a baby, 'does have some effect on what jobs she can do, because I would be very doubtful about giving a mother with a young baby posts which necessitated her, for example, having to go to the House fairly often at night.' Establishment Officers who were interviewed often expressed the same sentiments but then went on to say that in the tight labour situation of the last few years they had sometimes been forced to give such posts to women with family responsibilities. In all cases they expressed favourable surprise at the way the women had done the jobs, though they wondered aloud at the effect on the family.

It would be misleading to convey the impression that married women with children never break through the rank of Assistant Secretary. In 1955 there were 6 women Under or Deputy Secretaries of whom 2 were married, in 1960 there were 10 women above the rank of Assistant Secretary of whom 3 were married and in 1968, 11, of whom 4 were married, 2 of these 4 having children. The ratio between single and married women in each of these cases is affected by the operation of the marriage bar at an earlier stage in the Service's history. In fact it is only now that the cohort of women who have had the opportunity to marry and have children from the beginning of their careers, are beginning to pass into the age at which Under Secretary appointments begin to be made.

Until now no distinctions have been made between the kinds of accommodations between family and work life made by married women administrators. This is partly because of the limited nature of the information available, but it is also partly a result of the fact that work environment is not strikingly differentiated and therefore it does not encourage very obviously different patterns of accommodation.

Having made these qualifications it does seem that the 7 married women administrators aged over 30 and with children who featured in the investigation differed in their experience of the combination of work and family life. Three of them, 2 in their mid-thirties, both Principals, 1 with 1 child and 1 with 4, and 1 in her mid-forties, an Assistant Secretary with 2 children, experienced very stable combinations of family and career. When describing the development of their careers and home lives none of them dwelt on or indicated the presence of crises which had decisively marked either sphere of their lives. All enjoyed the work of administration a great deal and could see no reason, apart from an unpredictable emergency, that would make them alter their work pattern. None of them expressed very strong ambitions, rather they adopted a pragmatic attitude to the future. All felt that on their current running they might well, given the occurrence of vacancies at the right time, be Under Secretaries by the end of their career. When talking to other administrators the names of these women were mentioned more than once as examples of married women who appear to manage the combination of work and family successfully. The perceptions of other respondents coincided with those of the women themselves in characterizing them as rather cool, unsentimental characters.

It may well be that psychological differences are basic to the kinds of differences that are being elaborated. Certainly the 2 women who form the second grouping appeared very different psychologically from the first 3 women. They expressed their feelings more readily, they appeared more impetuous and less reserved than the first group. Both of these women when talking about their work expressed a sense of unsatisfied ambitions and frustrations. Both felt that their family commitments had led to difficulties in their work and indicated that at times they had been seriously at odds with other people in the work environment. One in fact said that other administrators had commented that she did not have the qualities best suited to administration and she saw herself as likely to get 'over-involved' in causes. In neither of these cases did the women see their domestic situations as having been smooth and easy to run: both had had 1 child very much separated in age from the rest of their children and had experienced difficulties in obtaining reliable domestic help. The total sense conveyed by these 2 women was one of lack of harmony—within themselves, within their work situation and in the relations between their home and work lives. Both women expressed discontent with the results that their combined lives had given them: one in quite despairing terms,

> 'I find myself conscious of a sense of failure all round. . . . I realize how much I missed not being with my children; they tell me that they did not think they suffered as they saw their father a great deal, accepted changing domestic help and felt my aura carried over sufficiently. . . . I feel that I have worked hard all of my life yet shall never reach the sort of level which might to some extent justify the strain to myself and my family of having done this. The decision to carry on working was I now think a wrong decision because the pressures are too great especially in the highly competitive early thirties'.

The remaining 2 women stand distinct from the other 5 for a mixture of reasons. They are both in their early forties, both Assistant Secretaries, but with different family experiences, one having married in her early twenties and had a large family and one marrying late and having 2 children. Both of these women are accounted highly competent by people at work and both convey a sense of managing their work well. But at a deeper level they feel a basic lack of commitment to their work and in this they differ from the other 5. Both, for different reasons, had invested a lot of time and energy in their work, but both strongly wanted more time to spend with their children and more time to develop other aspects of themselves apart from their administrative competence.

These last two sets of women appear to have unstable patterns of accommodation between their dual roles. All were dissatisfied with the balance of satisfactions that they derived from their experience of combining work and home. All were considering or had experienced other alternatives to the combination of a full-time, lifelong administrative career with their marital and family responsibilities. Their discontent generated a willingness to explore within themselves and their environment alternatives to this dominant pattern. The alternatives that are open to women administrators in this position will now be discussed.

3. *Alternatives to full-time administrative work*

Two of the 4 women just described were contemplating moving into schoolteaching. In both cases they felt that it would offer them a rhythm of work which would enable them to see more of their children: both saw opportunities to capitalize on their administrative experience and to gain headships. Their problems in this case centred around fitting such a transfer in with their husbands' careers and finding a post with a salary close to their present one.

Administrators, both men and women, tend to look to the public sector for alternatives to employment in the administrative class for they can, whenever they leave the Civil Service, transfer their pension benefits to a post in the public sector which includes *inter alia* university teaching, schoolteaching, the National Health Service, local authority employment and appointments in the nationalized industries. For transfers to other than the public sector it may be possible to transfer under 'approved employment arrangements whereby the Civil Servant receives the benefits for which his Civil Service qualifies him on retirement from the other employment. Approved employment terms normally apply to employment in the public service field in the UK or Commonwealth countries or with an international body. For those in the higher Civil Service (i.e. Assistant Secretary and broadly equivalent ranks above) virtually all employment may be approved including employments of a purely private or commercial nature'.[1]

Pension arrangements have two particular implications for women. First they provide an incentive for married women administrators to remain at work inside or outside the Service. All administrators can voluntarily retire from the age of 50 onwards and, provided they have ten years' reckonable service, the qualifying period for pension eligibility, receive at the age of 60 the pension and lump sum for which their service qualifies them. But before this age, or after when an individual has less than ten years reckonable service, a person leaving for no other paid employment, would not, unless the premature retirement were for certain specified reasons, for example health reasons, receive the accrued amount of their superannuation benefits. Hence there is every incentive for a married woman in early middle age who has perhaps worked ten years or more in the class, but who finds for some reason the continuation of family life and career a great strain, to try to weather the situation at least until she is 50, or to transfer to employment where she feels life will be less onerous and to which she can transfer her superannuation benefits. The Civil Service pension arrangements affect the freedom of a woman who has combined career and family for a number of years to decide that she has had enough and that she wants to try life without a career. She cannot do so without giving up superannuation benefits already accured as well as the salary.

The second implication is that women considering a move out of

[1] The Committee on the Civil Service, Factual Statistical and Explanatory Papers, London, HMSO, 1968, vol. IV, p. 28.

the Civil Service look in the direction of teaching. The private sector and many areas of the public sector appear less welcoming to women. Teaching, in both schools and universities, employs high proportions of women. But this is not to say that it is a particularly easy career for women administrators to transfer into. Again the problem is especially acute for the women who has served ten years or so in the Service and is likely to have a young family and to be at the most stressful period of the combination. In the administrative class she commands a salary of nearly £3,000 a year, she has a first degree and probably no teaching experience and hence would be lucky if she could earn much over £1,000 in any sphere of teaching. Her only hope of higher pay would be a post in teaching in, for instance, Public Administration, where her Civil Service experience would be more likely to count as direct qualification for the job.

In addition there is the possibility of moving not so much into teaching as to administration in the educational world. Several women Assistant Secretaries and Under Secretaries have become wardens of women's colleges and headmistresses of girls' public and fee-paying schools. Women's educational institutions apparently experience difficulty in recruiting administrative talent from the teaching profession and actively canvass women administrators with a view to persuading them to change careers. The kind of considerations operative in leading women administrators to change to teaching were expressed by one who had recently made the transition to a deputy headship:

> 'I shall have fewer hours away from home and can see more of my children in the early evening even if it means working later in the evening. I shall have school holidays—more important later on when I am likely to have to rely on an indifferent housekeeper rather than a good nannie. I hope to graduate to headship of a school or teachers' college or some such. It will leave me freer to engage in activities in the community which I cannot do as a Civil Servant. It will enable us all to lead a fuller family, social and cultural life I hope. I only drop £300 per annum at this stage in my career.'

Of the other 2 women mentioned above, 1 had experienced a break of six years in her career and the other was in the process of negotiating to work a thirty-five-hour week. They are amongst a very small number of women in the administrative class, who have experience which deviates from the norm, i.e. full-time, uninterrupted work. It is difficult to get exact figures on the total number of such 'deviants' because departments arrange such matters, but it is doubtful that altogether the number is much larger than 10 out of a total of 221 women administrators. This present small number is very much what one would expect. Married women were only allowed to stay on in the class after 1946. The years after this were hardly a time for women to gain concessions designed to help them to raise families and have administrative careers as well. It is the 1960s which has been the time of experiments with married women working part-time and resuming work after a break of a few years. These experiments are not due to any concerted pressure which married women as a group have organized, rather they have been due to the position of 'overwork' that the administrative class found itself in during the 1960s. The expansion of work experienced from the early 1960s onwards fell on a class which in the early and mid-1950s had not filled all of the vacancies it had advertised. These kinds of circumstances combined to make the administrative class more prepared to contemplate unorthodox methods of recruitment. In addition some departments have responded to initiatives from former married women employees and have re-instated them.

Reinstatement, like all procedures regarding personnel in the Civil Service, is governed by written rules. Departments are permitted to reemploy and to reinstate applicants at the grade at which they left the service, providing that their employment is considered as in the public interest and there is evidence that their capabilities have not diminished. Departments are felt free to devise their own procedures for deciding whether or not these two criteria are fulfilled by candidates. Prior to a revision of the rules in 1966 departments followed an informal guideline that to be eligible for reinstatement an applicant should have been away from the Service for not longer than his or her earlier period of service. In cases where individuals do not gain the reinstatement that they seek it is open to them to reenter the Service through the appropriate open competition.

Traditionally in the matter of reinstatement the Service has been prepared to give especially compassionate consideration to women who having left for reasons of marriage and family life have then encountered some setback. The roots for this lie in the marriage bar provisions. These no longer exist but the statements about the special consideration to be given to women disappointed by the vocation for which they left the Civil Service still appear in the rule book on personnel matters. It is impossible to gauge how far such considerations have influenced decisions to reinstate particular women candidates. In all only a very small number of men and women administrators have applied for and been granted reinstatement. The recent shortage of administrators, especially Principals, has probably led to an increase in the annual number of men and women administrators being reinstated at the level of responsibility at which they left the Service. But even so only a handful of administrators, most of them women, are involved each year.

In addition to rules about the procedure for reinstatement there are some very important ones attaching to the financial aspect of the process. Voluntary resignation from the Civil Service, before the age of 50 normally results in the forfeiture of accrued superannuation benefits unless the person is of the rank of Assistant Secretary or above or the resignation is to effect a change of employers in the public sector, e.g. from the Civil Service to teaching or employment under the federated superannuation system for the universities. Special rules, however, apply to the woman who marries while she is a permanent Civil Servant and who either resigns from her permanent appointment on marriage or resigns later for reasons connected with her marriage, for example, pregnancy, and, in either case, is subsequently reappointed to a permanent post. In such circumstances she may count her pre-resignation service for the Civil Service pension provided that any marriage gratuity paid is refunded on or shortly after reappointment. For married women reestablished before May 3, 1966 the arrangements were slightly more restrictive. Aggregation of service for pension purposes was not permitted if the break between full-time employment and reappointment to a permanent post exceeded seven years. Where the break did not exceed seven years it was normally a condition of reappointment that the gratuity was refunded. Also until a change of ruling in 1966 aggregation was not permitted unless a woman had been eligible for a marriage gratuity, that is to say had completed at least six years' service at the time of her marriage. Present rules make no such stipulation, nor do they place a limit in the break period. They also make the refund of the marriage gratuity optional and not a condition of reinstatement though pre-marriage service is not reckoned unless a refund is made. It is, however, worth noting that both current and old provisions governing the calculation of pensionable service, for women who return to the Service, do not allow a woman married at the time of her first appointment to a permanent Civil Service post to count years of service worked before her resignation towards her pension on her return to the Service.

A rehearsal of these complexities may appear rather boring but they can be extremely important. The rules relating to pensions are inflexible as people learn to their cost. The one woman amongst those contacted for interview in 1968, who had returned full-time after leaving, was married before she became a permanent Civil Servant.

When she returned to the Service, unaware of the intricacies of the rulings, she found herself unable to count her previous twelve years' service towards her pension. This woman had married whilst a temporary administrative Civil Servant in the 1940s. But the possibility of women being married before becoming permanent Civil Servants is not limited to the unusual circumstances of wartime. Any married women entering the administrative class for the first time faces the possibility, that were she subsequently to leave and then return to work, then she would not be allowed, as would a single woman resigning on marriage and returning later, to count her first term of service towards her eventual pension.

In brief the situation on women's reentry after a period of absence is that the Service has eased the various rulings by which it discouraged the practice. As things stand a woman who reapplies for entry to the administrative class now has a better chance than she had ten years ago of being readmitted without examination to her old grading. The exact nature of her present chances depends on (a) the labour situation in the department that she applies to—this is normally her old department, (b) her grade when she left, for most Establishments Officers interviewed expressed a preference for re-employing women who had served two or three years as a Principal, (c) the length of time she had been away. Many Establishments Officers made no firm statement about this, the most they were prepared to say was that the longer a woman had been away the more they would assume that it would count against her.

A handful of married women administrators have carved out part-time employment for themselves in the class. For instance in the Ministry of Agriculture, a married woman Principal has returned to work on a part-time basis. Her work is concerned with rewriting evidence for a Committee of Inquiry. The outcome of the Committee's work will probably be legislation and at this point her engagement will stop because she cannot follow through into the high pressure work of preparing legislation on a part-time basis. She hopes that engagement on another specific task will follow this one, and that like this one, it will be possible to organize the work so that another full-time Principal with whom she liaises carries the more immediate pressure work of Parliamentary questions and Ministerial letters. Altogether she works for 20 hours a week, Monday to Thursday, 9.30 a.m. to 4.30 p.m. and she receives 20/39 (hours) of a full Principal's pay: as a temporary Civil Servant she gets no superannuation benefits but she receives a proportion of the full allowance of annual leave and sick leave. She herself finds the arrangement worked satisfactorily and commented as follows:

> 'their are periods of pressure on this job—most of the time we are working to a deadline on papers which have to be produced at roughly two-monthly intervals or so. At such times it is sometimes inconvenient that I am only at the office part-time—I have sometimes worked at home in the evenings to get over this. The hours do not fit in well with meetings—I occasionally have to attend meetings which go on late. But in both cases (writing papers and meetings) the occasions when it is inconvenient being part-time are infrequent. So far we have not been behind or slow with work and on the whole this particular job can be done well in the hours —how much this would extend to other jobs I don't know.'

In enabling this woman Principal to work part-time the Ministry of Agriculture has been somewhat more accommodating than many other Ministries have yet shown themselves to be. The point still remains, however, that the job described derives from the 'research' aspects of administration rather than any other. In this sense the job represents an extension of the kind of temporary employment which the administrative class has occasionally made available to retired and married ex-administrators on a part- or full-time basis. These have been jobs concerned with matters peripheral to the mainstream of administration in a department—for instance acting as Secretary to an Enquiry on Football in the Department of Education and Science or researching into the history of the National Insurance Stamp in the Treasury. These kinds of jobs run for a specific period, administrators are employed in a temporary capacity and people work on a part- or full-time basis for a term of employment.

Chapter V
CONCLUSION

In conclusion this report considers what steps should and could be taken to affect the career experience of women members of the administrative class.

In a sense there is a question mark hanging over this exercise, for the next few years may well be ones of far-reaching change in the Civil Service. In 1968 the Fulton Committee on the Civil Service came to the conclusion that the Civil Service needed to be fundamentally changed in order to equip it for the tasks of government in the second half of the twentieth century. Since the publication of the Committee's Report there has been much debate about the accuracy of their analysis and the worth of their recommendations. The government has already accepted that classes should be abolished. Hence the administrative class will be replaced by an occupational group. In the future members of this occupational group will change posts less frequently than do present administrators and they may well, if the government accepts the Committee's recommendations, receive more formal training, specialize as either economic or social administrators, and have the opportunity to concentrate on long-term policy formation as opposed to the more day-to-day business of administration. The Committee also recommended that members of the administrative occupational group should have experience of other occupations and in particular industry, either before or after their recruitment to the Service.

At this stage it is difficult to assess how far and how quickly the administrative class will change. One can raise the question of whether any of the proposed changes will have special implications for women's careers, for instance concentration on more mature recruits might reduce the number of women entrants, but it is impossible to make any certain predictions. One thing it is possible to be definite about is that in the immediate future the Civil Service will be closely scrutinizing its organization of work and its utilization of personnel. It is therefore an appropriate time to focus attention on the Service's utilization of womanpower in its top jobs.

The Civil Service appears to adopt a non-committal stance over the recruitment of women to the administrative class. For instance in newspaper advertisements it invites applications for entry to the administrative class and avoids all mention of 'men' and 'women'. In 1968 the First Civil Service Commissioner in his foreword to *An Administrative Career in the Home Civil Service,* made a specific reference to women in the following terms:

> 'The traditional Administrative Class entrant has been an arts graduate; but scientists, mathematicians and social scientists are wanted just as much, and of course women as well as men.'[1]

The remainder of the booklet, however, makes no mention of employment provisions of special interest to women—maternity leave, marriage gratuity, opportunities for leaving the class and later returning. It is true that the Civil Service Commission has never regarded advertisements as the main means by which it disseminates information and attracts recruits. But the tenor of the advertisement's approach to potential recruits seems to infuse the other methods also. One feels that underneath the cool non-commital approach there is the hope that not too many women will catch on to the idea of the administrative class such that it becomes a woman-dominated occupation.

There are indications that the proportion of women in the class (8 per cent in 1968) may well grow noticeably in the next decade. Now 32 per cent of the applicants to the class are women and in the last few years their showing in the entrance examinations has improved considerably. In 1968 a quarter of the young recruits in whom the Service started to invest training were women. Such a statistic serves to underline the importance of asking whether the administrative class uses the talents and services of its women members to their fullest possible extent.

It is the conclusion of this report that it does not. It is recognized that it is impossible to settle conclusively on the kind of information readily available whether male and female recruits to the administrative class have similar distributions of ability, or whether this is so with male and female members of the class, or whether men and women of the same ability in fact get similar treatment. Nevertheless it does seem that within the rules of the formal organization of the administrative class which enshrine equality of opportunity for the sexes, the understandings, attitudes and mores which are part of the texture of the informal organization of the class operate to steer women away from the scenes of important action and hence lessen the likelihood of their being seen as candidates for top posts.

[1] Civil Service Commission, *An Administrative Career in the Home Civil Service*, 1968, p. 3.

There are features of the administrative class which make such an interpretation plausible. In entering the administrative class women have entered a stable unitary structure: they have not had opportunities to carve specialized spheres for themselves but have had to prove to a predominantly male audience that they can do as well as men what formerly men alone used to do. In addition the occupational world into which women have entered is one where decisions are taken about individuals' careers in a rather paternal fashion; chosen individuals are assigned posts, it is not a question of 'will all those interested please apply'. In the last twenty years a small number of women have broken through to the top ranks of the class. A noticeable feature of the careers of quite a few of them is that they have been given important, demanding posts during periods of crisis and manpower shortage. For instance the war years and the reorganization of economic departments including the establishment of the Department of Economic Affairs in the 1960s, seem to have been two occasions when acute shortage of talent has loosened up the informal structure and its sex-type-casting tendencies. In this sense the exceptions are evidence pointing to the existence of an informal 'rule'.

The experience of women in the administrative class drives home the point that the formal establishment of equality of opportunity does not necessarily result in equality of attainment between the sexes. The reason frequently given, both in the administrative class and other occupations where formal equality of opportunity exists, for the differences in men's and women's attainments is the 'facts of life': men and women play different roles in marriage and family life and this, it is held, inevitably affects their participation in the work situation. Other contributions to the PEP research on 'Women in Top Jobs' consider the question of men's and women's roles and possible changes in them more fully.[1] The major criticism that can be levelled at the Civil Service as an employer is that whilst it informally accommodates to the different social roles of men and women such that it does not expect the same flexibility and time commitment from married women as married men, it could do more to extend and regularize the formal opportunities for women administrators to have work patterns which fit in with a strong commitment to family life.

What one is asking for is that the Civil Service move to a position where married women administrators with children have the assured choice not only of leaving the Service completely or remaining at

[1] See M. P. Fogarty, R. and R. Rapoport, *Career, Family and Sex Roles*, PEP, 1970.

work full-time but also of taking part-time employment for a period in their total career span or of leaving the Civil Service for a period of years and then resuming work. Achieving such a situation requires a change of heart in the Civil Service. At present, as pointed out in Chapter IV, part-time work and reinstatement are not unknown. But essentially the attitude of the Service is that the provision of these opportunities is something to be kept in small print, and to be granted as hard-won concessions to women persistent enough to seek working arrangements which deviate from the standard pattern. Women administrators would benefit from the assurance that their choice would not be limited to going completely or staying full-time. One could make out a strong case that the Service would benefit also. In 1968 a quarter of the new recruits from the open competitions were women. If in later years these women were to be encouraged to consider part-time work or to resume work after a break in their careers, then some of the considerable investment made in the training of young women which is now lost would be conserved.

The Civil Service, in common with other employing organizations, is apt to weigh measures which increase the individual's variety of choice and room for manœuvre, in terms of the administrative complexity such measures create. In the case of the Civil Service this tendency is reinforced by the public bureaucratic emphasis of governing practice by rules. The immediate reaction of Civil Servants when faced by the demand for a range of employment opportunities for women is to be inhibited by the thought of the complicated regulations necessary to offer the opportunity of flexibility. Nevertheless, given the will on the part of the Civil Service to regard the accommodation of part-time and interrupted careers as part of the normal functioning of a work organization committed to the employment of women, then there seems no reason why means could not be devised to incorporate such opportunities into the structure of the Civil Service.

The rules governing the reinstatement of women have already been described. At present the reentry of married women to the class is regarded as a useful expedient in a time of labour shortage rather than something which the Civil Service should nurture and encourage. There seems no reason why the Civil Service should not provide a regularized place for married women returners in its recruitment structure for the administrative class and the subsequent occupational group. At present the Civil Service effects a balance of recruitment between Civil Servants from other classes, young graduates and mature recruits from other occupations. There seems no reason in principle or in practice why married women returners should not be included as a category in the recruitment process. It surely would be possible for Departments to keep registers of women who leave for family reasons and, in any one year, to invite applications for reinstatement from them. Guidelines could be established as to the level of previous performance necessary to ensure reinstatement. In addition women reentrants could be placed on a stringent probationary period of something up to two years. These two provisions should obviate the need for the women to reenter competitions which they have already passed through successfully. Late-entry Principals recruited through competitions aged anything up to 52 have been entering the class for a number of years so problems of orienting and fitting in older recruits are not completely new. Retraining of married women returners could well be included in the increased formal training facilities proposed by the Fulton Committee. A woman returning in her late thirties still has twenty years of service ahead of her: on the showing of late-entry Principals there is no reason why she should not attain the career grade of Assistant Secretary or where she is very good, experience accelerated promotion that takes her to the level of Under Secretary.

There are no rules governing provision of and access to part-time work in the administrative class. In the past the class has, occasionally, when hard pressed by labour shortage or persistent individuals, made part-time administrative employment available. The assignments created have been of the somewhat peripheral servicing nature described earlier in Chapter IV. As yet there have been no apparent attempts to create part-time work allocations which mirror full-time allocations in terms of the range of their responsibilities, but which are smaller and capable of being run on the lines worked by the part-time Principal in the Ministry of Agriculture described in Chapter IV.

Many administrators would react to the suggestion that this is possible by saying that administrative work is not capable of being performed on a part-time basis. This reaction is tied in with the 'total commitment' syndrome in administrative work. Part-timers are seen to suffer from the defects of married women magnified: they limit their availability whilst the demands made on the administrator cannot be so confined. The usual reaction of administrators in interviews to the subject of part-time working was 'it would so gum up the works if Mrs X didn't work conventional hours. A full-time administrator can drop what he is doing to go to a meeting, deal with a Parliamentary question or letter to a Minister; part-timers cannot be called from home and no-one else, despite the extensive filing system, can stand in for Mrs X.' One administrator quoted his Permanent Secretary as saying 'administrators are paid for being here rather than doing anything'. Outsiders, however, might wonder how important it is that all people with administrative responsibility are on tap all of the time. The level at which the question of the possibility of part-time work really arises is that of Principal. This is the basic working grade of the administrative class: levels above this are responsible for directing the work of full-time Principals and there are obvious difficulties in a part-timer running a full-time complement of staff.

One can also appreciate that dividing the work allocation of one full-time Principal between two part-timers would be a very inefficient way of conducting business. Most work allocations appear to be highly integrated and hence subdivision of one full-time allocation between two people could result in more time totally being spent in communicating and evolving agreements on policy. A few administrators, however, made the point that if one considered the work of departmental divisions headed by Under Secretaries, then in a rational process of work allocation there was no reason why one could not think in terms of half time as well a full-time Principal units, and they went on to point out ways in which the work in some divisions could be subdivided to provide a work allocation which because of the lack of pressure on it could be managed on a part-time basis. Such reallocations were mainly seen as devices to create additional labour power, three and a half units as opposed to three with the half-timer relieving the pressure on the existing labour force or doing work which just would not otherwise be done.

Given the will the Service could go further than it does at present in the direction of creating part-time employment for married women administrators. It is difficult to predict the proportion of married women who would avail themselves of the opportunities were they there but it is possible that the sense of strain experienced at some time by most women administrators working full-time with children would lead to a high proportion of married women wanting this option for a period of their working lives.

For women administrators to have the assured possibility of the flexible career patterns which many women with families appear to want, it seems essential that the Civil Service experience a change in its attitude to the employment of women. Historically the Civil Service has had to be pushed into granting women employment rights. In the past there have been in the administrative class elements of the feeling that women were inferior, troublesome substitutes for men, to be accommodated only when men were in short supply and when the Service eventually felt embarrassed by the shortfall between its employment policy towards women and the treatment demanded by influential and vociferous sections of the public. Having granted women formal equality of opportunity with men in entry, promotion prospects, pay and the combination of work and marriage, the Service now assumes that it can, in its formal rules and procedures, treat men and women as indistinguishable employees. Indeed it is a matter of Service pride that this is the formal attitude although the point has been made earlier in this report that, in the informal understandings which intertwine with the formal structure, men and women tend to be treated as different categories of employees.

What is wanted from the Service as employer is a wholehearted recognition of the fact that the career contingencies of married women administrators are likely to be different from those of men, and that it should strive vigorously to provide all of its women employees with a range of employment opportunities from which the individual woman can choose the one most suited to her personal needs. Such wholehearted recognition would involve the Civil Service's systematically reviewing and considering its employment and deployment practices specifically in terms of how they could be made to accommodate sizeable numbers of married women returners and part-timers.

For this to happen the issue of the treatment of women must be kept alive and not buried under a consensus of silence. The question is how this can be achieved. One result of the eventual granting of formal equality was that organizations specifically concerned with women—the women's organizations and ad hoc subcommittees of the Whitley Council on the 'Treatment of Women'—quietly dissolved. Another result was that any consideration of the position of women employees was completely absent from the deliberations of the latest of a long line of enquiries into the organization of the Civil Service, the Fulton Committee on the Civil Service (1968). Some reference was made to this subject in the earlier report of the Estimates Committee on Recruitment to the Civil Service,[1] but only because one woman witness, Lady Williams of Bedford College, directed the Committee's attention to it. Women's organizations of the type that disbanded in the late 1950s are not necessarily appropriate to the present situation. What does seem highly appropriate is that the subject of the employment opportunities of women should be placed in the context of general discussions about the recruitment and management of personnel. Despite the previous emphasis of this chapter it must not be assumed that by employment opportunities

[1] Sixth *Report* from the Estimates Committee, Recruitment to the Civil Service, London, HMSO, 1965.

one means solely opportunities for part-time work and breaks in careers. Some married women will undoubtedly wish to undertake uninterrupted full-time work. To these women other questions will loom large. These include both specific questions like that of maternity leave, which whilst relatively generous by British standards is not by those of Eastern Europe or Israel, for example, and the more diffuse question of relative promotion opportunities of men and women full-timers, which on the evidence contained in this report still appear to justify concern.

At present a National Whitley Council Joint Committee, drawn from the staff associations and the management side of the Civil Service, is discussing the feasibility of following the spirit and the letter of the Fulton Committee in reforming the Civil Service. It would seem appropriate to inject into their discussions, perhaps through constituting a subcommittee composed of men and women representing the staff and management sides, a consideration of the particular problems of women. The existence of such a committee might well help to focus the thought and attention to the career problems of women which now occurs in a somewhat diffused manner through government departments. The attachment of the subcommittee to the larger concerns of Whitley Council Joint Committee might help to ensure that a fruitful interchange of ideas results from a juxtaposition of the problems relating to the careers of married women—conditions of reinstatement, seniority on return, possibilities of part-time work—and those relating to Civil Service personnel in general, for example transferability of pensions and the possibilities of mobility out of and back into the Service.

This report has been concerned with the careers of women administrators. There is a traditional practice in the Civil Service, when considering conditions of employment, to treat all women Civil Servants according to the same rules. It is possible that the suggestions made in this report, about the need for greater flexibility in the career opportunities of married women administrators, apply to married women in other classes. Whether they do or not is a matter for discussion. If the conclusion is that they do not then the Service should be guided by the significant differences in the career contingencies of its female labour force and be prepared to differentiate between them.

Finally it remains to reemphasize a point made in the preceding pages. Change in the employment conditions of women is really part and parcel of broader change in the work environment. For instance in the case of the administrative class, the institution of the opportunities for sizeable numbers of women to undertake part-time work at some time in their careers implies a revision of attitudes to the allocation of work within the class. In crude terms the Service must be prepared to employ part-timers rather than increasing the workload of existing administrators to the point where another full-timer is needed. It is highly likely that a more judicious deployment of part-time workers could lighten the pressure of work felt by many full-time administrators both male and female. In part, the present perceived pressure of work is due to an increased amount of work in the 1960s falling on a static labour force. In part it seems due to bad servicing facilities—a difficult telephone service, inadequate secretarial assistance and working conditions that have recently been described as verging on 'squalor'. In part also it seems part of the cult of 'overwork' in the class, the tendency for political crises to be met by successive pile-ups of overtime.

There appears a tendency in the administrative class to drive and exhaust personnel resources rather than conserve them. Men as well as women suffer the adverse consequences of this. Public opinion which too readily associates expenditure incurred in the course of running the Civil Service with waste, bears a large share of the responsibility for the purse-conscious, cheese-paring attitude that often characterizes the management of personnel matters in the Service. It is to be hoped that the post-Fulton era will educate public, politicians and Civil Servants to the true costs of an efficient Civil Service. It is the conclusion of this report that measures improving the career opportunities of married women could readily be incorporated into the running of an 'efficient' administrative class. For these measures should be viewed not just as concessions to a minority of employees but should be undertaken as part of a concerted policy aiming at the efficient and humane utilization of men and women Civil Servants.

APPENDIX I

Non-Industrial staff in Civil Service, July 1969.
Analysis by staff group and grade of the Post Office.
Data supplied by the Central Staff Record.

	PERMANENT			TEMPORARY					TOTAL
				Male		*Female*			
Staff group and grade	*Male*	*Female*	*Total*	*Whole time*	*Part-time*	*Whole-time*	*Part-time*	*Whole-time + ½ Part-time*	*Whole-time + ½ Part-time*
1. ADMINISTRATIVE									
Permanent Secretary	—	—	—	—	—	—	—	—	—
Deputy Secretary	5	—	5	—	—	—	—	—	5
Under Secretary	27	1	28	1	—	—	—	1	29
Assistant Secretary	39	4	43	—	—	—	—	—	43
Principal	48	4	52	3	—	—	—	3	55
Assistant Principal	8	3	11	—	—	—	—	—	11
Others	5	2	7	1	—	—	1	2	9
	132	**14**	**146**	**5**	—	—	**1**	**6**	**152**

Appendix I—*cont.*

2. GENERAL EXECUTIVE									
Head of Major Establishments	4	—	4	1	—	—	—	1	5
Principal Executive Officer	12	1	13	—	—	—	—	—	13
Senior Chief Executive Officer	25	2	27	—	—	—	—	—	27
Chief Executive Officer	119	12	131	—	—	—	—	—	131
Senior Executive Officer	398	66	464	8	—	—	—	8	472
Higher Executive Officer	1,031	339	1,370	11	2	14	9	30	1,400
Executive Officer	2,886	1,378	4,264	60	—	29	—	89	4,353
Others	12	1	13	—	—	—	1	1	14
	4,487	**1,799**	**6,286**	**80**	**2**	**43**	**10**	**129**	**6,415**
3. Other Executives	3,702	235	3,937	62	1	43	25	118	4,055
4. GENERAL CLERICAL									
Higher Clerical Officer	744	721	1,465	—	—	1	—	1	1,466
Clerical Officer	6,691	10,996	17,687	1,323	42	2,027	372	3,557	21,244
	7,435	**11,717**	**19,152**	**1,323**	**42**	**2,028**	**372**	**3,558**	**22,710**
5. Other Clerical	2,209	538	2,747	10	—	3	—	13	2,760
6. Clerical Assistants	1,780	5,936	7,716	1,596	23	9,134	654	11,068	18,784
7. TYPING									
Senior Personal Secretary	2	20	22	—	—	2	—	2	24
Personal Secretary	5	137	142	3	—	101	1	104	246
Superintendent and above	4	125	129	—	—	—	1	1	130
Shorthand Typist	8	210	218	5	—	122	36	145	363
Typist	4	583	587	26	—	825	202	952	1,539
Audio-typist	1	33	34	3	—	27	1	30	64
Other (e.g. other departmental grades)	8	3	11	—	—	3	1	4	15
	32	**1,111**	**1,143**	**37**	—	**1,080**	**242**	**1,238**	**2,381**

8. INSPECTORATE	16	—	16	—	1	—	1	1	17
9. MESSENGERIAL									
Senior Messenger	1	—	1	—	—	—	—	—	1
Messenger	16	—	16	7	—	—	—	7	23
Paper/Record Keeper	1	—	1	—	—	—	—	—	1
Cleaner	2,972	1,345	4,317	1,879	723	772	2,474	4,250	8,567
Other (e.g. office keeper departmental grades)	556	16	572	195	5	94	105	344	916
	3,546	**1,361**	**4,907**	**2,081**	**728**	**866**	**2,579**	**4,601**	**9,508**
10. Minor and Manipulative grades (Post Offices) 1A	7,546	32,919	180,465	14,053	6,501	15,516	16,821	41,230	221,695
11. Professional and Scientific and Technical I	2,699	11	2,710	76	—	5	3	83	2,792
12. Scientific and Technical II	1,413	30	1,443	192	1	63	1	256	1,699
13. Ancillary Technical and Miscellaneous Supervisory and Manipulative grades in the Post Office	892	3,761	4,653	300	3	2,094	80	2,435	7,089
14. Cableship and Minor Engineering grades (Post Office)	96,138	629	96,767	21,456	68	1,070	84	22,602	119,369
TOTAL NON-INDUSTRIAL STAFF	**272,027**	**60,061**	**332,088**	**41,271**	**7,370**	**31,954**	**20,873**	**87,338**	**419,426**

Note: The figure in this table, being based on a count of cards held by the Central Staff Record, necessarily differ from those shown in the Quarterly Staff Return (which is based on departmental returns) for the same date.

APPENDIX II

Characteristics of enquiry undertaken for Women in Top Jobs, 1968

Because of the wish to gain information about women who, in terms of age, would be eligible for consideration for top jobs in the administrative class in the next twenty years or so, it was decided to choose informants through an entry cohort approach. The names, addresses and present employment, if any, of all women entering the Home Civil Service in 1947, 1948, 1949, 1953, 1954, 1960, 1961, 1962 and 1963 at the grade of Assistant Principal, were obtained from the Civil Service Commission. The years 1950, 1951, 1952 were omitted because all but 5 of the women entrants in these years had left the Service. Entrants during the early 1960s were included in order to provide some opportunity for comparing women administrators of different ages. This approach yielded a total of 36 women still in the home administrative class and a total of 23 who had left the Service.

In order to assist in the understanding of the work life and performance of women administrative Civil Servants it was decided to obtain information from men in the class. The Civil Service Commission supplied the names of 41 men, still in the administrative class, matched as far as possible with the women still in the class, by year of entry and present department. Where it was impossible to locate men who fulfilled both of these criteria precedence was given to year of entry.

Questionnaires were sent to the office address of the 36 women and 41 men in the Service and to the last known address of 22 of the 23 women who had left the class. After a period of six weeks, during which a reminder was sent, the response rate was as follows:

	Questionnaires Out	*Returned*	*Response rate (per cent)*
Men in the Service	41	34	82
Women in the Service	36	26	72
Women out of the Service	22	14	60

In all 23 males from the early entrants and 11 from the later entrants replied.

In the case of women still in the class, more replies came from the younger than from the older entrants and more from the single than the married women, as the following tabulation shows.

	Entry 1940s/1950s		*Entry 1960s*	
	Married	*Single*	*Married*	*Single*
Contacted	16	10	5	5
Replied	10	8	4	4

The questionnaire sought information on career experience, attitudes to aspects of work experience, and basic demographic data.

Subsequent to the return of the questionnaire 12 of the male and 19 of the female respondents were interviewed. Interviews were also conducted with 8 other administrators who were Under Secretaries and/or Establishment Officers and 4 of the women leavers.

In addition it was possible to obtain some information on the career progress of women who did not reply (10 in all) from central sources. This enabled a comparison to be made of aspects of the career success of 23 male and female administrators who were continuously in the class from the 1940s and 1950s onwards.

APPENDIX III

A report on information on male and female administrators contained in the Social Survey of the Civil Service, *Fulton Committee on the Civil Service, Surveys and Investigations, Vol. III, No. 1, Chapter III,* 1969.

A summary of the information on the social characteristics of male and female administrators presented in the Report on the Survey.

The men and women presently (1966) working as administrative Civil Servants are not markedly distinct in their basic social characteristics. The sample of administrative Civil Servants surveyed for the Fulton Committee in 1966 showed that both men and women administrators came predominantly (in the order of 75 per cent) from non-manual backgrounds, both sexes have the same substantial proportion (25 per cent) of fathers who were Civil Servants and were both for the most part (60 per cent) born in the Southern and Midland regions of England. In terms of educational experience men and women administrators are similar in that just over two thirds of them have a first degree from a university, the university being in the majority of cases Oxford, Cambridge or London, and the degree in the vast majority of cases being in Arts and the Social Sciences. Similar proportions of male and female administrators have entered the class directly (62 per cent), by transfer from another class (5 per cent) and promotion from other classes where graduate recruitment is not normal (33 per cent). The two populations do have their shades of difference. A slightly larger percentage of the women came from non-manual backgrounds, went to fee-paying schools, have a university degree and that in a non-science subject. The difference between the sexes is perceptibly stronger when one considers university attended; London has supplied something like one quarter of the women administrators, but only one tenth of the male administrators. The strongest difference between male and women administrators lies in their marital experience, over 80 per cent of the men are married but under 35 per cent of the women are. This difference in marital experience is not the result of a markedly different age structure between men and women, 11 per cent of male administrators are under 30 years of age as are 16 per cent of the women. In both sexes the largest group is that now aged between 46 and 50.

APPENDIX IV–A

Report prepared by staff of Civil Service Commission for Women in Top Jobs *PEP 1968.*

Fulton follow-up reports.[1] In connection with the Fulton enquiry, follow-up reports were furnished by Departments as at September 1, 1966, on all entrants to the Administrative Class, between 1948 and 1963, some 1,064 in all. A special report form was used, including a statement of the rank reached, an overall grading for efficiency at present duties, and an assessment of future promise in terms of the highest rank which the entrant was thought to be capable of filling successfully. The main criterion 'Combined Criterion Score', was a weighted combination of these three factors. Increasing service naturally improved the prospects of promotion to higher rank and thus tended to increase C.C. score. When comparing progress made by entrants over the full period of sixteen years, therefore, C.C. score was adjusted to compensate for length of service, this index being referred to as 'Adjusted C.C. Score'.

During the period 1948–63 some 118 female candidates had been declared successful in competitions for the Administrative Class, but through retirements, etc. follow-up reports were available on only 48 of them. This total of 48 comprises 22 who entered by Method I, 13 who entered by Method II, 7 who entered by limited competition and the other 6 who were direct entry principals. The unadjusted mean C.C. scores of the first three categories of these officers are compared with the similar scores of males in Table 1, overleaf.

The sample size in each cell was too small to allow any further statistical analysis. It would appear, however, that women have scored, on average about one point less then men.

Similar results were found when comparing the mean C.C. scores (as Principals) of 50 women promotees into the Administrative Class. Table 2 below presents the results.

Statistical Analysis

In order to obtain valid results on the basis of sufficiently large samples all the competition entrants (i.e. Method I, Method II and L.C.) were pooled together, and sorted according to sex, results being presented in Table 3, below.

[1] For Follow-up Form used in Fulton inquiry see Fulton Committee on the Civil Service, Vol. 3(2), p. 135.

TABLE 1 *Mean C.C. scores of entrants as Assistant Principal*

Period	Entry as A.P. years	Sex	Method I No.	Method I Mean C.C.	Method II No.	Method II Mean C.C.	Limited competition No.	Limited competition Mean C.C.	Total No.	Total Mean C.C.
		M	89	13·18	39	15·30	28	14·00	156	13·88
A	1948–51	F	5	11·20	1	12·00	3	10·33	9	11·00
		T	94	13·07	40	15·22	31	13·71	165	13·72
		M	74	11·58	46	13·37	20	13·05	140	12·38
B	1952–55	F	7	11·29	3	12·67	1	15·0	11	12·00
		T	81	11·56	49	13·33	21	13·14	151	12·35
		M	59	11·05	44	12·39	10	11·70	113	11·63
C	1956–59	F	4	9·75	4	12·50	1	10·0	9	11·00
		T	63	10·97	48	12·40	11	11·55	122	11·58
		M	53	9·61	77	10·06	15	9·20	145	9·81
D	1960–63	F	6	8·67	5	9·00	2	11·50	13	9·23
		T	59	9·51	82	10·00	17	9·47	158	9·76
		M	275	11·60	206	12·30	73	12·46	554	11·97
Total	1948–63	F	22	10·27	13	11·15	7	11·29	42	10·71
		T	297	11·50	219	12·23	80	12·36	596	11·88
	Mean Adj. C.C. Score	M		11·06		12·44		11·84		11·68
		F		10·05		11·54		10·86		10·64
		T		10·99		12·39		11·75		11·61

M = Males, F = Females, T = Males and Females.

TABLE 2 *Mean unadjusted C.C. scores (as Principals) for promotees*

	MALES		FEMALES	
Period	No.	Mean C.C. Score	No.	Mean C.C. Score
1948–51	61	12·9	5	10·2
1952–55	51	11·6	6	11·2
1956–59	113	10·3	23	9·0
1960–63	112	9·9	16	9·3
Total	337	10·7	50	9·5

TABLE 3

	MALES		FEMALES	
	No.	% of total	No.	% of total
Rank				
Assistant Secretary	157	28·3	5	11·9
Principal	330	59·6	30	71·4
Assistant Principal	67	12·1	7	16·7
TOTAL	554	100·0	42	100·0
Present performance				
Above Average	234	42·2	16	38·1
Average	262	47·3	22	52·4
Below Average	58	10·5	4	9·5
TOTAL	554	100·0	42	100·0
Future potential				
Under Secretary or above	312	56·3	14	33·3
Assistant Secretary	218	39·4	25	59·5
Principal	24	4·3	3	7·2
TOTAL	554	100·0	42	100·0

The differences between the percentages falling into various categories, on these three criteria, were investigated by the chi-squared test, results being summarized below:

(i) the differences on Rank and Present Performance, as criteria, were not significant at the 5 per cent level;

(ii) the difference on F.P. as criterion was significant at the 5 per cent level but not at the 1 per cent level.

WOMEN IN TOP JOBS

Summary of conclusions

Women's over-all progress in the Administrative Class would appear to have been slightly less than that of males, but the difference has approached statistical significance only with regard to estimates of Future Promise.

M. J. BHANSHALI
Assistant Statistician
May 16, 1968.

APPENDIX IV–B

Report prepared by staff of Civil Service Commission for Women in Top Jobs, *PEP, 1968. (For Fulton Follow-up Form see Fulton Report Vol. 3 (2), p. 135.)*

Administrative Class Follow-up, 1966: Supplementary Report. An Analysis of the Ratings for Women on Individual Components of Job-Performance

Objective

1. To compare between men and women rating on the seven aspects of performance (given in Part 2 of the Follow-Up Form).

Method

2. Of the 596 Open Competition entrants[1] only 42 were women. Since comparisons between samples which differ greatly in size are not theoretically advisable it was decided to extract a smaller sample of men, to be matched with the women on (i) Method of entry and (ii) Length of service, but to be representative of the male entrants in other respects.

3. Additionally, as a check on the sampling procedure, two such samples of men, equal in number to the sample of women, were taken and an examination made of the differences between them. No statistically significant differences were found, which indicates that the sampling procedure was adequate, and the two samples were pooled for the comparisons presented in Table 1, above.

Results

4. Table 4 compares mean scores for men and women on the seven aspects of performance. In order to allow some comparison between methods of entry figures are given separately for the different methods, whilst standardized mean differences are also given to allow some comparisons between the seven features.

5. Considering Over-All Means only (All Competitions), it can be seen that the values for men are always higher than for women. However the differences can be grouped in the following way:

(a) 'Stability' (difference significant at $P<0{\cdot}02$).

(b) 'Meetings' and 'Drive' } Marked differences but statistically not significant.

[1] The Main Report, on the Administrative Class Follow-up' (1966) by Dr E. Anstey.

TABLE 4 *Mean scores for men and women, and standardized mean differences, on the seven aspects of performance*

Aspect of Performance	TYPE OF COMPETITION						All Competitions (Over-all means)		All persons (M+F)	
	Method I		Method II		Limited Competition					
	M	F	M	F	M	F	M	F	Mean	Std. deviation
N =	44	22	26	13	14	7	84	42	126	126
1. Short term Contact	3·54	3·36	3·73	3·92	3·93	3·71	3·67	3·57	3·63	0·633
Std. Mean Diff.	0·284		−0·300		0·348		0·158			
2. Relations with Colleagues	3·73	3·59	3·74	3·92	4·12	4·00	3·81	3·71	3·78	0·743
Std. Mean Diff.	0·188		−0·242		0·162		0·135			
3. Paper Work	3·63	3·41	3·71	3·77	3·57	3·57	3·64	3·55	3·61	0·573
Std. Mean Diff.	0·384		−0·122		0		0·157			

TABLE 4—contd.

4. Figure Work	3·30	3·45	3·54	3·40	3·69	3·33	3·45	3·42	3·44	0·614
Std. Mean Diff.	−0·244		+0·228		0·586		0·049			
5. Meetings	3·54	3·41	3·69	3·69	4·07	3·57	3·68	3·52	3·63	0·718
Std. Mean Diff.	0·238		0		0·916		0·223			
6. Drive	3·62	3·32	3·66	3·77	4·07	3·86	3·70	3·55	3·65	0·786
Std. Mean Diff.	0·382		−0·140		0·267		0·191			
7. Stability	4·02	3·59	4·11	3·85	4·14	3·71	4·07	3·69	3·94	0·859
Std. Mean Diff.	0·501		0·302		0·501		0·442[1]			

[1] $P \leqslant 0{\cdot}02$

Notes: Std. Mean Diff. (Standardized Mean Difference)

$$= \frac{\text{Male Average} - \text{Female Average}}{\text{Standard Deviation for the item}}.$$

(c) 'Short-term Contact'
'Paper Work'
'Relations with Colleagues'
and 'Figure Work'
} Small differences again not statistically significant.

For (a) above this finding applied to all methods of entry, but for (b) and (c) the results were not consistent over the methods.

It can be seen (from Table 4) that in comparison with their male colleagues, the Method II women entrants have obtained rather higher mean scores on 'Short-Term Contact', 'Relations with Colleagues', 'Drive' and 'Paper Work', and that the Method I Women entrants have obtained a higher mean score on 'Figure Work'. Thus the performance of women seems to be dependent on the method of entry also. However, the effect of method of entry was not investigated statistically as the sample size was too small.

Conclusion

Women were awarded significantly lower scores than men only on the 'Stability' rating. This result may explain partly why they were awarded significantly lower scores on the 'Future Potential' grading also.[1]

M. J. BHANSHALI
Assistant Statistician
January 21, 1969.

[1] 'Progress of Women in the Administrative Class' by M. J. Bhanshali.

INDEX

For Product Safety Concerns and Information please contact our EU representative GPSR@taylorandfrancis.com
Taylor & Francis Verlag GmbH, Kaufingerstraße 24, 80331 München, Germany

www.ingramcontent.com/pod-product-compliance
Ingram Content Group UK Ltd.
Pitfield, Milton Keynes, MK11 3LW, UK
UKHW022011180926
475701UK00003B/300
* 9 7 8 1 1 3 8 2 8 0 6 5 6 *